THE BEAUCHAMP ALMSHOUSES
AND
ST LEONARD'S CHURCH, NEWLAND

THE BEAUCHAMP ALMSHOUSES AND ST LEONARD'S CHURCH, NEWLAND 1864–2014

Mark Dalby

A continuation of the work
of the late David Annett

Completed and edited by
Colin R. Brownlee

The Beauchamp Almshouses and St Leonard's Church, Newland 1864–2014
Mark Dalby

Research commenced by David Annett,
completed and edited by Colin R. Brownlee

Published by Aspect Design 2014
Malvern, Worcestershire, United Kingdom.

Designed and Printed by Aspect Design
89 Newtown Road, Malvern, Worcs. WR14 1PD
United Kingdom
Tel: 01684 561567
E-mail: books@aspect-design.net
Website: www.aspect-design.net

Copyright © 2014 Mark Dalby, David Annett and Colin R. Brownlee

All Rights Reserved.

Mark Dalby has asserted his moral right
to be identified as the author of this work.

This book is sold subject to the condition that it shall not, by way of trade or otherwise, be lent, resold, hired out or otherwise circulated without the publisher's prior consent in any form of binding or cover other than that in which it is published and without a similar condition including this condition being imposed on the subsequent purchaser.

A copy of this book has been deposited with the British Library Board

Cover shows the Quadrangle from the clock tower, 2013.
Photograph by Colin R. Brownlee.
Cover Design Copyright © 2014 Aspect Design

ISBN 978-1-908832-56-6

Contents

Foreword by the Editor 7
Foreword by the Chaplain 9
Preface. 11

The Beginnings 13
1. Beauchamp Family and the Countess Charlotte. 15
2. The Beginnings of the Almshouses. 20
3. First Vicar-Warden: James Skinner, 1861–1877 30
4. Plans and Preparations 36
5. Consecration and Dedication 54
6. Pensioners and the Almshouses 65
7. Choir School and the Chancel: Questions of Authority 76
8. The Church 95
9. Skinner's Resignation 108

The Consolidation and Continuation 115
10. Second Vicar-Warden: George Cosby White, 1877–1897. . . . 117
11. Third Vicar-Warden: Robert Wylde, 1897–1926 134
12. The Years to the Centenary, 1927–1964 150

The Last Fifty Years 171
13. Last Vicar-Wardens, 1965–1979 173
14. The Administrator: Mrs Vera Rowberry, 1980–1999 187

15. New Millennium, 2000–2014 207
16. Epilogue. 217

Illustrations 219

Appendix I, People. 233
    Trustees 233
    Vicar-Wardens, Chaplains and Families 236
    Churchwardens. 237
    Clerks to the Trustees. 238
    Curates 239
    Lay Wardens. 240
    Matron, Sisters and Nurses 240
    Medical Officers 241
    Porters. 241
    Servants and Domestic Staff 242
    Organist and Choirmasters 243
    Choir School Matrons 244
    Choristers of the Choir School 244
    Pensioners and General Residents. 250
    Priests in the Community. 276
    Altar Servers. 283
Appendix II, Church Ritual, Liturgy and Altar Servers 284
Appendix III, Church Organ 291
Appendix IV, Churchyard and Community Burials 293
Appendix V, the Grounds. 296
Appendix VI, the Chapel at Newland 303
Appendix VII, Principal Sources. 309

Foreword by the Editor

When I first visited the Beauchamp Community to research the history of the Choir School, little did I think I would end up living here and having the great privilege of completing Mark Dalby's book. He became not only a great friend but an invaluable source of knowledge and we shared information freely on our respective researches. Many a time the telephone would ring late at night and on the other end was Mark excitedly sharing some new nugget of information—and vice versa I have to say.

The main bulk of his book was completed before I arrived but there remained numerous facts to check and significant amounts of new information to be included, together with work on the layout. Mark would have long 'rest periods' from his book then update with the latest discoveries.

Shortly before his death, Mark and I had been engaged in a flurry of activity to have the book finished for the one hundred and fiftieth anniversary in 2014 and in fact the night before he died we had been discussing the latest updates which were required.

There is a sense of déjà vu as I write this preface, for as Mark had assured David Annett he would continue his work, so I assured Mark his book would be completed and published, as he was aware his time was running out.

So I offer this completed book as a testament to the work of two fine historians who had the vision to research and write the definitive history of the Beauchamp Almshouses and St Leonard's Church.

Colin R. Brownlee
2014

Foreword by the Chaplain

It is a great honour to be asked to provide this preface to Mark Dalby's *The Beauchamp Almshouses and St Leonard's Church, Newland*.

Mark Dalby was chaplain to the community from 2000 to the end of 2007. His death in 2013 was a great sadness to us all. He was a man of God, a sensitive and caring pastor as well as a scholar and teacher. Mark also had a keen sense of humour and a sense of fun.

His scholarship and sensitivity in his care for people are reflected in the way he has laid out the information in this book. It is very detailed and well researched, using the late David Annett's material as a basis.

This book will be of great interest and a reliable resource for the student of Victorian and twentieth century almshouses and their development. Mark also gives us a vivid picture as to church life in that period and it reflects much that happened in the Church in the period covered in the book. It will be of great interest to those who know the Beauchamp Community.

The Beauchamp Community is a major part of Newland's life

and history. Mark's book will certainly contribute to the history of the development of this part of Malvern.

Roger Watson
Chaplain to the Beauchamp Community
February 2014

Preface

David Annett, sometime headmaster of King's School, Worcester, ended his days as a resident of the Beauchamp Community[1] in Newland, living at St Christopher's, the former vicarage coach house where I myself now live. A devout churchman and a historian of no mean ability, he quickly interested himself in the history of the community.

There were already two books relevant to this. The first, published in London in 1883, was *James Skinner: A Memoir*, 'by the author of *Charles Lowder*' who was in fact a Maria Trench. The second, circulated locally in duplicated form, was *A History of St Leonard's Church Newland* written seriatim by Canon John Hunt *c.*1961–63. Both books contain much valuable information, but they were hagiographic in style and their contents were uncritical.

Mr Annett conceived the idea of writing a new and fuller history. He drew considerably on the earlier books but also did major research

---

[1] The name was changed from the Beauchamp Almshouses to the Beauchamp Community in 1974.

into the community's early years; he was kindly granted access by the Lady Morrison, the present chairman of the Trustees, to the Trustees' minutes and to a large archive relating to the community accumulated by the Honourable Frederick Lygon, later the sixth Earl Beauchamp.

At some points I acted as Mr Annett's assistant until illness put a stop to his work, but in his last conversation with me just before he died he expressed the hope that his researches would not be 'binned.' I assured him that they would not and that I would do my best to continue them. I have now sought to honour my promise. Two thirds of the first section is his work while the rest of the material is mostly mine.

I have been helped by Charles Allsopp, Meriel Bennett, Colin Brownlee, Tony Bullock, Jean Burrow, Jill Coleman, John and Olwyn Craze, John Flint, Father John Guise, Roger Hall-Jones, Paul Hodgson, Pat Hipwell, Peter Hughes, Father Gordon Ikin, Frank Kelsall, Elizabeth Palmer, Michael Peach, Father Nicholas Roberts, James Ruddock-Broyd, George Sharrock, Father Roger Watson, Cora Weaver and many others.

I am grateful to them all, but I must take responsibility myself for any errors. There are bound to be some, and I hope that readers will let me know if they spot any so that they can be corrected in any future edition. My final thanks must be to the Trustees for sponsoring the book, but any opinions expressed are mine and not necessarily theirs.

Mark Dalby
Principal author
2013

The Beginnings

Chapter One
The Beauchamp Family and the Countess Charlotte

Immediately to the southeast of Newland is the village of Madresfield and its famous Court. In 1260 William de Bracy is recorded as the owner of Madresfield, and his descendants continued to hold the manor until *c.*1419 when the male line failed and Joan, the heiress, married Thomas Lygon.

In the sixteenth century their descendant Richard Lygon married Anne, daughter of Lord Beauchamp of Powyke; she brought to the marriage both the manor of Powick and the 'Bear and Ragged Staff' which thereafter appears as a supporter of the Lygon arms. In 1713, William Lygon's daughter and heiress Margaret married Reginald Pyndar (or Pindar). Their son Reginald took the name of Lygon by Act of Parliament. His son William inherited a large fortune from his cousin William Jennens and in 1806 was created Lord Beauchamp of Powyke; in 1815 he was created Viscount Elmley and Earl Beauchamp. He died in 1816 and was succeeded by his son William. William died unmarried in 1823, and was succeeded by his brother John Reginald who, to quote Debrett, 'assumed for himself by Royal Licence the surname of Pindar only.'

In 1814 John Reginald had married Lady Charlotte Scott, daughter of the first Earl of Clonmell, Chief Justice of Ireland. Since Charlotte was an earl's daughter (albeit in the Irish peerage) and brought with her a dowry of £60,000, it might have been expected that the Lygons would consider this an acceptable match. But the reputation and character of her father had been marked by several controversial incidents, and his elevation to an earldom was the result of sedulous cultivation of the government of the day. The Lygons were unhappy to welcome such a colourful character to their family circle, and their unrelenting hostility led by the Dowager Countess was directed against the unfortunate Charlotte. The wedding took place not at Madresfield but at St Marylebone where the Scotts had a family connection.

When Charlotte arrived at Madresfield after her brother-in-law's death in 1823, she is said to have been distressed that the estate workers, when their labouring days were over, had to leave their tied cottages and, if they had no relatives to take them in, might end their days in the workhouse at Upton-upon-Severn. She therefore conceived a scheme for building almshouses to take in these retired workers, but she was unable to put this into effect because at that time, before the passage of the Married Women's Property Act, all her money had passed into her husband's control. But she discussed her plan with her husband who, despite the disapproval of the Dowager, agreed to use her dowry for the building of the almshouses. She died, however, in 1846 before anything had been done, and she was buried in St Marylebone where she had been married.

The third Earl's thirty-year marriage to Charlotte was childless, but the couple had a great affection for her nephew, Colonel Charles Grantham Scott, whom they seem to have treated almost as a son. A year after Charlotte's death, the Earl in his will left much of his unentailed estate to Colonel Scott. Two features of the will are of particular interest. In one, he bequeaths an eight acre 'parcel of pasture land' in Newland to Colonel Scott. In the other he writes,

And whereas, I have contemplated erecting and endowing Almshouses either upon some part of my estate or elsewhere in the hamlet of Newland aforesaid, for the residence of twelve or some larger number of poor men and women, members of the Church, who shall have been employed in agriculture, and have been reduced by sickness, misfortune, or infirmity, now, in case I happen to die without effecting such object, and any persons or person should within twelve months after my decease, at their, his, or her expense, purchase or give a suitable piece of land in Newland aforesaid, as a site for such Almshouses and with intent that the same should be devoted for such purpose, then I empower and direct the trustee or trustees for the time being of this my will, when and so soon as such land shall have been legally dedicated to charitable uses, provided they, he, or she, shall approve the scheme of the intended charity, and the rules and regulations proposed for the government thereof, to pay to the trustees of the said intended charity, out of such part of my personal estate as is hereinafter mentioned, the sum of sixty thousand pounds.

He concluded that, if the almshouses were not built, the legacy should go to St George's Hospital, Middlesex.[1] His intention was clearly that Colonel Scott should give the land he had inherited at Newland as a site for the almshouses, and this he duly did.

In 1850 the Earl married as his second wife a widow, the Honourable Catherine Murray nee Otway, who, it could be argued, tried hard to consign Charlotte to oblivion. This second marriage lasted only three years as the Earl died in 1853 and, as was his wish, he was buried beside Charlotte at St Marylebone. An obituary in the *Worcester Herald* stated that he 'was better known as an unostentatious country gentleman than as a public character' and referred to 'a certain degree of shyness of manner' But Catherine erected a grandiose monument to him at St Marylebone—'a bas-relief, which has been executed in Italy, and

---

[1] The will was conveniently reported in the 25 Law Journal Report, N.S., Chancery 33, Appendix.

is a fine work of art.' Surmounted by a cross, the Beauchamp arms and a mourning woman with the text, 'He is not dead, but sleepeth.'

There is no mention at all of Charlotte on the monument, who was the sole reason for the Earl being buried at St Marylebone, but she is mentioned on another tablet in the church which states 'In a Vault near this Place are deposited the remains of Charlotte, Countess Beauchamp.

Again, there is no mention of Charlotte on the large and handsome memorial brass which Catherine erected to her husband (originally in Madresfield church) which is now affixed to the west wall in the south aisle of the chancel of St Leonard's.[2] The east window of St Leonard's, given by Catherine in memory of her late husband, contains the heraldic badges of the Beauchamps and the Brayes along with the patron saints of the Earl and Catherine, but again there is no reference to Charlotte. The only place in the church or almshouses where Charlotte is mentioned is a small brass tablet on the north wall of the sanctuary. It is placed so high that it can neither be cleaned nor read from the ground and carries a Latin inscription which can be translated:

> To the honour of God and in memory of John Reginald Pindar, third Earl Beauchamp, who generously founded this church and almshouses, and also of his wife Charlotte, to whom this excellent work of charity was very dear, Charles Grantham Scott and Mary, their loving nephew and niece, undertook to set up the sculpture round this holy altar. Founded 1852—Completed 1864. Prayers and works of charity rise up to the presence of God.

---

[2] This contains Latin verses from the psalms as well as an inscription in English which refers to the Earl as 'the Provider of this Church, and the Founder of the Almshouses for decayed Agricultural Labourers in this Parish.' Also contains the prayer, 'May his soul rest in everlasting peace, and may perpetual light shine upon it.' Such prayer for the dead, revived by the tractarians, was still very uncommon in the Church of England as a whole at this time.

In 2004, in an early draft of this chapter, Annett wrote, 'All public credit for the foundation of the church and the almshouses is given to the Earl. Although they owe their existence to Charlotte's idea and her money, she has received no recognition, her contribution has been forgotten and—one suspects—wilfully obscured. It is good that at least her nephew remembered her.' But today Charlotte's significance is increasingly appreciated, and we should not condemn Catherine too harshly. Some women bitterly regret being 'second' wives, and she is not alone in wishing to erase the memory of the first wife; she lived till 1875 and did all she could to perpetuate the memory of her husband.

John Reginald, however, the third Earl, is still regarded formally as the founder of the Beauchamp Community, and his birthday, 21 November, is honoured as Founder's Day—or at least it used to be, since any observance of it has now sadly lapsed. In January 1867 the Trustees considered a letter from Countess Catherine asking to be allowed to erect a statue of the Earl in the centre of the Quadrangle. They referred this to their architect, P. C. Hardwick, for his opinion, but nothing more was heard of it. On her death, however, she bequeathed to the Trustees the marble bust portrait of him by Bertolini and the pedestal on which it stood, and this was placed in the boardroom where it still stands.

Chapter Two
The Beginnings of the Almshouses

After the third Earl's death in 1853 there were various legal delays and obstructions, and the effective life of the Foundation began with an Order of the Court of Chancery of 26 March 1859 sanctioning a 'Scheme for the management of the Beauchamp Hospital at Newland, Worcestershire.'

The scheme provided first for the appointment of twelve trustees:

George William, Lord Lyttelton, of Frankley
Henry Lygon, Viscount Elmley, of Powick (later fifth Earl); d. 1866
Charles Somers Cocks, Earl Somers, of Evesham
Sir John Somerset Pakington, bart, of Westwood Park
Sir Edmund Anthony Harley Lechmere, bart, of the Rhydd
William Dowdeswell, Esq., of Pull Court, Tewksbury
Revd George Shaw Munn, Rector of Madresfield
Hon. Charles Grantham Scott, of Cherbourg House, Malvern
Revd Thomas Philpott, of Belbroughton (incumbent of Newland church since 1831)
Rt. Hon. Earl Beauchamp, of Madresfield Court; d. 1863

Hon. Frederick Lygon, of Madresfield (later sixth Earl)
John Slaney Pakington, Esq., of Kent's Green, Powick

The Trustees were to meet at least once every six months. Three would constitute a quorum and before any business was conducted they were to elect one of their number as chairman.

The fourth Earl, General Henry Lygon, was elected chairman from 1859 to 1863, as thereafter was his eldest son, Henry, the fifth Earl, who died in March 1866. But right from the start his second son, Frederick, later the sixth Earl, was clearly the prime mover.

Frederick was born in 1830 and R. J. Olney suggests that 'Born to a somewhat elderly father, and losing his mother at the age of five, Frederick was perhaps a rather reserved and lonely figure as a young man' He quickly showed signs of a scholarly disposition. In 1852 he became a Fellow of All Souls, and he resigned in 1864 only because of his brother's illness and the desirability of his being in Madresfield. He was influenced in the tractarian[1] direction by his governess, Miss Marks, and at Oxford he met many leading tractarians including Canon H. P. Liddon and Dr E. B. Pusey. Throughout his life he continued to uphold tractarian principles. In 1858 he had published *The Day Hours of the Church of England* for use primarily though not exclusively in religious communities, while in later years he was one of the prime movers behind the foundation of Keble College, Oxford, and also of Pusey House.

He has been described as 'the ecclesiastical layman *par excellence*', but he was in no sense narrowly religious or academic. In 1857 he became MP for Tewkesbury and then, like other members of his family before him, MP for West Worcestershire. In 1859 he was appointed a Lord of the Admiralty. Later honours included Lord Steward of

---

[1] In 1833 John Keble preached an Assize sermon in Oxford, and this is generally regarded as the beginnings of the Oxford movement. His early followers were known as tractarians because of the tracts they published and disseminated throughout the country. His later followers were known as ritualists, Puseyites (after another leader of the movement) or anglo-catholics.

the Royal Household (a post from which he was allegedly dismissed after six years 'because of his haughtiness towards the servants'), Paymaster-General and Lord Lieutenant of Worcestershire. There are other hints of a difficult personality. Disraeli, though deeming him 'a disagreeable man', also wrote, 'Whatever may be his faults of manner and temper, he is a thorough good fellow', and E. W. Benson, Archbishop of Canterbury, described him as 'a bright gay man, very particular about his dress and brusque in his manner, and chimerical, but withal a faithful son of the Church.' A later writer has spoken of his 'grave personality' and of his being 'rather humourless and singularly reserved.'

Frederick was to exert a vast influence on his fellow-trustees both by virtue of his personality and commitment and also by his membership of first the building committee and then of the standing committee which he chaired. This latter was to prove a more significant body than the larger body of Trustees of which from at least 1865 he was treasurer and from 1866 the usual chairman. He accumulated a voluminous archive relating to the almshouses and the church. This contains correspondence with the warden, the architect, the clerk and the solicitor, and it indicates the firm and meticulous control which he exercised over every detail of the trust—in the planning stages, the construction of the buildings, and the early management and everyday life of the foundation. It also reveals that even when he was away from Madresfield he expected his lieutenant, G. S. Munn, a fellow-trustee and fellow-tractarian, to keep a careful eye on all that was going on and to report to him accordingly.

The 1859 scheme provided that the Trustees were to appoint a clerk at a salary not exceeding £50 a year. They were also to erect on the land given by Colonel Scott 'good and substantial Almshouses, to be called "The Beauchamp Almshouses" to contain a house for a Chaplain, a Board room, and other necessary offices and accommodation for twenty-four Almspeople.' There were to be 'eight sets of rooms for married couples, eight sets of rooms for single men or widowers, and eight sets of rooms for spinsters or widows (each set consisting of a sitting room, bed room, and a small pantry or wash house).' There was also to be accommodation for a matron and a porter, and appropriate furniture was to be provided throughout. The total cost was not to exceed £12,000.

The next clause provided that 'for the purpose of procuring a place of worship for the Almspeople' the Trustees might purchase and procure to be vested in themselves the advowson of Newland and then 'to repair and enlarge, or rebuild . . . the Church of Newland, so as to make the same available as a Place of Worship for the Almspeople.' None should be admitted as almspeople under the age of fifty, and no married almsman should be admitted whose wife was under fifty. The almspeople were to be 'poor persons of good, religious, and moral character, and members of the Church of England . . . who have been engaged in agriculture, either as employers or employed, and have been reduced to poverty by sickness, misfortune or infirmity.' A stipend of 16*s.* a week should be paid to each married almsman and of 10*s.* a week to each single one. Such stipends were to be paid weekly in advance, and the Trustees were empowered to provide two tons of coal annually for each set of rooms.

The Trustees were to appoint the first almspeople as soon as the accommodation was available, and when vacancies arose they were to give twenty-eight days notice in Madresfield, Newland and Worcester before proceeding to elections. All applications were to be made in writing on a form provided by the clerk, and the Trustees were to provide a minute book in which the details of those elected were to be entered, and also the date and cause of death or removal. The Trustees were empowered to make appropriate rules, and no almsperson was to be absent for more than twenty-four hours without written permission. Further,

> All the Almspeople and all wives of Almspeople who may not be prevented from so doing by sickness or other good cause, shall regularly attend daily morning prayer in the Chapel, and the public services of the Chapel on Sunday, Christmas Day, Good Friday,

Ascension Day, and the 21st day of November in each year (Founder's Day).

Each almsperson was to wear 'at Church and when beyond the precincts of the Almshouses' such distinctive dress as the Trustees provided.

Any almsperson who had been guilty, or whose wife had been guilty, of insobriety, immoral conduct, or wilful behaviour could be removed at the discretion of the Trustees. None were to underlet their premises or to receive any other inmate (except wives) without permission, and no trade was to be exercised. If anyone professing to be unmarried should, after his or her election, be proved to be married, that election should immediately be cancelled. As far as possible the original number of eight married couples should be maintained. In case of death of a husband or wife, the survivor should then be considered single, and the next single vacancy should be filled by a married person.

The Trustees were to appoint a priest of the Church of England as chaplain to the almshouses at an annual stipend not exceeding £200 a year, and he could be removed only by a two-thirds majority of the Trustees:

> The Chaplain shall read prayers every Morning in the Chapel, and shall perform there every Sunday two full Services, according to the ritual of the Church of England (at one of which, at least, a Sermon shall be preached,) and shall perform one full Service, at least, with a sermon, on every Christmas Day, Good Friday, Ascension Day, and 21st November. He shall also celebrate in the Chapel the Holy Communion on twelve days at least in each year, of which Christmas Day, Easter Day, and Ascension Day shall be three.

He was to visit the inmates 'in sickness, and at other times as there may be occasion', and he was to 'have the general management of the Almshouses, subject to the superintendence of the Trustees.' He was not to be absent for more than fourteen days at a time without written consent, and when absent must procure a duly qualified substitute.

The Trustees were also to appoint a matron and a porter/gardener, and their joint salaries or stipends were not to exceed £100 per annum. They were further to appoint, at a salary not exceeding £30 per annum, a medical practitioner residing nearby to attend on and supply all needful medicines to the sick and infirm. When an almsperson or his wife died, the chaplain was to provide that the deceased had decent burial at the expense of the Charity, 'and all the Almspeople, and wives of Almsmen, whose state of health will permit them to attend, shall attend the funeral.' As for their own responsibilities, the Trustees at least once a year were to 'view the state and condition of the Almshouses, and take cognizance of any complaints of the inmates touching the management thereof.'

The first meeting of the Trustees took place, with Viscount Elmley in the chair, on 29 September 1859 at the Star Hotel, Worcester, and this was their normal venue until the almshouses were opened although occasionally meetings were held at Madresfield Court or even in London. Charles Bolton Edgcumbe was appointed Clerk, and Sir John Packington gave notice that he would propose a motion that the Trustees apply to the Court for a revision of the scheme, 'principally with a view to building a Chapel as part of the Institution, and also allotting a portion of the Institution to the reception and treatment of sick persons.' A special meeting to consider this was arranged for 24 October 1859, and now Earl Beauchamp was in the chair. Sir John formally moved his resolution, but an amendment was passed to the effect that it would be unwise to apply to the Court again at this stage. It was then agreed 'that Mr Philip Charles Hardwick be appointed architect to prepare plans for the building.'[2]

Hardwick was born in 1822 and worked in the offices of the architect Edward Blore and of his father, Philip Hardwick, snr. He gained his

---

[2] The Madresfield Court archives contain three volumes of Hardwick's working drawings and designs for the almshouses and the church.

FRIBA in 1850, and took over his father's practice in 1852. He was architect to the Bank of England, and surveyor to St Bartholomew's Hospital, the Merchant Taylors Company, the Greenwich Hospital and the Charterhouse. His major works were the Great Western Hotel at Paddington and the buildings of Charterhouse School at Godalming. He worked at Madresfield Court between 1863 and 1875 Hunt describes him as 'a cultured and devout churchman, a man of wide imagination, considerable learning in Theology and Liturgiology, possessed of infinite patience, sympathy and tenderness . . . He gave generously of his time and substance, and allowed nothing shoddy to pass.' Later events were to show that he had need of his 'infinite patience' in dealing both with the Trustees and the warden.

The Trustees further agreed that Sir Edmund Lechmere, Colonel Scott, Mr Munn, Frederick Lygon and Mr Philpott should be appointed as a building committee, and that they should communicate with Hardwick and direct him to prepare plans and estimates.

In January 1860 the Trustees discussed plans for acquiring the advowson or patronage of Newland so that a joint appointment might be made of incumbent of the parish and chaplain/warden of the almshouses. This resulted on 20 August 1860 in The Beauchamp Charity Act—'An Act to enable the Trustees of Lord Beauchamp's Charity to purchase the Right of Nomination to the Chapelry of Newland in the County of Worcester, and to vest in them the Site of the Church or Chapel of Newland.' Hitherto the advowson of Newland had been vested in the vicar of Great Malvern, but indirectly the patrons of Great Malvern had an interest in Newland and the Act provided for the Trustees to pay £700 to the Court of Chancery for the purchase.

Meanwhile on 7 August 1860 Hardwick produced some rough estimates:

> Building 24 sets of rooms for Almspeople, the Gateway and rooms over, rooms for the Porter and Matron, the Cloister, the Chaplain's House and Board-room, the Laundry and Gardener's House £13,500

Furniture for 24 sets of rooms and the Chaplain's House   £1,000

Fittings for Wash-house, drainage and fencing   £800

The total here was £15,300, and it was clear that the sum of £12,000 allowed by the Court of Chancery in the original scheme would be inadequate.

The building committee continued their discussions with Hardwick, and on 5 September they reported to the Trustees. They believed that the existing church would be too small to accommodate the almspeople and suggested that, rather than rebuild it on its present site, it would be better to build a new church 'suitable for its double character' as both parish church and chapel of the almshouses on a new site adjoining the almshouses, where it would be 'readily accessible to the parishioners without entering the precincts of the Almshouses.' They further suggested that the warden's study be so placed as to give him a view of all the almspeople's rooms, and that these rooms be so arranged as to benefit from the maximum sunlight and be sheltered from the wind. They were also to be 'divided into three blocks, those set apart for married couples intervening between those destined for the single almsmen and almswomen. The propriety of this precautionary arrangement needs no explanation.'

The boardroom was to serve also as a library and for recreational purposes. A dispensary was to be provided adjoining the matron's rooms and, 'bearing in mind the age of the inmates and the number of deaths that must from time to time occur', the committee urged the desirability of the provision of a mortuary. Further, since hitherto Newland parishioners had been buried at Great Malvern, they also proposed provision for a graveyard on the site of the old church (after its demolition) together with an adjoining piece of land to be given by Earl Beauchamp. They concluded that 'less accommodation than they have suggested for each of the Almspeople would be a niggardly expenditure of the munificent funds of the Charity', and urged that it was 'better to expend a large sum at once upon a well-considered scheme than make expensive alterations at a later date.' They therefore urged the Trustees to ask the Master of the Rolls to approve an expenditure of £16,000.

The Trustees resolved unanimously that the plans submitted by the building committee be adopted and submitted to the Court of Chancery for approval. They further resolved 'that Mr Munn, Mr Philpott and Mr Lygon be appointed a standing committee to carry out the resolutions of the Trustees agreed upon from time to time, and to prepare business to be laid before the Trustees.' This standing committee appears to have taken over the function of the building committee, and since it was later to be the subject of acute dissension between Frederick and the warden it is worth remembering its terms of reference.

On 23 October a meeting of Newland parishioners was held in the old church, and Philpott, the incumbent, explained the Trustees' plans which were unanimously accepted by the parishioners, on the understanding that no expense for any part of them should fall on the parish.

On 20 December it was reported to the Trustees that the Master of the Rolls had rejected their application for additional funds for building, and had declined to give any reason for this. He had, however, allowed the sum of £4,200 for building the new church. Hardwick was now asked to suggest ways of reducing the building costs. He replied on 31 December that he would find it difficult to make any savings, but suggested:

Reducing the size of the rooms,
Leaving the 'dead house' and cloister to a future date,
Omitting the allowance for furniture, since this was not part of the building costs,
Omitting the upper part of the great gateway,
Reducing the sum allowed for fencing and draining.

These, together with other minor savings, would reduce the total to £11,950, and Hardwick was now asked to prepare revised drawings on the lines suggested and to secure tenders.

Meanwhile great frustration and delay had, over many years, been occasioned by what was deemed the lethargy and incompetence of the London solicitors, and the uncooperative attitude of the Court of Chancery and the Master of the Rolls in dealing with the purchase of the advowson, the release of funds, and the conveyance from Colonel Scott to the Trustees of the land on which the almshouses were to be built. On 20 January 1861 Frederick felt obliged to complain to F. W. Blake, the solicitor, that, 'The affairs of the Charity make very slow progress. Eight years have now elapsed since the death of Lord Beauchamp, and I cannot think that justice has been done to his benevolent intention.'

On 4 June 1861 the Standing Committee reported that they had received and studied six tenders for the buildings, and recommended the acceptance of that from Oliver Estcourt of Gloucester for £9,550 (which was in fact the cheapest). This was agreed. The committee then reported that the solicitors' firm of Westmacott, Blake and Rawlinson had dissolved, and they recommended the appointment of Messrs Fearon and Clabon as the Trustees' solicitors in view of their experience in dealing with the Court of Chancery. This too was resolved—and never regretted, for Fearon fulfilled all the hopes placed in him.

Chapter Three
The First Vicar-Warden
James Skinner, 1861–1877

Now that they had purchased the advowson of Newland, an essential element in the Trustees' plans and preparations was the appointment of the first vicar-warden. In spring 1861 Philpott resigned the incumbency, and on 31 May the Bishop of Worcester's secretary wrote to Fearon asking him to inform the new patrons of the vacancy. Frederick must have had advance warning of this as in April he was already in touch with James Skinner and even offering him the appointment of vicar and warden-designate. On 25 April Skinner wrote to him setting out the terms—responsibility, authority, etc.—on which he would accept the appointment, and Frederick replied accepting these.[1] There is no record in the Trustees' minutes of any discussion preceding the appointment, nor any formal indication of how Skinner came to be chosen, but it can be regarded as certain that the decision was largely that of Frederick, and it is generally believed that he was recommended to him by his tractarian friend, Dr Pusey.

---

[1] No trace of this letter can be found in the archives at present, which is unfortunate in view of Skinner's subsequent controversies with the Trustees as to the extent of his responsibility and authority.

On 18 June 1861 the Trustees agreed 'that the Revd James Skinner of Hillingdon be nominated Incumbent of the Perpetual Curacy of Newland, and also appointed Chaplain to the Almshouses, with a present stipend of £100 per year out of the income of the Charity.' This stipend was only half of the maximum allowed under the scheme, but since the almshouses were not yet in existence the Trustees presumably felt that his work at this stage would be primarily in the parish. But the benefice had endowments of only £60, so his total stipend at this point was only £160.

Skinner, born in Scotland in 1818, was twelve years older than Frederick. His father was Dean of Dunkeld and Dunblane, and both his grandfather and his uncle were Bishops of Aberdeen. At the age of fifteen he went to the University of Durham where he was remembered for his skill as an orator and his social exuberance. An undergraduate contemporary, Henry Press Wright, who later became a Canadian archdeacon and then rector of Greatham in Sussex, wrote of him,

> The habits of James Skinner were in no way studious—I might say quite the reverse. He would . . . read closely for the Debating Society, in which his powers as a speaker soon became notorious. Possessed of a discerning mind and great command of language, he had qualifications to render him an orator of no mean kind. His speeches were so powerful and his manner so quiet and self-possessed that few believed him to be a youth of sixteen. Dinners, dances, picnics and archery meetings were constantly tempting the young student, and certainly no one more enjoyed and, in his way, more adorned society than my dear friend. A Scotch reel was his delight and loud and hearty were his shouts when revelling in a Highland Fling. Good spirits, a strong sense of the ludicrous, a warm and loving heart, an able brain with a thoroughly honest learning combined to make him a favourite everywhere.

On leaving Durham, in 1839 he was appointed an assistant master at King William's College in the Isle of Man, despite the principal's disquiet at rumours that he was 'a violent Oxford Tract party man.' He was soon elected a Fellow of Durham, and in 1841 he was ordained deacon, serving as curate in Burton Agnes in East Yorkshire to Archdeacon Robert Wilberforce[2] who introduced him to many of the leading tractarians. Priested in 1842, he resigned his curacy a year later as, with a weakness of the lungs, he found the east Yorkshire climate difficult. After brief spells in Windsor, Southsea and Reading, where his health again gave way, he was appointed chaplain to the British Forces in Corfu where the climate was more congenial and where on one occasion he presented 193 candidates for confirmation. The High Commissioner, Field-Marshall Lord Seaton, wrote of his ministry there, 'I believe no Chaplain ever discharged his duties with greater profit to the soldiers than he did during the time I was in command.' In 1848 he returned to England briefly to marry Agnes Raymond, to whom he had been engaged for nine years, but in 1849 and 1850 his health broke down once more because of the excessive heat and he returned to England again.

He now became senior curate at St Barnabas, Pimlico, a daughter church of St Paul's Knightsbridge. He immediately appointed Charles Lowder, who later achieved fame as vicar of St Peter, London Docks, as one of his curates, and he was assisted by three others. Skinner described St Barnabas at that time as 'at the head of the Anglo catholic movement', and as such it 'aroused many feelings of hatred and hostility.' There had already been intimidation of the congregation, and of 1851 Skinner wrote,

> The whole of that memorable year [the church] was only held, as a beleaguered city is held, by armed men, against the violence of enemies who battered at the doors, shouted through the windows, hissed in the aisles and essayed to storm the chancel gates . . . It was

---

[2] Wilberforce, the second son of the famous William Wilberforce, subsequently joined the Roman Catholic church.

only by keeping a large body of gentlemen—regular members of our flock—on the roll of sworn special constables that we were enabled to preserve order during divine service.

The controversies, known as the St Barnabas Riots, reached the correspondence columns of *The Times,* but for six years Skinner and his colleagues fought a continual battle to defend the established anglo-catholic teaching and practices not only against evangelical opponents but also against the bishop. There were already those who thought him 'too stern and unbending', but there were others who appreciated his deep spiritual counsel.

Early in 1854 his health gave way again, and Robert Liddell who as vicar of St Paul's was nominally his superior wrote to him, 'For your own *health's*—perhaps I ought to say for your *life's* sake, I cannot consent to your doing *any duty whatever* at St Barnabas at present.' In the autumn he set out for an extended tour of Egypt and the Holy Land. He returned in June 1855 in good health to resume his duties, but his health failed again and in the summer of 1856 his doctor insisted that he give up work for two years. Liddell 'with deep grief' called on him to resign, and this he duly did. In March 1857 he went to Menton in Switzerland, and returned to England in the summer of 1858. He was still not well enough to undertake full-time work and settled in 1859 at Hillingdon, near Uxbridge, where he busied himself with the setting up of the (anglo-catholic) Church Protection Society, later to become the English Church Union, of which he became honorary secretary and also editor of its organ, the *Church Review.* In 1860 he was abroad again, and on 21 April—a measure of the esteem in which he was now held—he preached at Westminster Abbey at the invitation of the Dean.[3]

When Frederick contacted him, the parish of Newland contained only thirty-six families and he felt his new charge would be within his

---

[3] By coincidence the Dean, Richard Chenevix-Trench who later became Archbishop of Dublin, was the great-great-grandfather of Jonathan Chenevix-Trench, the son-in-law of Lady Morrison, the present chairman of the Trustees.

powers. Frederick for his part may have thought that he was acquiring the services of a distinguished theologian and liturgiologist,[4] and at the same time offering a well-deserved and peaceful haven to one who had worn himself out in battles for his faith. He may further have expected that, in view of his fragile physical health, Skinner would prove a meek and malleable subordinate, but in this he was greatly mistaken. Skinner's fighting days were far from over. As early as August 1861 he was concerned about the parish school, supported by private subscriptions, and his early enquiries convinced him that Newland parents valued this school; he later claimed that it had between forty and fifty pupils at that time. It was urged on him, not least by Frederick that, as the third Earl had left a considerable sum for educating the poor of Madresfield and the 'Hamlet of Newland', a separate school for Newland was unnecessary, and Frederick was anxious that it should be merged with the Madresfield one.

However, Skinner argued that the third Earl had envisaged Madresfield and Newland being served by a single clergyman, and he was unhappy with the idea of Newland children being educated under the aegis of another incumbent. He believed that 'next to the Church itself the parish school is the most essential and hopeful institution within it', and he added, 'I could no more contemplate a Parish without its own school, than a Parish without its own Pastor and its own Church.' In September he wrote to Frederick, 'I am very unfortunate in succeeding to a state of things at Newland, in respect of the school, which does not meet with the approbation of Mr Munn and yourself whom I regard as my best friends, and with whom it is my earnest wish to co-operate in all things.' He concluded, 'In all things, I must always do what my conscience tells me is right.'[5]

Although his official title as incumbent of Newland was that of

---

[4] The Bodleian Library contains ten sermons, tracts, etc. by Skinner published from 1840–60. An eleventh was published in 1861, probably before he moved to Newland.

[5] James Skinner, *The Newland School: A Pastoral Letter to his Parishioners and Friends,* November 1875, privately printed.

'perpetual curate', in practice this was the equivalent of a vicar and its holders were always known as 'vicar' by parishioners. But some clergy thought the title somehow demeaning and Skinner allegedly sent an eighteen-page letter to the bishop and then published a tract arguing that his true title at Newland was 'vicar.' The community archives do not contain a copy of either, but they do contain a handwritten memorandum on the subject dated 14 November 1861.

Pending the completion of the warden's house (on which work had not yet started), Skinner, his wife and their young daughter Agnes moved in October into Somers Villa, a rented house in Malvern Link, and he immediately immersed himself in parochial work. His wife wrote in her diary, 'The poor people seem to look forward with great satisfaction to having a resident clergyman among them. I believe it is forty years since the parish has had that blessing.' On his first Sunday she wrote, 'The little church was well filled, chiefly with poor; and oh, what a happiness it was to see dear James in his own church again.'

On his second Sunday he was ill, and the local doctor told him he must leave Malvern and go to Madeira for the winter, but he soon recovered and ignored this advice, and quickly obtained the help of a curate. In December the Trustees resolved that in consideration of the many expenses incurred in moving his family and furniture he should be requested to accept a present of £50. At this stage, despite the disagreements about the school, all was still sweetness and light.

With his tractarian emphasis on the centrality of the eucharist Skinner's 'great desire was to increase the number of Celebrations.' In 1862 there were twenty-three celebrations of communion as against seven in the previous year, while in October 1862 the Bishop of Worcester confirmed thirty-six candidates. Initially he continued his literary work. In 1863 he published *21 Heads of Christian Duty, with Directions How to Use Them* and also a hymn book, and in 1865 he published *A Plea for the Threatened Ritual of the Church of England*. But thereafter the demands of Newland were to prove too great, and his output ceased for a while.

Chapter Four
Plans and Preparations

The initial plans and preparations had been made by the Trustees, aided by their architect and solicitor, but from now on Skinner was to make a major contribution. Meanwhile Fearon was proving much more successful than his predecessor in dealing with the Court of Chancery. In December 1861 the standing committee reported that the Court had considered the revised plans for the almshouses and the church, and the various conveyances involved, that these were ultimately received (in Fearon's words) 'with something as nearly approximating to applause as the frigid ways of the Court of Chancery permit', and that an order had been obtained covering all the objects mentioned. They also reported that Estcourt had submitted a tender for building the church in accordance with Hardwick's specification for £4,610, and this was accepted.

A further concern now was the condition of the Newland brook on the southern boundary of the Trustees' land. This emitted a 'noisome stench' owing to the discharge of domestic sewage into its upper reaches, and there was the usual difficulty in discovering who was responsible and thus liable for 'abating the nuisance.' There were several threats of litigation, and the dispute dragged on for some years.

On 5 March 1862 the Trustees resolved that a revised version of the scheme should be submitted to the Master of the Rolls. A principal reason for this was Frederick's concern that the size of the pensions was excessive. He suggested that instead of a general rate of 16*s.* per week (or 10*s.* for single pensioners), a distinction should be made for those who were 'decayed farmers' and those who were decayed labourers, with a higher rate paid to the former. He explained,

> A labourer who has paid his rent and brought up his family on ten shillings a week would probably fall into mischief and evil habits if suddenly put into possession of a weekly income of 16 shillings (in addition to lodging and firing free) to maintain himself and his wife only. The Trustees therefore think that a just distinction may be drawn between the advantages offered to employers of labour and those offered to the employed.

On 3 September it was reported that the conveyance to the Ecclesiastical Commissioners of the burial ground and the site of the new church had been signed. At the same meeting a letter from Hardwick was read informing the Trustees that he had discussed with Skinner the plans for the warden's house, and that Skinner had requested alterations which would cost £150. The Trustees agreed to these, making the total cost of the house £2,975. In general Hardwick seems to have commanded the Trustees' confidence, but at least once he fell foul of Frederick who complained on 1 October, 'I am very much annoyed that the position of the Boardroom door should have been changed without orders from the Building Committee. I trust that nothing of this sort may be done again.' But Hardwick was not cowed, and on the following day he replied, 'I am not inclined to plead guilty to all the grave charges you make against me. A very little reflection on the part of the Clerk of the Works would have avoided the mistake with regard to the position of the door of the Board Room, as the intention of the arrangement was obvious.'

At last, on 22 October 1862, in the presence of many gentry and clergy, a dual ceremony took place at which the Bishop of Worcester, Dr Henry Philpott, consecrated the new graveyard and Countess Beauchamp laid the foundation stone of the almshouses and the new church. The *Worcester Herald* carried a full account of the occasion, but first the reporter explained that 'the plan of the buildings is for three sides of a quadrangle, the fourth side being open to the south, the yard having a garden in the centre and a terrace walk all round.' As many of the old trees as possible would be retained 'so that in every respect the site will be pleasing and picturesque.'

> Each of the almspeople will have his or her own sitting-room, bed-room, scullery, store-place, coal-house, and necessary outbuildings. There will be an entrance, with a porch, and one yard, for each group of four residences, as also a workshop, bakehouse, and wash-house, in common. Infirm inmates will live down stairs, and the hale ones in the upper story; and there will be a dispensary, in which a medical man will periodically visit all who require his attention. Accommodation for a matron, porters, etc., will likewise be provided.
>
> The chaplain's home will be at one angle of the establishment, and the church at another, being connected by means of a covered cloister. Already the chaplain's dwelling is in an advanced state, and will probably be roofed in by Christmas next. It is built of brick with Bath-stone dressings, ornamental barge-boards to gables, and the style is 'Domesticated Gothic.' It also includes a board-room for the trustees, 35 feet long by 18 feet wide, with open timber roof, and where the inmates of almshouses will assemble on festive and other occasions. This structure is now nearly ready for the roof.

The reporter then turned his attention to the church,

> This edifice will be in the Early Decorated style, with Chancel, chancel aisle, nave, and bell turret: no bells are intended at the present. The walls will be of rubble, with Bath-stone dressings. There will be a porch on the north side of the nave for the public entrance

of the parishioners, and on the south side of the chancel aisle a porch, forming a kind of campanile underneath which the almspeople will pass from the cloister into the church. At the east end of the aisle an organ is to be placed. The chancel will be arranged after the manner of collegiate churches, as set apart for the body attached to the establishment; so that the almsmen will occupy the chancel, and the women the aisle adjoining, while the general parishioners will sit in the nave. Altogether there will be 230 sittings. The east window will be of three lights, with Geometrical tracery, and the font from the old church will be placed in the new structure.

He deplored the planned demolition of the old church, 'hoped that the interesting little structure will be preserved as there are but one or two other specimens of ancient timber churches of this kind in the diocese' and asked 'could it not be allowed to remain as a mortuary chapel?' One wonders if this suggestion was inspired by a briefing, possibly from Skinner. He went on to praise the architect, adding 'Strange to say, the Court of Chancery threw no obstacles in his way nor crippled his designs, the Master of the Rolls merely disallowing certain decorative work which would have rendered the church more ecclesiastical in appearance.' One wonders again what the disallowed features could have been; there is no comment on them in either the Trustee's Minutes or in Skinner's correspondence.

The ceremony began at 11.30 a.m. when the bishop and clergy went in procession to the old church, 'being headed by the Eastnor choir, chanting antiphonally as they went.' Again, the reporter gives a good description, and this can be supplemented by the order of service preserved in the Trustees' minute book:

> The petition for the consecration having been read to the Bishop by the registrar at the entrance to the church, his Lordship signified his consent to the consecration, and the congregation having entered the church, the Litany was read by the incumbent, and the anthem, 'Man that is born of woman' was sung; after which they returned to the

churchyard, and went round it in procession, chanting antiphonally the 49th and 115th Psalms. Then the sentence of consecration was read by the Revd R. Sarjeant, pro-Chancellor, and signed by the Bishop. A hymn ['Earth looking on this hallowed ground'], a prayer, and a benediction, concluded the service.

From the burying-ground the whole party proceeded to the site of the new church,[1] where every preparation had been made for laying the first stone, and awnings erected in case of foul weather. Fortunately, although the morning had brought in a regular sou'wester, both in wind and rain, it cleared up, and a tolerably bright day resulted. Prayers having been read by the incumbent, the Countess Beauchamp proceeded to lay the stone, by the instruction of the Architect. Underneath it was deposited a bottle, containing a copy of the Act by which the Authority for erecting the parish church was obtained. Her Ladyship performed the ceremony with a silver trowel, on which was the inscription: 'Presented to the Countess Beauchamp on the occasion of her laying the foundation stone of the Beauchamp almshouses and parish church of Newland, Worcestershire, by Oliver Estcourt, the contractor for the works. Oct. 22 1862.'

The reporter concluded rather acidly that after the conclusion of the service,

A selected party (from which newspaper reporters were excluded) went to the Board Room . . . where Mr Hambler of this city had laid out an excellent luncheon. Some good speeches, as we are informed, were made by the Bishop, Sir John Pakington and others, but these we were not allowed to have the means of recording.

---

[1] Psalm 84 was sung as the party proceeded from the churchyard. After the initial prayers there was a lesson from 1 Corinthians 3:9–15, then another hymn, 'O Lord of hosts, whose glory fills.' After the laying of the foundation stone, Psalm 87 was sung, more prayers were said, and Psalms 112 and 150 sung in recession.

On 25 November Skinner engaged the Trustees—or rather Frederick—in his second battle. In the original design of the church the pillars separating the chancel from the aisle were to be of marble but, when economies had to be made, it was proposed that Bath stone be substituted and also that deal be used in place of oak in the chancel. Skinner now wrote passionately to Frederick,

> I beg . . . to be allowed to point out that the Parish Church of Newland ought not to be lost sight of in the Chapel of the Beauchamp Almshouses. I suppose that the intended substitution of deal fittings in the chancel for the more 'decent' oak, and the plain Bath stone columns for shafts of various marbles is a necessity laid upon the Trustees by order of the Court. I exceedingly regret that economy should show itself in this direction, for it is hardly possible to exaggerate the appearance of poverty and meanness which it will impose upon that part of the church which ought to stand out from the other parts with the mark of beauty and magnificence upon it. But if the Trustees can do no more than they propose to do, I beg to put in a plea in my own name and the name of the parish against them doing what they propose . . . I ask the Trustees to allow me to put forward my insuperable objection as Incumbent of the Parish to have the chancel of my Parish Church furnished with deal, and the columns of its arches without constructional distinction.

Skinner's letter does not seem to have reached the Trustees, but at a Trustees' meeting on 28 August 1863 the committee referred to a letter from Hardwick in which he 'strongly urged that the ornamental character of the church would be much more enhanced if marble pillars were substituted for Bath stone to support the arches between the chancel and the aisle.' The committee reported that they had replied that they were 'unwilling to resist the urgent appeal of Mr Hardwick' and had sanctioned the outlay of £205. They were fully satisfied that the beautiful result will amply justify the expenditure.' One supposes that Skinner had nobbled Hardwick and thus secured his objective. The matter of the deal fittings was passed over for the moment, though it was understood that they were only temporary and would be replaced with oak when funds permitted.

Hardwick was also concerned about the effect of economies on the almshouses, and on 27 November 1862 he wrote to Frederick, 'I am a little anxious about [the bricks] for the chimneys, on which so much of the effect of the building—cut down as it is in ornament—will depend. It is very important that they should be of a good colour.' The elaborate chimneys are indeed a delightful feature of the buildings, and it is good that they were not sacrificed on the altar of economy. His letter also reported concern by Skinner about the warden's house, which was to prove another bone of contention. In the design of this, again in the interests of economy, the bedrooms had been placed partly in the roof-space, and there was to be no layer of felt under the tiles. Similarly, there was no provision for a bathroom—which is not surprising as in the 1860s most bathing took place in a hip-bath or bath-pan before the bedroom fire. But Skinner was not happy and complained to Hardwick who reported to Frederick,

> Mr Skinner has written to me once or twice lately on the subject of a bath for his house, the lack of which he seems to feel very much. He wrote with what appears to me an unnecessary degree of irritation about the bath, and from the tone of his letter one would rather suppose that I was the person who prevented his house being larger and provided with a bath and other matters. I really am only desirous that his house should be as comfortable as possible, but I cannot do more than was authorised by the Trustees.

On 29 November the committee reported that Hardwick had stated that he usually included felt, but that with tiles as thick as those used here he had considered this unnecessary. Felt would, however, 'form an additional security for the bedrooms' and the extra cost would be £110 while the cost of installing a bath would be £93. The Trustees considered this report, and Frederick's proposal that the extra expenditure be not approved was carried unanimously.

This provoked a vigorous response from Skinner who wrote to Frederick on 6 December,

> Mr Hardwick informed me that the Trustees have declined to apply to the Court for the cost of lining the roof of my house over the bedrooms with felt. I must ask you to excuse my saying how exceedingly I regret this determination on the part of the Trustees, and how much I wish they would reconsider it. I hardly think that, possessing ample funds for providing everything necessary, a good and reasonable cause can be given for condemning the Chaplain and his family to live in the roof of a house which is not even to be protected from the extremes of heat and cold. I am sure you will bear witness that, in providing a new residence for the Chaplain whom, I suppose, it is desirable to retain, there is every reason why his health and safety should as far as possible be secured.

Frederick replied on 15 December that the Trustees did not feel able to sanction additional outlay on his house, and that its cost had already exceeded that of an ordinary parsonage. Skinner ignored this last point, and replied the next day with a long and vehement letter, stating among other things,

> When my medical adviser sanctioned my acceptance of a house in Worcestershire, he laid great stress upon the absolute necessity of my house being dry, airy, and inaccessible to extreme variations of heat and cold. I earnestly hope that the absence of a felt lining may ultimately prove of as little consequence as you think it; but if it should be otherwise, there will probably be some regret that my proposition was so positively rejected.

If these letters ever reached the Trustees, they appear to have remained unmoved for the minutes contain no mention of a change of heart. But Skinner's attitude here is interesting. He mentioned more than once that Newland was a poor living, and that with a further £200 from the Trustees his annual stipend still amounted to only £260 (this would equate to around £12,000 today, which is less than half the stipend of a parish priest). On the other hand, despite his many generous benefactions to the church and the frequent sojourns abroad which we shall notice later, he was still able to leave on his death £7,431, the equivalent of £359,000 today. It seems that he was happy—and able—to spend money where he thought this right, but that he was not happy to spend it on things which he thought should be provided by others, not least by the Trustees.

It was on 29 November again that the committee reported that Catherine Lady Beauchamp had offered to fill the east window of the church with stained glass at her own expense as a thankoffering to God for her husband, and also that Skinner was prepared 'to undertake the expense of a fit and becoming reredos on behalf of certain who wish to have the privilege of setting it up.'[2]

On 8 April 1863 the Trustees met for the first time in the new boardroom at the almshouses, but soon after Skinner picked up his acid pen once again. He had apparently not been consulted in all the stages of the designing of the east window, which was to be made by the well-known firm of Hardman to a design by their Mr Powell. On 3 May he wrote to Frederick,

> I must say how sorry I am that the original design has not been carried out, and will also venture to urge my most earnest hopes that Lady Beauchamp will not insist upon so much heraldic development in juxtaposition with so utterly unearthly a subject as the Court of Heaven. I cannot trust myself to find words in which to express the incongruity, as it presents itself to my mind, between the Holy Angels worshipping the Majesty of God and the 'Hemp-Crusher' [or bray,

---

[2] The brass on the north wall of the sanctuary states that 'the sculpture round this holy altar' was given by the Hon. Charles Grantham Scott and Frances, his wife, in memory of their uncle, the founder, and his first wife, Charlotte, who was also their aunt, but it seems strange that they should have used Skinner as an intermediary.

the crest of the Brayes, Lady Beauchamp's family] and the Bear and Ragged Staff [crest of the Beauchamp's] surmounted respectively by the Braye and Beauchamp shields. Surely the geometrical tracery over such an unspeakably sacred picture as Our Lord in Majesty should be filled with Angels' faces, and every token of the Earth should be avoided there . . . The board-room and its windows is a field for heraldry to run riot in, but do let us keep the Church of God for the things of Heaven.

Frederick showed this letter to Lady Beauchamp, and on 14 November she told him that she would put Skinner's objections to Powell. A week later she wrote that Powell agrees with some of the suggestions in Mr Skinner's letter, but not with all, and he will write his opinions to me when he has considered the various points fully. The border round the three lights will be replaced as suggested by Mr Skinner, and he will remove the poor Bear and Hemp-Breaker from the tracery. Mr Powell seems keen that Mr Skinner should be pleased like myself.'

In the event, Skinner seems to have been satisfied, though still not wholly pleased, and years later he wrote, 'The insertion of the medallion of the founder [the third Earl] with his patron saint (St John) on his right, and that of the donor (St Katharine) on his left, is quite according to conventional propriety, though their *absolute* fitness, in such a place may be doubted.' But these, though prominent, are not the main features of the window, which is dominated by the figure of Christ in majesty in the centre with twenty-four elders on both sides and figures of angels above it.

Meanwhile, although no bells had been contemplated in 1862, on 23 May 1863 G. Mears of the Whitechapel Foundry submitted estimates for the supplying and hanging of (a) five bells and (b) three bells. In the event he was asked to supply only one bell, which he duly did in 1864, but Estcourt's bill includes an item of £10 'for rehanging old bell'; this was a pre-reformation (*c.*1370?) one inscribed 'Sci Thessiliay' and taken from the old church which may have acquired it from the previous parish church of St Thomas.

The Trustees met again on 28 August. The committee reported that the Court of Chancery had accepted most of their proposed amendments to the scheme. The amended scheme allowed the Trustees to meet annually instead of half-yearly, and to 'pay such share of the expenses of performing Divine Service in the Church of Newland as they shall think fit.' The title 'chaplain' was changed to 'warden', and 'almspeople' became 'pensioners.' The Trustees were given discretion to deal with each application on its merits, without regard to the relative numbers of each sex or to the proportion of married people.

Married pensioners were now to receive 10s. a week and single ones 7s. 6d. but the allowance to former employers could be augmented up to 15s. Notice of vacancies was also to be given at Powick, and strangely the notice at Newland was omitted. The prohibition of trade was qualified by the addition of 'without the permission of the Warden', and a new sentence stated that 'Each, according to his or her ability, shall be ready to employ themselves usefully according to the Rules and Regulations of the Almshouses.' Whit Sunday was added to the days when the warden was required to celebrate Holy Communion, and the limit of £30 to the remuneration of the medical practitioner was removed.

On the practical side an agreement with the Malvern Link Gas Company for the supply of gas was suggested, as was an insurance policy on the buildings for £5,000 at an annual premium of £16. 9s. 8d. The committee also recommended the provision of an organ for the church and reported that Nicholson of Worcester, 'an excellent organ builder', had produced an estimate of £175 for a suitable instrument, capable of later enlargements. They further reported that George Ure Skinner, the warden's brother (a noted traveller and botanist, and now a widower), had asked to be allowed to defray the cost of £70 for a 'window communicating from the Matron's house with the church, to enable sick persons to attend

Divine Service.'[3] This is the church's Oriel window.

As to the election of the first pensioners, the committee recommended advertising initially for six 'employers of labour', married or single, and six agricultural labourers, married or single. Preference would be given to inhabitants of Newland, Madresfield and Powick. The filling of the remaining places would be suspended until it was seen how best to adjust the proportions of classes and married states, but in the meantime steps should be taken to engage a porter and matron, while Skinner should be paid the full stipend of £200 from midsummer. In the event, the Trustees decided to advertise for eighteen places at this stage, and agreed that the badge of the almshouses should be a Swan, one of Lord Beauchamp's Supporters.

But the most radical feature of the committee's report was their statement that 'It would be very desirable for the Charity to use some of the surplus income in the maintenance of a small Choir School "upon the industrial system",' and that,

> Eight or ten children of the agricultural class should be boarded and educated by the Charity. The musical education would be undertaken by the Clerk, who would also exercise a general superintendence over their conduct, and to whom they would be apprenticed. He would also provide a Pupil Teacher to instruct the boys in reading, writing and arithmetic and the rudiments of a solid and useful education. The boys would learn gardening under the Porter.

Such a school, they suggested, 'would not only contribute to the stately character of the Foundation and increase the beauty of the services in the church, but become a valuable and truly charitable

---

[3] There was formerly an inscription inside the window, i.e. looking into the church, 'In Honorem Dei et in Consolationem Infirmorum fieri curavit corporis sui sani memor atquque gratissimus G.U.S.' (To the honour of God and the comfort of the sick G.U.S. had this work done, mindful of his own healthy body and most thankful for it). Hobhouse's article describes this window as connecting 'the infirmary with the church in the manner of Philip II's bedroom at the Escorial'.

addition to the institution.' The total cost of maintaining it, including books and clothes for eight boys, was estimated at £231. 10s. 0d. p.a. The warden had offered to contribute £40 p.a. from the collections in the church, and it was thought that some parents might be willing to pay a premium for such an education for their sons. The Trustees approved the establishing of the school, provided that its annual cost to the charity did not exceed £200, and that the Court of Chancery approved; they agreed to spend £145 on alterations to the fuel-house, bake-house and laundry in order to accommodate the school.

It is an indication of the energy and authority of the standing committee that this proposal for the establishment of a choir school, with all the details worked out, should have been adopted so promptly and unquestioningly. But the Trustees' minutes record only committee reports, legal and commercial transactions, and resolutions of the full body, and there is rarely any mention of discussion or dissent, though these must surely have occurred. It would also be fascinating to know who the prime mover behind the proposal was.

Choir schools were much loved by Tractarians[4] since they enabled more stately worship. Skinner would have been aware that there had been a short-lived choir school at St Barnabas Pimlico just before his arrival there,[5] and he would have been further aware of the choir school only twenty miles away of St Michael's, Tenbury. Skinner very much wanted his own choir school at Newland, while Frederick may have hoped (vainly) that the establishment of such a school would soften Skinner's opposition to the merging of the village schools at Newland and Madresfield.

The first residential building to be completed was the warden's lodge,[6] and Skinner and his family were able to occupy this in

---

[4] *Tractarian Choir Schools* by Colin R. Brownlee, now a Beauchamp resident.

[5] David Bland, Ouseley and his Angels. I am indebted to Colin R. Brownlee here as for many subsequent references to the Newland choir school. Ouseley resigned from St Barnabas in November 1850 and took the choristers to Langley Marsh in Buckinghamshire. Skinner began his ministry at St Barnabas on Lady Day, 1851.

[6] According to one of Hardwick's drawings in the Madresfield archives, the

[*See opposite page for n.6 cont.*]

November 1863.[7] With a preface dated Christmastide that year, and, he later claimed, at the request of Frederick and at a cost to himself of £300, he now published *The Daily Service Hymnal*.[8] He had probably been working on this ever since his appointment. *Hymns Ancient and Modern,* a tractarian book, had been published recently, but he did not regard this or any other current compilation as definitive and explained 'That the necessities of my own parish and collegiate institution of poor, with daily and constant Services, require some immediate provision which I cannot find ready to my hand.' [9] He further stressed that 'There is no place for private and subjective Hymns in the public worship of the Church', and such hymns were avoided at Newland for many years. Meanwhile, at this stage the association of words and tunes was not as 'fixed' as it often became later, and books of words and books of tunes could be published quite separately. *The Daily Service Hymnal* contained only words and, in view of the likely establishment of a choir school, this is surprising. Being the man he was, Skinner would certainly have made diligent provision for the music but we have no details of this.

On 15 January 1864 the committee was hoping that the rest of

---

ground floor of the Warden's Lodge comprised: drawing room, dining room, study, schoolroom, pantry, back kitchen/scullery, front kitchen/servants' sitting room, brew(?) and wash house, larder, fuel store, and three WCs. The first floor comprised nine bedrooms (two designated 'guests'), servant bedroom with no fireplace, one WC. There was also a cellar, but no bathroom. Adjacent to it was a coach house comprising harness room and stable on the ground floor, and loft, living room and bedroom on the first floor.

[7] His family at this stage consisted of himself, his wife, their daughter, Agnes, his brother George, George's two young daughters and some servants.

[8] Julian's *Dictionary of Hymnology,* second edition, 1908, p.340, states that a 'revised small-type edition' was published in 1864 'with an article explanatory of Commemoration Days, and introits and anthems'. For other references in Julian to Skinner, cf. pp.39, 448, 793, 872 and 1084. Like many works of this period the *Daily Service Hymnal* has now been scanned and reprinted; this, though not in small-type, seems from the preface to be the first edition, but it contains the items ascribed by Julian to the revised edition. One wonders whether Julian was confused.

[9] *Daily Service Hymnal,* prefatory notice, p.iv.

the buildings would be fit for occupation by the end of March, and it reported that many applications had been received. The Trustees directed them to fix a date for the consecration of the church and the dedication of the almshouses, and to appoint a porter, matron and medical officer. They also resolved that the motto of the charity should be that of the Lygon family, 'Fortuna mea in Bello Campo' (My lot is cast in a fair ground).

On 31 March the committee reported that the Master of the Rolls had approved the scheme for the choir school, and the scheme was now further amended by the addition of eleven new clauses, beginning:

> The Trustees shall establish and maintain on the premises a School of Industry for ten or more children, orphans of parents who may have been employed in Agriculture. These children (hereinafter called Foundation Boys) shall reside on the premises, and be boarded, clothed and maintained by the Trustees free of charge.

They were to be admitted at an age of not less than eight, and were not to remain on the foundation after they had reached sixteen. Children or descendants of pensioners, if living with them, were entitled to receive free instruction in the school, and 'The Trustees may also admit other children as day scholars in the School at a head-money of not less than sixpence, or more than eighteen pence a week.'

A schoolmaster was appointed at a salary not exceeding £60 a year or, if the master was the clerk, £40 in addition to his clerk's salary. An assistant teacher could be employed if the Trustees deemed it necessary at a salary not exceeding £40 a year. Such an assistant should be appointed by the master with the consent of the Trustees, and the master should be responsible to the Trustees for his conduct and efficiency. Instruction was to be provided in the principles of the Christian religion, reading, writing, arithmetic, English grammar, history, geography and other things that the Trustees thought expedient 'so as to give the boys a sound moral, religious, and useful education.'

The boys were to assist in the gardening, and the foundation boys were also to be taught vocal music and should 'assist as Choristers in the celebration of Divine Service at Newland Church, as the Warden shall from time to time direct.' The last clause stated that 'Subject to the preceding Rules, and to a general control on the part of the Trustees, the government and regulation of the School shall be vested in the Warden.'

It was also at this March meeting that the committee presented samples of the pensioners' uniform to be worn for ceremonial occasions and services: for the women, a blue duffle coat and black silk bonnet; for the men, a gown of blue cloth of the same colour as the women's coats, with a silver badge with the Beauchamp crest on the left shoulder. There was no mention of staffs at this stage. A letter was read from the warden, recommending as matron 'a Miss [Barbara] Fleetwood, a *Lady* by birth and education, and one accustomed, more or less, to the kind of work. She is of "a certain age", and would, I think, cooperate with me in organising the Establishment and imparting to it a good Church tone.'

The date for the opening of the almshouses and the consecration of the church was fixed for 9 June. The election of the first eighteen pensioners was arranged for 24 May. Advertisements were approved for applications from *bona fide* members of the Church of England, specimen application forms were agreed, to be countersigned by the incumbent of the applicant's parish, and candidates were informed that 'Those elected must produce their baptism certificate, and married couples must show their marriage certificate.'

The standing committee was authorised to proceed further with the scheme for a choir school, and again an advertisement was approved with appropriate information prior to elections on 24 May. The committee was also to proceed with the appointment of a porter, matron and medical officer.

In May the first twenty-nine pensioners were elected:

Thomas and Jane Barker, 7*s*. 6*d*., St John's, aged ? and seventy-eight.

Francis and Mary Barnes, 10*s.*, Madresfield, aged seventy-five and seventy-six.

John and Sarah Batchelor; 10*s.;* Newland; both aged seventy-four.

James and Sarah Biscoe; 12*s.* 6*d.*; Eldersfield; aged seventy-two and eighty-one.

Anne Boulton; widow; 12*s.* 6*d.*; Forthampton; aged seventy-nine.

Elizabeth Bruton; 7*s.* 6*d.*; Madresfield; aged seventy-five.

William and Sarah Cooper; 12*s.* 6*d.*; Crowle; aged seventy-four and fifty-nine.

James and Maria Drinkwater; 10*s.*; Newland; aged seventy-eight and sixty-eight.

Thomas Fowler; widower; 7*s.* 6*d.*; Powick; aged eighty.

William and Dorothy Griffiths; 12*s.* 6*d.*; Claines; aged ? and seventy-two.

William and Jane Heaven; 12*s.* 6*d.*; Bromsberrow; aged seventy-two and seventy-one.

Margaret Howells; 7*s.* 6*d.*; Leigh; aged eighty-six.

Sarah Jones; widow; 7*s.* 6*d.*; Claines; aged sixty-three.

Samuel and Elizabeth Kings; 10*s.*; Powick; aged fifty-eight and fifty-seven.

Michael and Mary Stallard; 10*s.*; Powick; aged seventy-seven and seventy-five.

James and Catherine Stokes; 10*s.*; Great Malvern; both aged seventy-nine.

Isabella Walker; spinster; 12*s.* 6*d.*; Cheltenham; aged seventy-eight.

James Williams; widower; 7*s.* 6*d.*; Newland; aged seventy-five.

There were thus ten employers (four married couples, one widow and one spinster) from Bromsberrow, Cheltenham, Claines, Crowle, Eldersfield and Forthhampton, and nineteen employed (four married couples, two single men and three single women) from Claines, Great Malvern, Leigh, Madresfield, Newland, Powick and St John's. Their ages ranged from fifty-seven to eighty-six, the average being seventy-three to seventy-four. A form of service for their admission and clothing was devised by Skinner, and many of them were already in residence when the almshouses were officially opened. We should note, though, that the use of the term 'pensioner' varied; sometimes it referred to all the inmates, while at other times it did not include the wives of those who had been elected. On this latter reckoning there would have been eighteen pensioners and eleven wives. But when a pensioner (in the strict sense) died, it became normal either to elect the widow as a pensioner in her own right or at least allow her to remain in her flat.

Also in 1864, eight foundation boys were elected to the choir school:

William New; aged twelve.
Charles Hill; aged twelve.
John Howse; aged twelve.
Herbert Vaile; aged eleven.
William Arkell, aged eleven.
John Barnes; aged ten.
Alfred Tansley; aged nine.
William Stuart; aged eight (probationer).

Chapter Five
Consecration and Dedication

By summer 1864 all was ready, and the staff consisted of Skinner, the vicar-warden; Miss Fleetwood, the matron; Edgcumbe, the schoolmaster (who was also organist and clerk) and a porter, possibly William Moulden. Because of the illness of the (fifth) Earl, the consecration of the church and the dedication of the almshouses had to be postponed to 21 July, the last service in the old church being on 17 July.

The weather throughout the day was 'delightful; light clouds shadowing the sun, and refreshing breeze prevailing throughout', and the reporter from the *Worcester Herald* opened his account with a lyrical description of the setting:

> Hard by the little ancient church of Newland—which every antiquary will hear with extreme sorrow is to be destroyed, and for no valid reason whatever—is the charming site (about eight acres) of the new foundation, which forms three sides of a quadrangle, the fourth being open to the south, commanding a near view of the Malvern range. A large garden occupies the open space of the quadrangle,

surrounded by terrace walls. With the cold winds thus excluded, and the still chillier blasts of poverty, with a noble landscape in front, the abodes of comfort all around, the house of God, with its spire directing the mind to heaven, and the manse where spiritual advice and consolation may be obtained in the hour of need—all this in one little charmed circle, close at hand—forms in the imagination a retreat so paradisical that in a temporary fit of envy one almost regrets the fact of not being a 'distressed agriculturalist' with a nomination to so delightful a sinecure.

He then explained the general layout of the almshouses, the church, the 'covered wooden cloister (temporary, but hereafter to be of stone and brick)', the chaplain's residence and the 'large and handsome board-room.'[1]

The reporter next turned his attention to the church. Unfortunately he did not mention a large number of heads—some of them crowned—carved at various points on the exterior and believed to represent royal and other saints. At a distance these seem too homogeneous to be of particular people, but recent photographs reveal a greater individuality though as yet their identification remains a mystery.[2] At some points the general description simply records the fulfilment of what had been envisaged a couple of years before, though it also makes a distinction between the permanent and the temporary as where 'the present seats in the chancel are only temporary, and oak stalls will be provided; for the nave chairs.' But it is particularly helpful in its listing of the makers and suppliers of various fittings and furniture. Thus the organ was by Nicholson. The columns to the arcade dividing the chancel aisle from the chancel were 'of fine pieces of Pyrenees marble, polished; the bases, bands, and caps, are boldly

---

[1] Hobbhouse writes of 'its hammer beam timber roof, its founder's portrait framed in Gothic leaf tracery, and its fireplace complete with encaustic tiles decorated with the Beauchamp arms.'

[2] No reference to them has been traced either in Hardwick's drawings or the Beauchamp archives.

carved alabaster'; these latter contrasted very beautifully with the marble which had been presented by G. Skinner who brought it from Italy. The north and east walls were lined with 'bands of Mansfield stone, alabaster, and different coloured marbles' and the marble work was by Mr White, of Vauxhall-road Westminster. The nave, 49 feet, 6 inches long, by 24 feet wide, was roofed with open timbers, and the cornices and brackets supporting these were carved by Mr Purdy of Gloucester.

There was 'a splendid stone reredos, representing the crucifixion, by Boulton the figures being in high relief.' The decoration of this was by Clayton and Bell, and it was sculptured in Caen stone with, on the left, the beloved disciple, the Blessed Virgin Mary, Mary the mother of James and another woman. And, on the right, Mary Magdalene kneeling, Joseph of Arimathea, the converted centurion and his attendant. On either side were emblems of the passion. The reporter continued,

> Lady Beauchamp gave the east window, in memory of her husband, the noble founder; it is by Hardman, and in its three lights and geometrical tracery is represented Christ in Glory, adored by Thrones, Principalities, and Powers, the angelic host playing on instruments of music, and at the base of the window the Beauchamp arms. In the north wall of the chancel are two windows by Clayton and Bell, presented by members of the Skinner family, whose initials are given as MRS, MED, KES, ARS; and Saints Simeon, Elizabeth, Mary, etc., are depicted, bearing scriptural sentences.

Skinner later explained that,

> The Chancel Windows (in couplets) represent those four typical conditions of life which God blessed, through the Incarnation of His Son (as represented by St Ambrose), in the persons of Ss Simeon, Anna, Elizabeth and the Blessed Mary—the man, the widow, the wife and the virgin—all of whom were rewarded in their faithful

waiting upon the first coming of Christ. The design is to teach the aged Pensioners of the Charity that the old men, and widows, and wives and virgins, for whose benefit it exists—if they shall wait, in a like spirit, in this temple, for the second coming of our Lord, shall, in like manner, yea in a higher manner, be crowned by blessing.'[3]

Other windows were considered next, along with further features of the chancel and nave,

> Cathedral glass of very agreeable tints fills the nave windows, and at the top of the west wall is a wheel window. Beneath this window, and close to the SW angle of the building, is a large projecting oriel or bay window, opening into the church from the sick ward of the establishment, and which is so arranged that the patients can hear the service in the church without the fatigue of going there. This oriel is supported by a marble shelf on handsome brackets, and around the base of the window are represented the acts of mercy, Christ healing the sick, etc.
>
> The chancel arch is supported by marble shafts, sinking into the wall, and on the western face of the stone screen diving the chancel from the nave are sunk panels, with incised figures of Temperance, Fortitude, Justice, and Prudence, and the screen is enriched with beautiful specimens of California and Belgium marble. The ancient font (circular and cylindrical) from the old church has been placed on a new base of steps at the west end. The fitting-up, accessories, and furniture, are gorgeous: there is a brilliant brass lectern, splendid altar railing, two lofty brass stands for candles on each side of the altar,[4]

---

[3] *Newland Parish Church and the Beauchamp Charity.* The reference to St Ambrose here is puzzling. It could be that Ambrose had referred to these four typical conditions of life in one of his writings on the incarnation. On the other hand it is almost certain that there were originally frescoes on the jambs of the windows, and these could have been based on Ambrose or on the incarnational passages in the 'Te Deum' which was at one time attributed to him.

[4] These stands were converted in the late 1920s by the removal of the twelve-branch

[See p.58 for n.4 cont.]

two beautiful candlesticks on the altar itself,[5] with two immense nosegays placed between them. The church is heated with hot water. Both chancel and nave have been covered with beautiful encaustic tiles, by Mr Godwin, of Lugwardine; and, with the marble, alabaster, stained-glass windows, brass-work, and fine carving, which meet the eye in all directions, the effect is exceedingly rich. The only item to which we have any objection is the spire, which is crocketted to such an extent on the angles and canopies as to destroy its outline.

The altar itself would have been covered, so the reporter would not have known that it was of oak, with an altar-slab of Sicilian marble. Similarly he might not have seen the detail of the faldstool which in the earliest-known photograph was also covered; this was the gift of a penitent and richly carved in oak by Forsyth; the northern panel represents Mary Magdalen at the feet of Jesus and the southern the post-resurrection words 'Noli me tangere'. The top panel contains an ebony cross with the instruments of the Passion in the interstices. Another original feature he would not have seen was the richly carved oak frontal chest which was first located in the sacristy area but is now in the cloister. The bier in the cloister may also have been an original feature.

The writer next turned his attention to the almshouses and, while there is some repetition here, his account is worth quoting in full,

> The principal entrance to the buildings is from the north, fronting the Worcester road. It is by a lofty arched gateway. A porter's lodge opens into the gateway, and within the quadrangle on the east side between the gateway and the church there are the matron's apartments, with

---

candle corona which surmounted each stand into the pair of floor standards which you see today on the steps of the high altar. The pair of candle coronas have been found and are undergoing restoration.

[5] Skinner states that 'some of the altar vessels, the candlesticks, the flower vases, and the twelve-light candelabra (by Hart, of Wych Street, London)' were given by another member of his family, C. B. Skinner of Ipswich.

dispensary attached. West from the gateway are the almshouses. The rooms for the single men are in the south wing, for the single women in the north wing, and for families in the west. The rooms for families or married couples are similar in plan to the other, with the exception of being a little larger. The entrance hall is open from the quadrangle, with side doors to the basement set of rooms. And a staircase leading to those above. There is one entrance, porch, and yard, for each group of four residences, also a work-shop, bakehouse, and wash-house in common. Infirm inmates will live down stairs, and the hale ones in the upper story. Provision is made for comfortably supporting sixteen single persons and eight married ones, and of these latter it is stipulated in the will that the wife must not be under fifty years of age, the age of the husband being fifty-five. For each occupant there are a sitting-room, bedroom, and kitchen, those rooms for the married being made rather larger. The sitting-room is fitted up with a central table, an easy or arm-chair,[6] and other necessary furniture. Each window is fitted with maroon-coloured cloth curtains. The bedroom contains an iron bedstead, with all requirements, a chest of drawers, wash-stand with a towel-rail combined, beside carpets and window curtains.

The residence for the porter consists of three rooms, but somewhat larger than those provided for the pensioners, is fitted up with similar articles of furniture, only of superior workmanship. The apartments for the clerk consist of three bed-rooms and two sitting-rooms, with a larger kitchen, and all necessary apparatus, and the quality of his furniture is superior to that of the porter. The rooms for the matron are four in number, three bed-rooms and one sitting-room. Provision is made for eight boys (choristers), for whose accommodation there is a dormitory, with a separate bed for each boy. They have a clothes-box, which answers for a book-stand as well. The apartments for the master are fitted up with all necessary articles, and the window of his

---

[6] In 1995 Mrs Rowberry claimed that the twelve wooden chairs then (and now) in the library 'were given to the first people who came to live here'.

bed-room overlooks the dormitory, so that he has the boys under his eye. A portion of his bed-room is arranged as a study, and the sitting-room he occupies is that belonging to the clerk. The school-room is a fine airy place, admirably adapted for its purpose. The whole of the apartments are lit with gas, supplied by the Link Company, and the articles of furniture have been supplied by Mr C. Fildes, cabinet maker, of this city.

Nearly a century later, Hunt recorded that 'The water for the community is drawn from its own well, the power provided by a donkey', and that was doubtless the case from the beginning.

After paying tribute to Hardwick, and to Estcourt who had 'carried out the intention of the architect in excellent style', the reporter noted that 'the gas fittings, grates, bed-stead, &c were supplied by Mr Lingham, of this city.'

The reporter then gave an equally detailed description of the ceremonies, though again this can be supplemented by the copy of the order preserved in the Trustees' minute book. Sixty or so surpliced clergy and the choristers, headed by James Gurney, for many years clerk at the old church, carrying 'the splendid banner of the Charity, on which was emblazoned the Beauchamp crest and motto "Fortuna mea in bello campo",' formed up in the cloister and from there proceeded to the great gate to meet the bishop and his chaplains, singing Psalms 112 and 113. After prayer there, the procession moved round the east and south sides of the quadrangle singing Psalms 103 and 72. A halt was made in the middle of the south side for further prayers by the bishop, and they then moved round the west and north sides singing Psalms 115 and 111. Arriving again at the great gate, Skinner offered more prayer, a lesson (Matt. 25:31–41) was read and the 'Veni Creator' was sung. The bishop read further prayers, including one for the community specially composed by Skinner,

> Vouchsafe, O Lord, out of the fullness of thy gifts, to all who shall dwell here receiving Thy bounty, grace according to the need of each.

To the aged men and women grant contentment and peace, humility and thankfulness, and a true love for Thy House of Prayer and all the offices thereof.

Make the married to live together so that their prayers be not hindered; the single to rejoice before Thee in chastity and purity; and the widows to be 'widows indeed'.

Bless the children who shall be trained to minister here, that they may ever praise Thee with clean lips and pure hearts.

Grant instruction to the ignorant, perfect renewal to the sinful, and comfort to those who have sorrow.

Send down Thy Holy Spirit to dwell continually here, that all the inmates may live in unity and brotherly love, having compassion one of another, so an entrance may be ministered unto them abundantly into the everlasting Kingdom of our Lord and Saviour Jesus Christ, Who liveth and reigneth with Thee, O Father, and Thee, O Holy Ghost, one God for ever and ever, Amen.

The bishop then pronounced the formal act of dedication,

Forasmuch as it hath pleased Almighty God to allow this Charitable work, and to accept these Almshouses for the comfort of His poor, we hereby pronounce this House of Prayer and of Alms to have been in all things duly completed, and we declare the same to be for ever open: In the name of the Father, and of the Son and of the Holy Ghost.

Singing psalms 122 and 132, the procession then moved to the north door of the church where the registrar read the petition for consecration. The bishop signified his willingness to consecrate, and Psalm 24 was sung as the procession entered the church and the bishop proceeded to his seat in the chancel. There he received the Deed of Conveyance and laid it on the altar. He then gave an exhortation to the congregation and offered prayers. The chancellor of the diocese then read the Sentence of Consecration, which the bishop now signed.

The hymn 'Blessed City, heavenly Salem' followed, being sung 'with a rapidity', the reporter noted, 'which totally destroyed its fine effect.' After further prayers, there was a choral communion, with readings from Revelation 21:1–7 and Luke 19:1–11 and a sermon by the bishop on the Exodus 3:5, 'The place whereon thou standest is holy ground', of which the reporter gave a lengthy summary. There was a 'Special Offertory for the benefit of the Church mission in British Columbia', and 152 communicants. After the blessing, the procession moved out of the church into the cloister singing the 'Te Deum' and Psalm 150. Thereafter, 'A substantial luncheon was provided by the Trustees for the Bishops, clergy and visitors in the Board-room, while the lady visitors were entertained by Mrs Skinner at the Warden's Lodge.' The bill from the caterers, William Hopkins of Worcester, shows that sixty-three persons were supplied, at a cost including wine and travelling expenses, of 7s. per head.

Further planned festivities were cancelled because of the fifth Earl's illness, 'and there was little or no speech making for the same reason.' There was, however, evensong at 4 p.m. with a sermon by the Bishop of British Columbia, a friend of the warden, on behalf of missionary work in that country, where church workers had to contend with 'an alien spirit, blasphemy, hardness of heart, excitement, gambling, violence and recklessness' of which the bishop gave instances from his own experience. He also spoke of the 'Indians, or native savages of Vancouver and Columbia' describing their 'gross ignorance, cruelty and superstition—brutal, bloody and destructive.' After this harrowing recital a collection on behalf of the mission raised £50.

A short description of the day in the *Church Review* for 26 July concluded,

> The whole ceremony, which was necessarily lengthy, was conducted with great solemnity and beauty, and without a drawback. The musical services were under the direction of Mr Edgcumbe the organist and choirmaster: and, considering the very recent formation of the choir, and the short practice they had, were rendered with

wonderful accuracy and precision. The service in church was choral throughout.

This tribute to Edgcumbe was well-deserved. When he was appointed as clerk the establishment of a choir-school had not even been considered. To take on the further role of choirmaster, and in such a short time to train his 'rustic orphans' with no previous musical experience to cope with the elaborate and demanding programme of these services, was a very remarkable achievement.

As for the costs, the principal items in Estcourt's bill to the Trustees were:

Tender for church and tower	£4,610. 00s. 00d.
Marble columns etc.	£211. 00s. 00d.
Stone screen between nave and chancel	£90. 00s. 00d.
Repairs to old font, fitting desks, altar rail, table slab, etc.	£102. 12s. 00d.
Tile and marble floor to chancel and nave, instead of wood	£106. 17s. 07d.
Deal seats covered with cloth in chancel	£41. 03s. 07d.
Marble sink and window, and marble shelves in sacristy	£38. 00s. 00d.
Oak door and screens and closets and altering ditto for organ etc. (estimated in deal)	£84. 00s. 00d.
Screen to sacristy, oak door and stonework to same, oak closets, and fixing old oak ceiling (estimate in deal)	£105. 00s. 00
Oak vestment chest and ironwork to door	£31. 19s. 09d.
Fastening together the chairs in church, stool for organist	£3. 09s. 06d.
Taking four benches out of old church, altering and refixing[7] in new one	£5. 01s. 05d.
Rehanging old bell	£10. 00s. 00d.

---

[7] Where these were refixed, and for how long they were retained, is not clear.

The total amount of £16,319. 09s. 09d. comprised:
Church £5,010. 17s. 10d.
Almshouses £7,695. 06s. 09d.
Chaplain's House £3,613. 05s. 02d.

Chapter Six
The Pensioners and the Almshouses

On 20 September 1864 Skinner gave his first report to the Trustees. These reports always started with a general conspectus of the state of the community—numbers, absences (each pensioner was allowed to be absent, with permission, for up to thirty nights a year), illnesses, deaths, etc.—followed by a detailed description of individual cases of illness, hardship, indiscipline, etc. Administrative matters were discussed next—nursing arrangements, amount of pensions and so forth. Only after all these had been dealt with did he raise his more personal concerns.

There were currently twenty-nine pensioners and wives in residence. Of those elected in May Thomas Barker had died before coming into residence, and there had been one death subsequently—William Griffiths who had come to the community 'a hopeless cripple and in very destitute circumstances. Up to the hour when he lost consciousness he never ceased to thank God for the temporal and spiritual blessings which sweetened the last three months of his life in this place.' But the numbers had been maintained by the election of William Moulden and his wife Sarah (Moulden, provisionally appointed as porter, had been found 'unequal to the duties' and was now an ordinary pensioner). There were thus ten married couples, two single men and seven single women. Nineteen sets of rooms were occupied, and there were five vacant. The pensioners were comfortable in their quarters, but Skinner felt they should be provided with window-blinds, and that steps should be taken to prevent their fires from 'back-smoking.' He also recommended that a wheel-chair should be bought.

In general, conduct had been 'excellent' but there had been one case of misconduct,

> On the evening of Monday last, the 19 September, in the sight of the whole body of Pensioners returning from Evening Prayer, Thomas Fowler, who was only formally admitted on the fourteenth of this month, was brought into the Almshouses in a state of drunkenness. The publicity of the exhibition has added to the guilt of it, and the Warden has been compelled to magnify the importance of treating it seriously. He has suspended the Pensioner from all privileges, deprived him of his gown and badge and staff, and confined him to gates until the pleasure of the Trustees shall be declared. Thomas Fowler is a very old and feeble man, and the painful position in which he now stands is perhaps not incapable of explanation. A brother seems to have paid him a visit after many years of separation, and induced him to join him in 'a glass' at the Swan. Probably unaccustomed to such indulgences, he fell a victim to his own feebleness and his brother's mistaken kindness, and became drunk without any excess at all . . . The Warden has not thought it necessary hitherto to insist upon the pensioners wearing the dress of the Charity when they are outside the Gates, but he is now inclined to believe that the dress would not only protect feeble old men against the evil disposed, but that it would also sometimes support the sense of duty against themselves. And he would be glad to have the instructions of the Trustees upon this subject.

The Trustees resolved that Fowler 'be mulcted 5s. per week for four weeks and deprived of his Gown, Staff and Badge for the like period, that he be seriously warned by the Warden against any repetition of such misconduct.'

On 21 November, Founder's Day, the pensioners were entertained to dinner by the Trustees in the boardroom, and by this time seven more pensioners had been elected; one had been an employer, but the others had been employed as were almost all of those admitted subsequently.

On 10 January 1865 Skinner reported that the full complement of twenty-four pensioners was now in residence, that their conduct was 'in all respects satisfactory' and that the total number of residents was thirty-eight. Their average age was seventy-one, and only four were prevented by infirmity from attending church. He wrote warmly of the new pensioners who had 'brought with them a most excellent spirit which will be of the greatest use in moulding the permanent character of the Institution', and commented that even those who were crippled, blind or bedridden were 'not only perfectly happy and contented, but are grateful for the blessings they enjoy.' He also stressed the need for some domestic help for the infirm and requested the engagement of a 'handy and able-bodied women to scrub, clean and cook for the very helpless', this being beyond the abilities of the matron, 'she being a lady.' He also recommended that a record be kept not only of the pensioners but 'of all events which go to make the History of the Institution.' A book was duly purchased and, though it recorded names rather than events, it is an invaluable source for the period up to the end of the century, though sadly it was not used thereafter.

At the end of their meeting the Trustees visited the boardroom, as they did each year, and here 'the Officers, Pensioners and Foundation Boys in their respective distinctive dresses were assembled.' The chairman 'addressed a few observations and asked if any Officer or Pensioner had complaints to make touching the management of the Charity.' No complaints having been made, the Trustees then made a full inspection of the buildings.

In April the warden reported four deaths, including that of Ann Boulton who had been buried at Forthampton, her native village in Gloucestershire, by special request of her daughter; however, 'the funeral was attended by so many inconveniences and involved expenses so inconsistent with the circumstances of the deceased' that he 'had signified to all the Pensioners that for the future the interment of Pensioners will be restricted to Newland.' The Trustees confirmed the election of three new pensioners.

Skinner was also concerned about the position of the matron and reported that 'The Matron being a lady, and chosen because a lady was thought to be the fittest choice, fully and diligently discharges those duties which a lady may fairly be called upon to perform.' But since much of her work is 'not the kind which a lady ought to be asked to do', he suggested the employment of 'an able-bodied woman' to do the heavier domestic work and the cooking and cleaning for the sick.' The matron could give up £10 p.a. of her salary towards the cost of such assistance. This would give time for the Trustees to consider the advantages of ultimately employing 'two able and efficient nurses bound together by the ties of blood or grace.' The matron in an appended report detailed her duties as:

1. Visiting each pensioner every morning to see who is likely to require assistance.
2. Nursing sick pensioners through the day and sitting up at night (or paying others to do so)
3. Carrying out doctor's directions regarding medicines, dressings, etc.
4. Reporting to the warden on the state in which pensioners' quarters are kept.
5. Recording the pensioners' attendance at church, and supervising their twice-weekly cleaning of the church.

But the Trustees resolved that,

A person of the present Matron's rank of life is not the most suitable for the work which, according to her Report, devolves upon her; and though they are satisfied with her conduct in all that concerns herself they think that the duties should be entrusted to someone more easily approaching the standing of a nurse, with such assistance as she may require; they therefore propose to dispense with Miss Fleetwood's services from 1 August 1865.

Miss Fleetwood duly retired on 22 July, and in November Skinner reported to the Trustees that, empowered by the treasurer, he had entered into a 'temporary arrangement' with the community of St Margaret, East Grinstead, whereby a lady, accustomed to the work and devoted to it for the love of Christ, had given her nursing services to the charity. This sister has been helped by 'an able-bodied servant', and the arrangement had proved highly satisfactory.[1] This was good news, but there had been four more deaths and there was a lengthy report by the medical officer, Dr Archibald Weir, analysing the illnesses and causes of death of pensioners since the opening of the almshouses. He felt that a death rate of 20 per cent in a community where the average was 78.8 was not unacceptable. Nonetheless, the incidence of illness was higher than it should be, and he had had to make 177 visits. Inadequacies of diet were partly responsible, but 'the principal cause of illness is the small and badly-ventilated bedrooms.' The amount of fresh air available was far below the accepted standards for barracks and hospitals, and he urged the Trustees to take immediate action to remedy the situation. The Trustees asked the standing committee to look into this, but in January 1867 Dr Weir complained that nothing had been done to improve ventilation, and that there was more sickness than there should be; at this same meeting Skinner recommended the purchase of two portable beds for use when a very sick person needed an overnight attendant, also one

---

[1] From this point, 1865, until 1939 a small number of Religious Sisters—not always from St Margaret's—attended to the nursing side of the community.

or two Monks Patent Chamber Commodes for pensioners confined to their bedrooms.

Nothing had been said about a porter since Moulden had been found inadequate, though presumably someone had undertaken the duty, but in November 1865 the Trustees elected John White of Shelsley Beauchamp as porter and resolved that he 'be placed (except as to Stipend) on the footing of a Pensioner', that his stipend be 5s. per week, and that he be relieved of his duties as a gardener 'until such time as it shall appear how the experiment works.' In the following January, however, Skinner reported that within a fortnight of his appointment White, 'being extremely weak in body and mind', had taken fright at his responsibilities and, despite his entreaties, had left the community. He had subsequently apologised and had been allowed to return as an ordinary pensioner. Meanwhile, another pensioner, Robert Laurence, had discharged the duties very well, but Skinner now urged that,

> For a permanent appointment, it will be necessary to entrust them to a married man, without family, who is not too infirm for the many little active works which the Porter appears to be the proper person to undertake No single man can be expected to be always at home; and yet it is needful that the Gate should never be wholly left. And no very infirm man can be expected always to be equal to the tending of the Church fires and gas, the cleaning of windows of Almshouses and the like, requiring energy more or less; and yet, it is needful that these duties should be done.

He recommended that it would be well to advertise the post in order to enable a choice of persons. In 1867 Thomas Hurd applied for the post and, although there is no record of his appointment, it seems that his application was successful. He was certainly porter in 1871 and living with his wife in the porter's lodge. He continued as porter till 1882, so for the first time there was the permanence that Skinner desired.

The 1871 census[2] shows fifty-four residents in all: eleven in the Warden's Lodge, seven family and four servants; two in the Porter's Lodge; six in the Clerk's Lodge, five family and one servant; and thirty-five in the Almshouses. Unlike the community's own register, the census does not indicate the previous place of residence but it does give the place of birth:

James Skinner	Head	Marr.	52	Vicar of Newland	Forfarshire
Agnes Skinner	Wife	Marr.	50		Middleton Sudbury
Margaretta B. Skinner	Niece	Unm.	24	Annuitant	Barnes
Mary E. Skinner	Niece	Unm.	22	Annuitant	Chipperfield
Eliza Henderson	Ser.	Wid.	40	Domestic servant	Winchcombe
Miriam Glover	Ser.	Unm.	21	Domestic servant	Haughley
Henrietta B. Haines	Ser.	Unm.	15	Domestic servant	Healing
Joseph Caswell	Ser.	Unm.	14	Domestic Servant	Madresfield
Katharine Green	S-in-L	Wid.	49	Annuitant	Middleton Sudbury
Agatha G. H. Skinner	Niece		13	Scholar	London, Eaton Place
Mary B. Green	Niece		12	Scholar	Bury St Edmunds
Thomas Hurd	Head	Marr.	62	Porter	Colthampton
Elizabeth	Wife	Marr.	46	Hartey	
Ethelbert West	Head	Marr.	43	Clerk to the Trustees	Eltham
Elizabeth W. West	Wife	Marr.	42	Powick	
Marian E. West	Dau.		6	Scholar	Knaresborough
Louisa C. E. West	Dau.		5	Scholar	Somersetshire
Bertha G. West	Dau.		2		Newland
Jane Mackie	Ser.	Unm.	19	General servant	Saint Clements

Those in the Almshouses were described, unless stated otherwise, as 'Pensioner of the Beauchamp Charity' (abbreviated below to Pensioner):

---

[2] Public Record Office RG10/3055. Initials, personal names and place-names are often difficult to read, and there are almost certainly inaccuracies in the above list. Future censuses from 1881–1911, now in the public domain, are only summarised in the text, but the names of pensioners are listed in the appendix.

Ann Williams	Head	Wid.	55	Pensioner	Bishampton
John Holt	Head	Wid.	82	Pensioner	Cradley
Sarah Cooper	Head	Wid.	66	Pensioner	Dymock
Nancy Bayliss	Head	Unm.	76	Pensioner	Ledbury (deaf)
Louisa Walker	Head	Unm.	78	Pensioner	Shrawley
Sarah Jones	Head	Wid.	65	Pensioner	Martley
Elizabeth King	Head	Wid.	65	Pensioner	Nuneaton
Elizabeth King	G-dau.		11	Scholar	Madresfield
Francis Barnes	Head	Marr.	82	Pensioner	Didbrook
Mary Barnes	Wife	Marr.	81	Pensioner	Leigh
James Charles	Head	Marr.	71	Pensioner	Leigh
Ann Charles	Wife	Marr.	66	Pensioner	Norton
William Moulden	Head	Marr.	71	Pensioner	Spilsbury
Ann Moulden	Wife	Marr.	66	Pensioner	Bodenham
William Heaven	Head	Wid.	78	Pensioner	Featham
Elizabeth Bate	G-dau.		12	Scholar	Alvechurch
Richard Pritchard	Head	Marr.	73	Pensioner	Severn Stoke
Ellen Pritchard	Wife	Marr.	71	Pensioner	Wormsley (deaf)
Hannah Morris	G-dau.		11	Scholar	Becups
Elizabeth Adams	Head	Unm.	66	Pensioner	Cleveley
James Mason	Head	Marr.	64	Pensioner	Grimley
Mary Mason	Wife	Marr.	77	Pensioner	Worcester
William Shrites	Head	Marr.	82	Pensioner	Clifton
Betsy Searle	Nurse	Wid.	41	Nurse	St Clements
James Body	Head	Wid.	87	Pensioner	Bidisham
Sarah Cooper	Head	Wid.	64	Pensioner	Addingley
Elizabeth Caswell	Head	Wid.	71	Pensioner	Powick
Robert Laurence	Head	Mar.	80	Pensioner	Hawling
Sarah Laurence	Wife	Marr.	80	Pensioner	Hawling
Ruth Cook	Dau.		49	Seamstress	Martley
Ann Bowcott	Head	Wid.	68	Pensioner	Powick
Maria Drinkwater	Head	Wid.	75	Pensioner	Upton-upon-Severn
Elizabeth Judge	Head	Wid.	83	Pensioner	Leigh
Sister Maritas	Head	Unm.	36	Sisters of Charity	Whitwell
Rosey A Allisbone	Serv	Unm.	15	General Servant	Tamworth

Excluding the seven who were not pensioners, the age range varies from fifty-five to eighty-seven, which was much the same as when the first pensioners were elected. It is interesting that not a single pensioner had been born in Newland and only five had been born in the adjacent parishes of Leigh, Powick and Madresfield, though presumably many had worked on the Madresfield estate before coming to the almshouses. There were no longer any choir boys living *in situ*, but in three cases young children were living with their grandparents and in one case an adult daughter was living with her mother. In the formal charity scheme there was no provision for an adult daughter to be resident, and this would seem to be an early illustration of the generosity of interpretation which has been an on-going mark of the charity. But this generosity was not unlimited. Skinner later referred to the Trustees a case where two pensioners had been visited by their son whose health was such that he was unable to find any other accommodation and who had stayed with them so long that he was now more of an inmate than a visitor, but the Trustees felt that the accommodation provided was not sufficient to harbour further grown-up persons and that the son ought to be removed as soon as possible.

Meanwhile the Trustees were anxious to improve the environment of the almshouses, and in August 1868 Lord Beauchamp, as Frederick had now become, had referred among other things to the necessity for building a perimeter boundary wall, erecting a permanent cloister and completing the tower. In 1871 the iron gates opposite the Tower were bought—originally, it is said, for Madresfield Court—and it has been claimed they were 'part of the c18 Choir Gates of Cologne Cathedral.'[3] But no early source supports this attribution, and an inventory probably *c.*1877 states that they were 'formerly of St Mary's Church, Oxford.' R. L. P. Milburn, a distinguished scholar and at that time a resident in the community, may have had this in mind

---

[3] The earliest reference I have traced to Cologne is in Stroller, 'Worcestershire Villages IV', *Berrow's Journal*, *c.*1927.

when he stated in 1989 that the Earl 'topped them with a coat of arms bearing not the swan with its coronet, but the open book and three crowns of Oxford University' Further research at St Mary's Oxford has shown that the gates were not from there and almost certainly made for Keble College, Oxford.

In 1876 the Earl was authorised to obtain tenders for building the cloister according to Hardwick's designs, and to accept one provided that the cost did not exceed £900, and the cloister was duly completed in 1876. Above the entrance is the text, 'Blessed are those who dwell in your house, O Lord.'

In May 1872 Skinner was concerned that, in view of the nursing care needed by the infirm, more assistance should be provided for the sister who filled the post of matron. At present she had the help only of a young girl, and he felt that a more able-bodied woman was needed. The Trustees agreed that they would meet the costs of employing such a person. A Mrs Grogan was appointed, and for a time all was well but she resigned after a year and for a while a local woman, Mrs Batchelor, took her place. In January 1875 Skinner proposed a permanent replacement for Mrs Grogan, and recommended that Mrs Batchelor be confirmed in her post. Quite apart from 'abundance of work of a higher kind',

> There are three widower pensioners of the ages of 91, 84 and 84 respectively for whom everything dressing, cleaning, cooking had to be done. There is one married couple aged 87 and 86 for whom the same service is necessary. And there are four of the age of 85, 85, 80 and 74 for whom almost the whole of the more severe work of the house had to be discharged. Day by day at least eight beds have to be made; five grates to be cleaned, and fires to be lighted and breakfasts to be prepared before nine o'clock.

The Trustees resolved that Skinner take immediate steps to supply Mrs Grogan's place, and there was further discussion of the nursing arrangements in September 1875, but we have no record of the outcome.

More generally, in January 1873 Skinner reported that a robbery—the first to be recorded—had taken place at the clerk's house the previous October and that a considerable sum of money had been stolen, though there was no suggestion that anyone in the almshouses had been involved. In November 1874 he complained to the Trustees that the pensioner Widow Kings 'is not a fit inmate of the Almshouse . . . she is quite out of her mind, grows more and more crazy, and Dr Weir does not think that she will ever be any better. She has to be constantly watched, and wanders about in the night with a light. It is clear that something must be done to provide for such cases.'

The Trustees apparently ignored this plea, but in January 1875 Skinner reported that she had been removed to the County Asylum. He also reported that, while attendance at church was 'good and regular', there were one or two women whose attendance 'is by no means equal to their powers', and he thought that these 'might be brought to a sense of their duty if the Trustees would issue an order, that every absence from Church on Sundays and for more than a stated number of times in each week, without a medical certificate sent unto the Warden, or his permission gained, would entail a fine upon the pensioner.' The Trustees resolved that the warden be empowered to levy fines not exceeding 5 shillings per week for non-compliance with the rule regarding attendance at divine service.

To conclude on happier notes, three widower pensioners—James (or John) Williams in 1866, William Moulden in 1871 and Joseph Trapp in 1876—remarried in Skinner's time. None of their brides were fellow-pensioners but were presumably friends from their pre-pensioner lives. In each case the brides were allowed to join their husbands in the almshouses.

Chapter Seven
The Choir School and the Chancel
Questions of Authority

On the day of the consecration and opening seven orphan boys were formally admitted to the choir school, and an eighth as a probationer. Skinner reported in September 1864 that 'A very good Assistant Master, Mr John Harmer, has been secured to carry on the general work of the school.' But already he himself and Edgcumbe, the master, were not relating well, and he added presciently, 'In the interests of the School it will be well if the position of the Warden, the Master and the Assistant respectively shall be somewhat more accurately defined.' The present understanding seemed to be,

> That the Master of the School is to take no share in the work of the School; and yet to hold himself to possess authority for regulating the work done and the manner of doing it.
>
> The Assistant Master is to have the whole of the work of the School to do; and yet he is not allowed to have authority over the boys whom he instructs, or over the subjects in which they are to be instructed.
>
> The Warden is stated in the Scheme to be invested with the

'Government and Regulation of the School' and yet the 'Master' claims to exercise his office, both over the Assistant and the Boys, subject to no control but that of the Trustees.

He concluded that 'It does not appear to be possible to carry on any corporate work, but least of all an educational work, when the seat of the administrative power is not clearly ascertained and accepted', and that 'In the present case, the Warden's authority over the Foundation School is suspended; the Master's authority is not experimental and the Assistant Master's is nowhere.' He then asked the trustees to consider two suggestions,

> First, and generally, whether the administration of the affairs of the Charity as regards the Church, the Almshouses and the School had not best be committed to the Warden as the executive head of the institution, subject to the Body of Trustees. For indeed it seems difficult to say how the Charity shall be well and harmoniously governed while one of its officers claims to be beyond the Warden's control and to owe no allegiance but directly to the Trustees.
>
> Secondly, and specially, that the government and regulation of 'the School', which is said to be 'vested in the Warden' should mean, and really be, that the Warden has not only the power but the duty of defining and imposing the rules of instruction and discipline . . . And that the Mastership of a school of eight or ten boys should be in the hands of one who, through direct communication with the Warden and by his own personal labour shall apply those rules.

It was surely 'no great question' whether in so small a school a 'Master', who does not undertake to work the school, does not rather disturb the work of others, and obscure the view of authority and obedience which to the eyes of the boys should always be clear.

But the Trustees were not convinced, and they passed unanimously a resolution proposed by Frederick,

That the ordinary discipline and authority of the School is vested in the Master, the authority of the Warden being so grave as to require sparing exercise except in cases of serious inconvenience and mischief.

That it appears from the Scheme that any exercise of authority in the School by the Warden must pass through the hands of the Master, who is solely responsible for the conduct of his Assistant.

That the Trustees will always be glad to hear that the Warden and the Master have taken counsel together in the affairs of the School, and are unwilling to believe that necessity will arise for a more precise definition of their respective authority.

This was the first engagement in the long-running battle between the warden and the Trustees regarding the extent of his responsibility and authority. From the resolution quoted above it is clear that the Trustees were not prepared to grant the warden the over-riding authority over the school which he desired. From later developments it is equally clear that their optimistic hope that the warden and master should work harmoniously together was not fulfilled.

Meanwhile on 21 October Skinner wrote to Frederick,

Of course, if the Trustees have the power so to interpret the words of the Scheme as to deprive the words 'government and regulation' of their ordinary significance, and to declare that it is not my Office to 'regulate' as more commonly understood 'to regulate', I have not another word to say.

At a special meeting of the Trustees on 10 November Lord Lyttleton who was chairman on this occasion reopened the discussion. Edgcumbe was called in and examined by Lyttleton, Sir John Pakington and Frederick. A long discussion reached no conclusion, but Frederick wrote to Skinner on the same day, 'I cannot easily express the pain with which I read your letter this morning. Lord Lyttleton induced me greatly against my will to read it to the Trustees, and I now very much regret having done so.' On the other hand, on 19 November

Lyttleton wrote to Skinner (?), 'I need hardly say I agree with your view, but I cannot yet say exactly what course to adopt... You seem to have a copy of [the scheme] and no one else has but Lygon, and I am not sure that he will let me have it.' It seems extraordinary that a leading Trustee should not have a copy of the scheme and extraordinary again that Frederick might not let him see one, especially since the scheme expressly provided that a printed copy should be given to each Trustee.

On 26 December Skinner wrote to Frederick protesting against the restrictions on his exercising his authority in the school, and for the AGM on 10 January 1865 notice was given of a motion to be proposed by Lyttleton and seconded by Colonel Scott,

> That application be made to the Court of Chancery with a view to the revision of the clauses in the Scheme relating to the Choir School, in order to make them more entirely consistent with themselves than they now appear to be; to make more effectual the provision of the 62nd clause giving the Warden power of management and regulation over the School, and subordinating the Master of the School to the Warden, subject to an appeal to the Trustees.

This motion was duly discussed, but in the event was withdrawn. A report on the school by the Reverend William Lea was then read. Lea commented that on the whole the boys were 'carefully and efficiently taught, and considering the short time they have been under tuition they acquitted themselves very satisfactorily.' They were equal to the standard of National Schools in reading and writing from dictation, but below it in arithmetic and scripture, though 'I was much pleased by the intelligence of their answers on the meaning of the Church Catechism.' He suggested that the warden should catechise the boys in church every Sunday afternoon, having prepared them in the subject during the week, and also that he examine them monthly in secular knowledge. There was more reference to the school in Skinner's report, but it was proposed by

Frederick and seconded by Pakington that 'The paragraphs relating to the Foundation School be omitted from the Warden's Report, that the chairman be requested to acquaint the Warden thereof and the Report as amended be entered in the Minute Book.' We thus have no means now of knowing what Skinner had written.

In a letter to Skinner in September Frederick touched on another matter which was to lead to a second controversy regarding the extent of Skinner's responsibility and authority. It would seem that Skinner's household had been sitting in the south aisle seats along with the female pensioners. Unfortunately we do not know what 'household' involved here. Apart from himself, there were at least five others in 1863 and 10 others (including servants) in 1871. If it was only the female members who were involved, there would still have been at least five in 1863 and nine in 1871. Frederick now wrote,

> Widow Stokes made a complaint today about the seats, and I regret to find the great crowding to which the women have been subjected in the church aisle which was built for their accommodation. In conjunction with Mr Munn I have assigned to each pensioner and wife of pensioner a distinct place, and written her name on the back.
>
> The space not required by those for whom the aisle was built may of course be occupied by your household. I am sorry to have to speak so plainly, as I thought the matter would have been properly settled when previously brought under your notice.

On 29 September Skinner, writing from Ireland, sent a very long and indignant reply,

> Every honourable and right-minded man in the position which I have the privilege to fill—having worked in the ministry a quarter of a century—may be (ought he not to be) indulged in the feeling that his work is committed to him with confidence in his power his will to accomplish it. You have thought it your duty, more than

once, to write and to act as if this indulgence was not to be extended to me, but that my work and responsibility are such that you, at your pleasure, interfere—not as a friend and adviser consulting with me, but as a superior authority overruling and rebuking me. If I know myself at all, I can declare sincerely that I object to this kind of interference not because I have a jealous preference for my own way, but because I have a respect for my office and the influence over others which it may fairly claim to exercise for good.

I have never in any way been led to think it possible—still less have I ever been informed by the Trustees of the Charity—that in regard to any of the duties imposed upon me, least of all the duty of ordering what concerns Divine Service in the Church of which I am Incumbent, the 'Chairman of the Standing Committee' disappointed to rebuke me and, without notice, to alter my arrangements at his pleasure during my absence from home. If it be the will of the Trustees to invest 'the Chairman of the Standing Committee' with this authority, and to take from me all discretionary action, not only as Warden, but even as Incumbent of the Church, I will not now venture to dispute their power. But, first, they would surely announce their determination to me: next, I will venture to doubt whether any right-minded man would accept my position so defined. Certainly such was not the position which was offered to me. I venture to complain:

(i) That you have made a change without due inquiry—that is inquiring of me ('the women's aisle has been greatly crowded . . .').

(ii) That you have rebuked me for not attending to your wishes, without once inquiring whether your wishes had been attended to. ('I am sorry to have to speak so plainly . . .)

(iii) That upon this charge thus made and believed, and this rebuke thus grounded and administered, you have proceeded to alter my arrangements in the aisle, not only without my consent, but against my assigned . . . and written the name on the back.')

The point involved in these three complaints is one and simple, viz. whether the Warden is a Constitutional Officer, serving under the general authority of the Trustees, or an officer without any discretion serving under the arbitrary will of the 'Chairman of the Standing Committee.'

Frederick replied on 2 October. We have only the draft of this, and he stated there,

> I do not see how the allotment of seats in a chancel aisle built for a specific purpose (viz. the accommodation of female pensioners and the wives of pensioners) has any bearing upon 'Divine Service', interference with which I should not think of attempting. The Perpetual Curate of Newland can (as such) have nothing to do with a chancel aisle built under the sanction of Chancery for a particular purpose. The Warden of the Beauchamp Charity is bound to carry out the objects for which the building was provided . . . I certainly conceive it to be my duty as Chairman of the Standing Committee to take care that effect is given to the intentions of the Trustees for the comfort of the inmates.

He then explained why he took action to remedy a complaint—'that while the women pensioners were greatly crowded together, space intended for them was either unoccupied or occupied by others than those for whom it was provided.'

Skinner replied on 4 October,

> Nothing contained in your note of yesterday convinces me that you have acted either fairly to me or wisely to the Charity in the matter in question. The present result is the utmost dissatisfaction and confusion among the old women, from all I can learn. It will be most unwillingly, if my duty so compels me, that I shall submit the question between us to the Board of Trustees. I should greatly prefer to arrange it in a private and friendly way with you, if I could only hope that this were possible.

Frederick showed Skinner's letter to Munn who commented on 6 October,

> It is quite impossible that we can move one inch backwards, tho' I think we must in the other direction, and provide most directly against the crowding which still exists, and consequent dissatisfaction—'confusion' there cannot be. I see no token of succumbing, but as he invites to a friendly meeting, you must use your discretion.

Skinner sought to enlist the support of Philpott who wrote to Frederick on 10 October,

> I could not help wishing, as there must be abundance of room in the aisle of the chapel for the female parishioners while the Warden's family are absent that the arrangements you deem necessary had been deferred till his return, then if he refused to deal properly with it, a formal statement of the complaint and the grounds for it, would be laid before the Trustees at a meeting. I do not conceive that, strictly speaking, the Standing Committee have power to interfere in such a case. . . . Mr S, who has called upon me, is evidently much disturbed by what has been done, but hopes to arrange matters with you in a quiet and friendly way. Open and serious contentions on small derangements could scarcely fail to expose to ridicule the whole management of the Charity. . . . I have long felt . . . that as a member of the Standing Committee I am in a false position. It would be most painful to me if I should ever find myself unable to go fully with you, and I think that when this matter has been adjusted it would be better for all parties that I should retire.

At the Trustees' meeting on 23 January 1866 Philpott duly resigned from the standing committee, as (probably for different reasons) did Munn; Frederick and Sir Edmund Lechmere were appointed as the committee for the ensuing year. But Philpott was not the only Trustee to feel uneasy, and on 29 January Lyttleton wrote to Frederick,

> The meetings of the Beauchamp Trust Committee are very unsatisfactory and I have half a mind to give them up. It is impossible for us at a distance really to know what is going on, and we come expecting to find a small amount of business, instead of which all sorts of questions turn up on a little enquiry, which we have not had the time or the means to elucidate. It is very useless to make suggestions which can lead to nothing and only give trouble and annoyance: and I believe the best way would be to make you Dictator and Mr Munn Master of the Horse.[1]

Meanwhile on 16 October Skinner, now on holiday in Lowestoft, sent Frederick a long letter of complaint and asked him whether, when he accepted the points he had outlined in April 1861 prior to his acceptance of his appointment, he was then acting for the Trustees, or expressing a personal opinion. Frederick in a reply (of which we have only a draft) of 29 October refused to accept Skinner's complaints or his interpretation of his status and authority, and he charged him with misrepresentation and exaggeration. Skinner replied the following day. He complained that he was never informed of the existence of a standing committee,

> with powers to interfere in the internal discipline of the Almshouses, which I thought was committed to me. I have nevertheless been subjected to the arbitrary exercise of this power . . . If it is thought better, I am quite willing to confine myself to spiritual ministration, and to give up the charge of the Discipline of the place to you, or I am willing to take charge of both the spiritual ministration and the ordinary Discipline, and to submit myself heartily and faithfully to the Body of the Trustees.

---

[1] In ancient Rome a Dictator could be appointed in times of emergency, and his second-in-command was entitled Master of the Horse, i.e. cavalry.

Frederick replied on 6 November with a firm but conciliatory restatement and justification of his position and actions. On 8 November Skinner replied,

> I cannot express how grieved and distressed I am by your line of self defence on the question between us as contained in your last letter. You have now made matters worse than ever . . . There is now no possible choice but for a thorough investigation of 'all the facts of the case', and to that investigation I must now invite the Trustees.

Frederick replied on 9 November, 'You are entirely mistaken in supposing that I have attempted any self-defence. None was needed.'

It was on this date that the Trustees met, and Skinner in his report made a lengthy statement of his grievances against the chairman of the standing committee and asked for the Trustees' ruling on 'certain points connected with his position and the powers of the Standing Committee and its Chairman.' Frederick, the chairman in question, read to the Trustees some of the correspondence between Skinner and himself on this matter. The Trustees decided that, as there were only five of them present, this ought to be discussed at a better attended meeting. Meanwhile it was agreed 'that the latter part of the Warden's report be not now entered in the Minutes.' A special meeting was now fixed for 20 November. Here, Lord Somers was in the chair, and eight other Trustees were present as well as the warden. After discussion and 'upon division' it was resolved,

> That the Trustees, having considered the objects for which the chancel aisle of the church at Newland was built and the present number of women Pensioners and wives of pensioners, desire that from this date no person other than the Matron, the women Pensioners, wives of Pensioners and persons duly permitted to live with them be accommodated with seats in the chancel aisle—the Organist of course excepted.

Meanwhile there had been continuing problems with the choir school. In January 1866 Skinner reported that of the eight foundation boys only six were available for choir duties, and added that 'The warden has no control over the management of the boys and is unable to give any account of the failure of two boys which is now of longstanding.' He considered this an inadequate number, and asked the trustees to consider increasing the number to the minimum number 10 as laid down in the scheme.

The Trustees responded by directing the standing committee to report on the expediency of increasing the number of foundation boys, including the possibility of admitting some day boys. At the same time Lea submitted a report which was less enthusiastic than his previous one. Religious knowledge was now very good, reading was fluent and writing was good. But reading was 'deficient in expression: more attention should be paid to the pronunciation of the letter H', there were too many spelling mistakes in dictated writing, and arithmetic was below average.

On 27 January Edgcumbe wrote to Frederick that, having received Lea's report,

'I cannot but consider it . . . a censure on my government, and beg to say that if this opinion is shared by the Trustees I cannot hold my position here longer than would be convenient for them to supply my place.' In March he gave notice that he would resign his office of clerk and schoolmaster at Michaelmas. But till then his skirmishes with Skinner continued, and on 16 May Skinner wrote to Lygon, who had now succeeded to the earldom,

> It gives me great concern to be obliged to ask your Lordship to stay Mr Edgcumbe summarily from the extraordinary course upon which he has entered, of interference with me in my spiritual functions in this place. One of the boys is a candidate for Confirmation and ought to have been with me today to receive my private instructions and guidance.

Mr Edgcumbe has, in a manner most offensive to me, distinctly refused to allow the boy to come, unless he is permitted to be present! I cannot of course consent to any such claim on his part. I am simply amazed at this notion of his authority over the institution of which I am both Warden and Incumbent. I fully confide in your Lordship's power and willingness to settle this difficulty at once—by disabusing Mr Edgcumbe of his notion.

On 27 June the Trustees advertised in the *Guardian*,

Wanted for an endowed Charity in a healthy agricultural neighbourhood, a Person qualified for the combined offices of CLERK to the Trustees, Schoolmaster and Organist for daily choral services. Salary about £110 p.a. with house and good garden. An allowance to be made to a pupil-teacher. The Clerk will have to board the Choir School, for which a proper payment will be made.

On 12 July Skinner wrote to the Earl claiming that the duties of warden and vicar were too much for one man, arguing that he needed a priest—not a deacon as at present—to assist in the maintenance of the services and suggesting that one or more of the duties of the clerk, schoolmaster and organist should be undertaken by an assistant priest. He suggested the following salaries: clerk £50, master £60, assistant £40 and organist £25. The Earl replied on 16 July that this was financially unacceptable. But, though the Trustees' minutes contain no reference to this, Ethelbert West was duly appointed to the three posts occupied by Edgcumbe, and was soon in residence with his family. In January 1867 Skinner reported that he had 'entered on his duties with much earnestness and success.'

But now the Trustees, still smarting from wounds received in their battle with Skinner over the running of the school, found that they had not the financial resources to carry out some desired improvements to the church and community buildings. They had the ingenious idea of solving both these problems with one stroke by closing the school.

The reactions of Skinner to this proposal could be foreseen.

In his report for a Trustees meeting on 17 September 1868 Skinner made six main points:

(i) In the scheme the Trustees are directed to maintain—so as to lodge, board, clothe and educate—ten or more orphan children.

(ii) The number of children has never reached the 'statutable' number of ten.

(iii) The annual cost of the school has been on an average under Mr Edgcumbe about £266; under Mr West not more than £225 p.a.

(iv) 'It has been found more convenient to contract with the Master for the Maintenance of the School (including salaries of Clerk to the Charity and Organist of the Church) for £300 p.a. than to pay a salary to the Schoolmaster and be responsible for the details of expenses in education and maintenance.'

(v) It would be possible to reduce the cost per head by enrolling a number of fee-paying boys, or to charge the relatives of the existing boys a small fee (but this would raise difficulties).

(vi) No further reduction or closure of the school should be made without applying to the Court of Chancery to vary that part of the Scheme relating to the school.

He concluded that 'for the purposes of a school, which shall "assist Divine Service in Newland Church", the existing school cannot be brought down lower than it is at present.' He supported his points with two memoranda—a statement of the expenses of running the school, and an estimate of the annual income and expenditure of the charity. But the Earl in a counter-memorandum rejected these figures, and argued that at least £2,500 was required for the desired improvements. This sum could be raised only by selling stock and so reducing income by £100 p.a. or by economies like temporarily closing the school as he recommended. It was therefore resolved,

> That in order to clear off the present liabilities of the Charity and to provide for certain necessary works such as the Cloister and Boundary Wall, the Choristers' School be suspended until such time as the Trustees may consider it desirable to reopen it, and that the School be accordingly closed on and after 1 January 1869.

It was further resolved 'that notice be given to Mr West to terminate the present arrangement as to the School and the Organistship on 31 December 1868.'

At another special meeting on 5 November Lyttleton made an (unminuted) statement 'as to his communications with the Warden.' The Earl then reported that Fearon had advised that the Trustees submit to the Charity Commissioners a memorial regarding the choir school, and he now submitted a long draft which he had approved and which the trustees accepted. The draft, which was fully minuted, included the surprising statement, that the school 'was intended, amongst other purposes, to serve as the nucleus of a superior class of day-school for the populous district of Malvern Link, but from circumstances which need not now be entered upon, this expectation has not been fulfilled.' This intention had never been mentioned in the minutes: how could a superior prep school be combined with a 'school of industry', and what were the 'circumstances'?

The Earl then read a letter from the clerk, and it was agreed to appoint West organist at a salary of £50 p.a. in addition to his salary as clerk and his occupation of the premises as at present, except for the school-room. It was further agreed,

> That the school being suspended, as far as the Trustees are concerned, from 1 January next, and consequently the school-room being at the disposal of the Trustees from that date, it was resolved that the

Warden be allowed the use of the room for the purpose of a Choir School.

The warden's report as minuted contains no reference either to the closure of the choir school or to the possibility of his starting a private school on his own initiation. Had this proposal been contained in his letter and paper to Lord Lyttleton?

On 25 November 1868 the Earl wrote to Fearon complaining that Skinner, writing as incumbent rather than warden, had sent to the court a 'counter-memorial' about financial matters,

> Although I cannot find time to follow him through that lengthy document, I must take advantage of the opportunity to call attention to some other erroneous impressions which it is calculated to convey . . . That Mr Skinner should fall into such serious errors in dealing with this [financial] part of the subject is not to be wondered at, for he has never had anything to do with the expenditure and is in no way responsible for it.

He then moved on to the proposed closure of the school which, he claimed, was originally established for twenty boys, including day boys, 'It is true that day boys were not at first admitted, for Mr Skinner contrived to establish relations with the then Master which occasioned much embarrassment and prevented the development of the school.' Now, the necessary retrenchment could be achieved only by reducing the number of pensioners or by closing the school. But since the maintenance of the pensioners was the prime object of the original foundation, and the school a later addition, and 'in view of the unsatisfactory state of affairs at the School and the relations with the Warden concerning it', he felt that the school should be closed and that this would cause little disturbance particularly since there were currently only five boys in the school. As an example of the warden's interference, he continued,

The Warden, without reference to the Trustees, has seen fit to require the attendance of the boys every day at a Choral Celebration of Holy Communion, and to dispense with their attendance at the daily Morning Prayers at which the Pensioners are by the Scheme bound to be present, and to sing at it, which was one of the principal objects of the establishment of the Industrial School.

The original choir school ceased to exist on 1 January 1869, but shortly afterwards Skinner, in his annual pastoral letter to his parishioners, referred to the 'maintenance and education of poor orphan children' as 'an object of mercy not inferior (most would think it superior) to the relief of the aged poor', and noted how 'with the help of such children, duly instructed in vocal music, it was provided that Divine Service should be sung in Newland Church "as the Warden should from time to time direct".' As a result 'Divine Service at Newland was *commenced* upon a type and standard so very far beyond the reach of an ordinary village Church.' The Trustees had withdrawn their support from the choir school, but 'I have pledged myself to keep it up.' Only four boys now remained, but I shall make them 'the *nucleus* of a Choir School, to which I must add gradually as my means and opportunities grow.'

Clearly something had gone wrong since the Trustees resolution of November 1868, for Skinner now regretted that they had not seen fit to grant him the use of the original choir school premises unless he agreed to the master being appointed by them, and his suggestion that they should have a power of veto over his own choice had not been accepted. They had been unwilling to continue the services of an organist and choirmaster unless he conceded to them 'my discretionary power to order what Divine Offices of the Parish Church should be sung chorally, and what should be said plain', and they had insisted that Morning Prayer should be fully choral every day. They had even denied him the use of the boys' old caps and cassocks. But one of his curates had agreed to take charge of the boys for the time being, and for the future he asked those who were able to give him some substantial financial help.

Evidence for the next few years is scanty. At the Trustees meeting on 17 January 1871 an order from the Court of Chancery was read and minuted. This sanctioned the suspension of the choir school 'until such time as [the Trustees] may consider the resumption thereof to be expedient.' But it appears that West was still serving as organist in 1874 with an allowance of 7s. per week. It was said that 'the choral service was still maintained in the greatest excellence', but—despite the claims of Hunt—it is doubtful if the choir school functioned in any significant sense in the rest of Skinner's time, and his sorrow must have been increased by the closure of the village school in 1875 when it was no longer judged efficient. For children under eight, Skinner was willing to establish a Dame's School in a suitable cottage, but the Earl's agent had required him to return the key to the cottage, and the Earl proposed himself to open such a school for the children of his 'cottagers' without any reference to himself.

Skinner and the sixth Earl were both ardent tractarians, and together they were responsible for the establishment of the anglo-catholic tradition in St Leonard's and the almshouses. It might have been expected that they would have worked happily together, but as we have seen this was not the case. In Lygon's archive, there are large numbers of letters from Skinner, many of an outspoken and aggressive nature, expressing grievances against the Trustees, the standing committee, Lygon himself and anyone else who crossed his path. It seems that these letters of complaint did not always reach the standing committee, let alone the Trustees. The committee's minutes—if they kept any—have not survived, and all we know of their deliberations is contained in the lengthy reports which they submitted to the Trustees. It is frustrating to have only Skinner's side of his correspondence since sadly Lygon's replies have not been preserved except occasionally in draft form.

But there does seem to have been a structural weakness in the scheme. Skinner submitted a written report to the Trustees prior to each of their meetings and this was read to them, but he was not himself 'in attendance.' His day-to-day contact with the Trustees was through the small standing committee which was dominated by Lygon and which, it could be argued, sometimes exceeded its remit as in the matter of the chancel seating. In December 1876 he wrote to Munn, who was acting for the Earl in his absence,

> Except when the Trustees communicate any of their proceedings relating specially and personally to myself through the chairman, I have now no means of knowing the results of their meetings as they deal with my reports or affect the Charity. May I ask that, as formerly, the Minute Book may be sent to me when the proceedings shall have been entered that I may become acquainted with the decisions, from time to time, upon which I have to administer the Almshouses. It would, obviously, be a great means of promoting a good understanding, and of assisting the Warden, as enabling him to become familiar with the mind of the Trustees (with some of whom He is not even acquainted by sight now) and enabling the Trustees, through questions, to become familiar with the Charity, if he were allowed to be present at all the Board meetings (except when he is himself to be discussed) although he has no right of vote.

The Earl replied by sending him the minute book and its key but, as to his attendance at the Trustees' meetings, he thought the advice of Fearon was sound when he had suggested at the original establishment of the charity that its officers should not normally be present.

There can be no doubt that Skinner was most assiduous and considerate both as warden and as parish priest, and even while indulging in his controversies he had his times of personal grief: In January 1867 his brother George died in Panama, and in February 1868 his only daughter, Agnes, died. But there can be no doubt again (though Hunt minimises this) that he could be extraordinarily difficult, and his relationship not only with Lygon but also with Edgcombe was poor. And while anglo-catholic clergy were usually totally dedicated in their parochial duties, as Skinner was, and often much loved and respected by their parishioners, as Skinner was again, there was often something in their psyche that relished battles with authority, and this would seem to have been true of Skinner.

As we noted earlier, he was not the only person who found the Earl difficult, and it is clear that the Earl's fellow-Trustees and even the other members of the standing committee did not always agree with him. Nonetheless the fact that the Earl seems to have related perfectly well to Skinner's successor suggests that it was Skinner who was largely to blame for the poor relationship.

More happily, though, Skinner had occasional moments of self-awareness. In referring to the sad aftermath of the closure of the choir school, he wrote, 'I am very sorry if this result was my fault. I am but a poor hand at "managing" men.' He could also at times be generous even in his comments on his adversary. In 1869 he wrote that 'We were mainly indebted for the blessing of this Choir School, under God, to the unceasing and persevering zeal of the Treasurer of the Charity, the Honourable Frederick Lygon, now the sixth Earl Beauchamp', and in 1877, just before the end of his ministry at Newland, he wrote warmly of 'the present Earl Beauchamp, whose zealous labours in the early history of the Charity, while Mr Lygon, entitle him to be considered as almost a second founder of the Hospital.'

Chapter Eight
The Church

Shortly after its consecration the church was visited by members of the Worcester Diocesan Architectural Society. They thought that 'the general effect of the interior is very good, and many of the details are extremely elegant.' They particularly commended the chancel screen, the faldstool and the reredos, but regretted that the east window was 'too narrow for so wide a chancel' and added that 'its squeezed-up appearance is no doubt increased by the reredos and altar being of the same width, and thus carrying the outer line of the window opening down to the floor.' They noted, though, that Hardwick's original design had been for a five-light window. Externally they also thought the church satisfactory—except for 'the bell-turret, which must be pronounced a failure from whichever point of view it may be seen', and they particularly objected to the 'innumerable crockets.' But the public at large were delighted with the church, and in the summer of 1864 such crowds came to the Sunday services that some could not even get into the porch. To ensure places for parishioners, no visitors were allowed to take seats until the bell had stopped ringing.

In January 1865 the standing committee was 'requested to see to the removal of the Old Church, and the erection of a lych-gate [at the grave-yard] with old materials.' On 20 September, however, Frederick wrote to Skinner,

> Mr Hopkins came over today, and after some consultation it appeared that the best way of dealing with the old church would be to move the chancel against the temporary cloister and make it good for a Dead House. This would cost little more than the Lych-gate, and would give us something we really want instead of a merely ornamental appendage. There would remain material enough for a lych-gate, and perhaps the old porch might be adapted to some such use.

This suggestion was put to the Trustees, and on 9 November they resolved 'that in lieu of the Lych-gate to the burial ground a Dead House be erected out of the materials of the Chancel of the Old Church.' The stage was now set for the final demolition of the old church, and a large stone cross was erected on its site in what was now the churchyard. This was designed by Skinner and made by Forsyth of Worcester. The Latin inscription reads in translation:

> To God, the best and greatest, our Saviour, who for the joy that was set before him endured the Cross. As a sacred memorial of the Chapel of St Leonard, Newland, since the fourteenth century still standing but lately pulled down, upon whose altar here the priests of Newland during five centuries were wont to celebrate the Holy Mysteries; of them the last and least J. S. dedicated this cross. Erected by the munificence of the faithful AD 1866.

The dead house, later described as a mortuary chapel, was duly erected, although it was less than half the size of the original chapel. The boarded ceiling of the old chancel was used in the sacristy of the new church, and Hunt states that the altar from the old chapel was now placed in the new chapel. Also, in the centre of it there was a stone catafalque on which the bodies of the pensioners could rest until their burial.[1] Soon windows, by Clayton and Bell, were added, all with appropriate themes. The east window has Christ in the centre, with the text 'Victor over death', and adoring angels on either side. On the south wall are Dorcas (Acts 9:36) and Eutychus (Acts 20:9 ff.); then Jairus' daughter (Mark 5:41), the son of the widow of Nain (Luke 7:11–15) and Lazarus (John 11:44). On the north wall are the man revived by Elisha's bones (2 Kgs. 13:21), the widow's son of Zarephath (1 Kgs. 17:22) and the son of the Shunammite (2 Kgs. 4:34).

As for the new church, those who know it will recognise the *Worcester Herald*'s description even though many of its most distinctive features were not yet present. In the earliest known photograph, which must have been taken soon after the consecration, the pulpit is small and insignificant, the walls on either side of the east window were bare except for the text, 'I am alive for evermore', and there was no hint of spirit fresco. Under Skinner's guidance, however, enhancement proceeded apace. Work on the spirit-frescoes began almost immediately, and on 26 November Hardwick wrote to Frederick, 'I begged [Mr Preedy] to keep the colouring quiet but I think it shouldn't be too subdued—I think some colour in the scroll and about the letters would be an improvement.' But Preedy's work proved unsatisfactory, and on 1 August 1866 T. Gambier Parry,[2] who had invented the spirit-fresco technique, wrote to the Earl,

> I suppose it was there [at Newland] that some wall-painting was done a year or so ago by a man named Davies—sent to you, I think, by Mr Preedy. I have been vexed to hear of its failure, more especially as it was done on a system recommended by me. The fact so annoyed me that I have most strictly enquired into it—and find, as I supposed, that it was not done on the conditions which were necessary—that the

---

[1] Moved to the main entrance under the tower.
[2] 1816–88. An artist and art collector, also a tractarian, who developed this method after studying Italian frescoes and who resided at Highnam Court near Gloucester. He was the father of the composer, Sir Hubert Parry.

plaster was not of the sort properly prepared, and moreover that one half of the gable wall had a very little time previously been saturated by the overflow of some neglected gutter or gargoyle. The system of 'Spirit fresco' is quite certain of success if only the conditions are properly carried out.

There was further disappointment when the 'Doom' or Judgment scene, given by the Earl and executed by Preedy in its traditional place over the chancel arch, prematurely fell to pieces and in 1877 was in the course of being repainted.[3] At the top is Christ in Majesty, his right hand raised in blessing and his left displaying the symbols Alpha and Omega. On his right is the archangel Gabriel and on his left Michael, and below are the twelve apostles. On the north stands St Peter with his keys at the gate of heaven, beckoning towards Christ the souls of the saved who are guided forward by an angel. On the south the damned are barred from heaven by the 'angel with the flaming sword.' It was probably in 1877 that the impact of this scene was softened. An early painting in the community library shows very vividly the damned being cast into hell, but this apparently caused great distress to worshippers, and the present fresco is gentler, though the damned still express their misery, loneliness and despair. Beneath the Judgement scene, on the north side stands the Blessed Virgin Mary with a lily and the texts, 'Righteous through the obedience of one person' and 'Holy Mary, Mother, the handmaid of the Lord', and on the south side Eve with the texts, 'Sinners through the disobedience of one person' and 'Mother Eve deceived by the serpent.'

In August 1868 the Earl referred to the necessity for providing permanent fittings for the chancel. Skinner urged this again on the Trustees in January 1870, and in 1872 Hardwick was instructed to prepare designs for stalls there. These were duly provided, richly carved

---

[3] Hunt strangely claims that this represents 'not the General or Last Judgment (Matt. 25) but the Particular or First Judgment, i.e. of an individual soul at the hour of death. It is secret, but takes place in the presence of the saints and angels.' This is clearly wrong.

in English oak, by Messrs Rattee of Cambridge. The north and south stalls, for the male pensioners, each bore as a legend 'an appropriate Christian virtue, by which the pensioner, who occupies it, may study to improve his life.' On the north side were Contrition, Gratitude, Unity, Temperance, Truth, Chastity and Humility, while on the south side were Religion, Justice, Compassion, Prudence, Patience, Obedience and Charity. The seats in front were for the choristers, men and boys, but there were three further stalls on either side for the clergy. These had richly carved *Misereres*, each of a different design and bearing some of the spiritual gifts as their legends—on the north Understanding, Ghostly Strength and True Godliness, and on the south Wisdom, Counsel and Knowledge.

Meanwhile from 1868 more and more spirit frescoes were executed. The work was now entrusted to Clayton and Bell,[4] and Skinner thought that there was no more successful example of it in England.[5] In the sanctuary, above the east window, are the texts 'Worthy is the Lamb that was slain' and 'Blessing and Honour and Glory and Power be unto Him that sitteth upon the throne, and unto the Lamb for ever and ever.' On the roof the elements of earth, air and water are painted in rich colours. On the right was the resurrection and on the left the ascension; both these were thankofferings by Skinner and his wife 'for an only and beloved child' (their daughter Agnes) who died in 1868.

In the chancel, on the north is the palm-sunday procession of Jesus to Jerusalem with the text 'Hosanna, blessed is the son of David who comes in the name of the Lord. Hosanna in the highest', while an arcade below depicting various virgin martyrs—Saints Dorothea,

---

[4] Interestingly in 1973 Farrer Bell, grandson of Alfred Bell who had overseen the original work, was unfamiliar with the phrase 'spirit fresco' and maintained that there was nothing mysterious about the work of Clayton and Bell: 'They simply use ordinary oil paint, but with a matt (dull) finish instead of a gloss (shiny) one'.

[5] In 1865 Clayton and Bell had executed a similar series of spirit frescos at St Michael's, Garton on the Wolds, North Humberside; these latter have been conserved by the Pevsner Memorial Trust. The only ones executed by Gambier-Parry himself were in the church which he built on his estate at Highnam, near Gloucester.

Margaret, Agnes, Katharine, Barbara and Etheldreda. These were given in memory of George Ure Skinner by his two daughters. On the south is the procession of the magi with representations of the nativity and the text 'And the Gentiles will walk in your light and Kings in the splendour of your rising'; over the credence are medallions of the early priests, Melchizadek and Aaron, by the organ St Cecilia, and in the bases of the soffits of the arches of the chancel aisle six doctors of the church—the eastern doctors, Athanasius, Basil and Chrysostom, facing east, and the western doctors, Gregory, Augustine and Ambrose, facing west. All these were given by Skinner in memory of his brother Benny.

On the north side of the nave the corporal works of mercy are represented in the arcade below. All these were described by Skinner as 'private offerings of love to God' and they frequently refer to 'kindnesses bestowed'; one would love to know more of the modest donors. These are giving of alms (CW and EW), feeding the hungry ('some of the anonymous'), giving drink to the thirsty (in memory of F. Dawkins, husband, father and brother AD, AND, MCSD and RPD), taking in the stranger (KG and FEG), clothing the naked ('for his mercies dispensed to a penitent, most grateful and lowly woman'), visiting the sick ('for his highly deserving handmaid Mary C. Gresley, FML.), consoling the prisoner ('his sons and daughters . . . in memory of our greatly beloved father EVR and LER and HWR.) and burying the dead (EW). In the compartment above are miracles of mercy: the miracle at Cana of Galilee, in memory of a daughter ('her mother MBC., who still misses her, rendering thanks . . . for Albinia A. Gibbs, his most deserving servant'), the miracle of the loaves and fishes, a thankoffering for a wife ('her loving husband AG. . . . for his most deserving servant ABG) and the raising of Lazarus, a thankoffering for a mother (her grieving daughter AIS. . . . for her most beloved mother, I. A. Selby).

On the south side the Beatitudes are represented in the arcade below, and all these, wrote Skinner, were 'offerings of grateful love by private persons—sons and daughters, husbands and wives, brothers and sisters, and penitents': The persecuted—St Stephen (CGH); The peacemakers—Esther at the feet of Ahasuerus, bringing peace to her people ('the sons and daughters of IB, priest and their beloved father'); The pure in heart—the annunciation (executed personally by Bell, and his own gift, 'the sons and daughters of HAB., their beloved mother, offering praises in her memory'); The merciful—Pharoah's daughter saving Moses; Those who hunger and thirst after righteousness—Mary at the feet of Jesus, and Martha serving (GIH); The meek—Jacob humbling himself before Esau (TE and MW); Those who mourn—Mary Magdalen at the feet of Jesus ('the penitent AGA'}; The poor in spirit—David in the sheep fold ('some of his friends grieving together and praying . . . for his most unworthy servant J. S[kinner].' Above are four parables: the Good Samaritan, an offering for a mother (her grateful and loving daughter MT, rendering praises now and forever for her sweetest mother, C. Trench); the Great Supper, for a son (his most grateful father WC, rendering thanks . . . for his servant, William Gibbs, greatly loved and highly deserving son'; the Talents for parents ('their most grateful daughter ML rendering thanks . . . for his servants Baldwin and Mary Leighton, greatly beloved parents), and the Pharisee and the Publican (for his mercies bestowed on us on the Feast of Pentecost 1877, MEBC).

At the west end, the arcade below represents Jesus with the wise virgins on his right and the foolish on his left—another offering by Skinner and his siblings for 'our sweetest and most highly deserving mother', Innes Skinner who died in 1872. The miracle of the pool of Bethesda above was a thankoffering by the architect, Hardwick. Below the oriel window Jesus is depicted healing the sick man let down from the roof, and there is the inscription, 'GUS caused this to be erected to the honour of God our Saviour, who cures every weakness and every infirmity.' Between the oriel window and the wall are St James and St Leonard whom Skinner describes as the patron saints of the church. This is not strictly true, since the church is formally St Leonard's, but the feast of St James on 25 July fell within the octave of the dedication, so he was sometimes regarded in the early days as a co-patron. The decoration of the upper stage of the western wall, on either side the baptismal window, illustrates the healing leaves and sustaining fruits of the life-giving Spirit.

All the frescoes mentioned so far were listed by Skinner in his pamphlet 'Newland Parish Church and the Beauchamp Charity. His priority was the completion of the nave frescoes, and in 1877 he 'assumed to himself the responsibility of the cost' of the last of these. But there are now others at the south of the chancel, and the full scheme was completed only by his successor.[6]

There were also additions to the glass which at the consecration was restricted to the east window and two chancel windows. The window at the north of the sanctuary was a memorial by J. S. and A. S[kinner] 'to the memory of their most beloved mother Anne Raymond.' It depicted St Leonard, on either side and underneath St Anne teaching her daughter, the Blessed Virgin Mary, to read. Hunt states that 'When the frescoes were added two other deacons famous for their devotion were placed on the jambs of the windows; those of St Stephen and St Laurence.'

The nave windows were by Clayton and Bell and depicted on the south side the apostles, each bearing his emblem and a scroll with a clause from the Apostles' Creed, with the text, 'I have built on the foundation of the apostles.' Some of these were given *c.*1869–70 by a number of priests as a thankoffering 'in this house of duly consecrated holy retreat for priests', and on the north side the Old Testament prophets and leaders—Moses and David, Samuel and Elijah, Isaiah and Jeremiah, Ezekiel and Daniel—with the text, 'I have built on the foundation of the prophets.' The four major prophets all carry scrolls bearing the opening words of their prophecies, and all these windows Skinner described as 'private thankofferings for mercies received in this church.' The inscriptions refer to 'Walter Devereux, most sadly

---

[6] Unfortunately, Clayton and Bell closed in 1993 and most of their records were destroyed by Second World War bombing.

missed brother—HBD', 'AV', 'MRS.' and 'KES.' The baptistery window in the west, by Lavers Barraud and Westlake of London, was the offering of occasional members of the congregation. There were four circular lights representing the Holy Ghost, the baptism of our Lord, the passage through the Red Sea, and the saving of Noah and his family by water. Three further perpendicular lights represented Ezekiel's vision of the waters.

Again, there are five windows in the south not mentioned by Skinner. The two dormer windows were definitely added later. Of the other three, Hunt states that the first two were given by Skinner, and the third also dates from Skinner's time:

> 1. In the east wall the round window above and behind the organ represents the Agnus Dei surrounded by the emblems of the evangelists, and in the surrounding lights eight angels carrying the ascriptions given to the Lamb—power, riches, wisdom etc. (Rev. 5:12).
>
> 2. In the west wall another round window contains four alleged scenes from St Mary Magdalene—at home with Martha, penitence, anointing the feet of Jesus, and her presence at the empty tomb
>
> 3. In a window beside the organ is St Cecilia, patron saint of music.

Other new features were:

> 1. The pulpit, carved by Forsyth's of Worcester, with a sculpture of John the Baptist preaching in the centre, supported by two richly cut panels containing the emblematical olive tree and wine. This was a thankoffering from WCA and EA, and the wreath of passion flowers was copied from a natural flower actually blooming against the west wall of the Chancel aisle.
>
> 2. The illuminated iron chancel gates and the cresting of the screen,

the work of Messrs Skidmore of Coventry and the gifts of friends of Skinner.

3. The font cover, surmounted by a copper dove in silver-gilt by the same artist and offered to the church in the same way.

4. The brass lectern, made by Messrs Hart and the gift of a friend in 1864, through the Reverend G. R. Adam, an early curate.

5. The processional cross given in 1867.

Despite the absence of the frescoes and windows at the south of the chancel, the church at Skinner's retirement in 1877 was very much the distinctive and almost unique church that we know today.[7] Clearly the concept underlying the frescoes and the windows was his, and from them one could preach the whole of the Christian faith. His scheme was that of a genius, and one notes how generous he and his family were in their donations. One also notes, though, the mock-medievalism. No doubt some, though not all, of the pensioners were literate, but it is unlikely that any could understand Latin. Yet all the inscriptions were in Latin.

As for the worship of the church, in 1863–64 Skinner published the hymnal we have already noted and in 1868 he introduced a daily eucharist, 'without which all else seems like "sounding brass or a tinkling cymbal".' He explained that 'I am far from meaning this of other places; only of this place it would have seemed so, if, having so many other Services continually, we had persisted in omitting the greatest Service of all.' At Easter 1868 he presented the church with a full set of silk eucharistic vestments which were 'henceforth used by

---

[7] Significant later features were a new sedelia, erected by Mrs Skinner in memory of his ministry as vicar and warden and of their life together, the colouring of the reredos, the ugly paint covering up decayed original work at the bottom on the chancel and nave, (restoration of this is planned for 2014) and the aumbry where the Blessed Sacrament is reserved.

him, without the least opposition from bishop or parishioners.' The *Newland Almanack* for 1869 gives the services as:

Sundays	8 a.m.	Holy Communion
	11 a.m.	Matins, followed by sermon
	12 noon	Holy Communion (last in the month only)
	3.30 p.m.	Litany, with Baptisms or Catechising
	7 p.m.	Evensong, followed by sermon
Daily	7.45 a.m.	Holy Communion
	8.45 a.m.	Matins
	12 noon	Litany (Wednesdays and Fridays only)
	5 p.m. or 7.30 p.m.	Evensong
Festivals	7.30 p.m.	Evensong and sermon (Eve of Festival)
	7.45 a.m.	Holy Communion
	10.30 a.m.	Matins
	11.30 a.m.	Holy Communion

Sermons also preached at evensong on
Wednesdays and Fridays in Advent and Lent.

Skinner's pastoral letter for 1869 pointed out that the total parish population was under 210, that apart from nine farmers all were of the labouring poor on an average weekly wage of 12*s*., that the church could not hold more than two hundred people, and that the extraneous congregation was very fluctuating. He then gave some statistics based for the first three years from one Dedication Festival (July) to the next and for the last for eighteen months, i.e. from the previous Dedication Festival to the end of December:

	No. of celebrations	Communicants	Offertories	Amount
1864–65	93	3,277	190	£333. 16s. 5½d.
1865–66	101	3,451	210	£295. 17s. 2d.
1866–67	105	3,684	213	£324. 8s. 4½d.
1867–68	457	7,696	359	£465. 19s. 3d.

It was a sign of God's blessing that all this had happened 'in a small village church in a little country place, where fasting early Communion had been before all but unknown, and the *principle* of giving to God, weekly, had never been practised.' As for the offertories, more than £230 had been given to foreign missions and more than £320 to charitable and religious works at home.

The numerous services were possible only with the aid of curates and of other clergy living nearby, and their ritual was firmly anglo-catholic. Gordon Lansdown Barnes, in a list of vestments in use at Skinner's retirement, notes four figures silk chasubles, four plain alpaca chasubles with appropriate orphreys, eight plain alpaca tunicles and dalmatics, again with appropriate orphreys, twenty stoles, twelve maniples and four linen albs. The presence of tunicles and dalmatics indicates that what was later called High Mass was celebrated at times, and this was most unusual at this period. There were also three sets of sacred vessels. The most ornate, consisting of chalice, ciborium and paten, was given to Skinner by 'the faithful worshippers at Newland' on his retirement at Michaelmas 1877, and on his death it was presented to the church. The other sets consisted only of chalice and paten, with the hallmark 1863, and these too may have been gifts of the Skinner family. There was also a large flagon, hallmarked 1857, and another 1863 paten given as a 'small thankoffering' by one Henry Carter.

It is a tribute to Skinner that, as Hunt points out, 'the restoration of a church to the fullness of Catholic worship and practice was accomplished without discord.' He continues, 'It was the dynamic ministry of the Vicar, the great impression which his personality made upon everyone, the power and flaming sincerity of his preaching, that drew crowds . . . to this church.' His voice was weak and unattractive. He was not a great 'popular preacher', his preaching made great demands on the attention, understanding and even more the consciences of his hearers, and his sermons were 'packed with biblical and patristic lore, sometimes of inordinate length.' But Hunt considered that, apart from the passionate sincerity of his preaching, it was the 'beauty of holiness' manifested in the services especially the Eucharist, and the example of his personal ministry which combined to make Newland a lively centre of Christian life and worship.' Hunt also mentioned that 'His proficiency of knowledge in some of the arts and crafts and a sensitive appreciation of beauty drew around him craftsmen who counted it a privilege to execute his noble conceptions.'

In 1870 the first two retreats were held at Newland, the second being conducted by Father R. M. Benson, founder of the Cowley Fathers, and it is thought that Skinner had hopes of a retreat house being built on the site.[8] Other famous visitors included Edward King, later to become Bishop of Lincoln, Bishop Forbes of Brechin, William Bright, an ecclesiastical historian, and his former colleague Father Lowder. It was also in 1870 that Skinner was asked by a committee of clergy to produce a 'Synopsis of Moral Theology' for which there was felt to be a great need. It was shortly before his death that he completed this, and in the event it was published posthumously. During his time at Newland he had been too busy to undertake much writing, and apart from the two noted the Bodleian Library includes only one tract from this period.

---

[8] Skinner did in fact purchase and furnish a house in West Malvern as a retreat house for priests and church societies. It later became known as St Edward's, and later a boys' home was added to it. Eventually it passed to the Convent of the Holy Name.

Chapter Nine
Skinner's Resignation

Gradually Skinner's health problems reasserted themselves. In 1872, even after an absence from work, he was able to preach only when sitting. In 1873 he was away in Italy from March till September, but the cold and damp he experienced on his return undid the good of the warm summer. In December 1874 he succumbed to bronchitis, and in January 1875 he submitted to the Trustees a medical report on the basis of which he requested leave of absence 'from Feb. 1st to May 31st in order that he may go to the south of France or Italy.' He assured them that his work would be ably discharged by the Reverend Thomas Humphries Clark. Leave was duly granted but, before it had expired, the Earl wrote to him on 29 April,

> I hope that you have gained permanent benefit from your stay abroad, and trust that the predictions of your doctor as to the need of your residence away from Newland for so much of each year may not be justified, for an Institution such as the Almshouses cannot but suffer materially from the repeated and protracted absences of the Warden.

He also touched on the nursing arrangements at the almshouses, and Skinner replied from Biarritz,

> Your letter, which was forwarded from Newland, caught me up at Pau, from whence we have just arrived at this place. I am much obliged by your kind enquiries after my health. I thank God for having thus far prospered fairly, considering the exceptional severity, even in the south of Europe, of the past winter and spring. My cough has almost entirely ceased, and has indeed troubled me little since I left Cannes; in other respects I believe I may say also with truth and thankfulness that I am stronger, so that I expect DV to return to my work the first week of June, with every hope DG of abiding in it. How far this hope will be permanently fulfilled under the trials of an English winter and spring is of course in Higher Hands than mine, and to Them I humbly commit it.

After discussion of nursing arrangements and of the warden's lodge, he concluded,

> May I add that what is much wanted—the renewal of at least three of the outside blinds [at the Warden's Lodge] which after ten years service are reduced to rags in many places. The arrangement originally was to divide the expense between the Charity and myself, but now in view of my uncertain life and tenure of office it would not probably be an unfair arrangement for the Charity to renew their fixtures.

Skinner returned to Newland in the summer, but he relapsed in the autumn, and on 19 November a letter from him dated 8 November was read to the Trustees,

> He felt that he owed it to the Charity and to his family to submit himself to a second examination by a Physician who should be a stranger to him personally, and of undoubted distinction in his profession. The report of Dr Andrew Clark [Senior Physician to the London Hospital] is herewith enclosed.

Under the circumstances the Warden has no choice but, respectfully, to ask for leave of absence from Dec. 1 1875 to June 1 1876, and to intimate that on his return to England DV in June he will as soon as is possible for him to make the necessary arrangements to resign the office of Warden of the Beauchamp Charity.

He proposed committing his office during absence to the Reverend Nigel Fowler Nash. Dr Clark's report certified that Skinner,

> is suffering from chronic bronchitis, emphysema, some secondary congestion of the lung, and from slight hypertrophy of the right ventricle of the heart; that it is necessary not only to prevent extension of disease but to avert peril to life that Mr Skinner should winter abroad, and that change to a more genial climate should be made without delay.

In the light of this Skinner's request was not unreasonable, but the Trustees feared that his intimation of his intention to resign as warden did not extend to his resigning as vicar of the parish. As long ago as 1869 Skinner had referred inaccurately to his being 'by accident' warden as well as vicar, and stressed with only partial accuracy that 'this position is altogether irrespective and independent of his *parochial* position.' It was therefore agreed that,

> The Trustees, in considering the Warden's application for six months leave at short notice on the ground of ill-health, with an offer to resign next year, desire to record their conviction that the separation of the Wardenship from the Vicarage of Newland would entail such serious inconvenience on the Almshouses and parish that they decline to be partial to the proposed arrangement, and will not withhold their assent on the present occasion from the application for leave made by the Warden. At the same time they think that his certified incapacity to be at his post for six months in the year affords serious reasons for his resigning the Vicarage as well as the Wardenship.

The Trustees further agreed that this minute should be transmitted to the bishop, and they accepted the nomination of Nash as deputy on condition that he resided in the warden's lodge.

Shortly after his return to England Skinner, 'in his anxiety simply to know and to do his duty . . . placed himself, absolutely, without reserve, in his Bishop's hands', a course which, he claimed, had 'seemed to be suggested by the Trustees themselves when they sent a copy of their resolution to the bishop.' On 18 August the bishop replied that,

> I have no hesitation in saying that if your medical advisers certify me that it is necessary for the preservation of your health that you should be absent from Newland during the ensuing winter and early spring for a longer time than the law allows for the absence of an Incumbent, I shall think it right to give you leave of non-residence accordingly, upon the condition that you provide a satisfactory substitute for the care of the parish in your absence.

In September Skinner reported this to the Trustees, adding that while it might be necessary by medical order to apply to them for such leave of absence, he could not say this with precision at the moment. He hoped, though, that when the necessity should arise the Trustees would kindly endorse the bishop's permission. The Trustees, however, 'saw no reason for departing from the opinion that the interests of the Beauchamp Charity required a resident Warden, and that incapacity for residence is incapacity to perform properly the duties of this office.' They noted that over the past four years Skinner had had formal leave of absence for no less than eighteen months, and they considered that if they were further to permit the pensioners to be deprived of the benefits of a permanently resident warden they 'would be guilty of a breach of the trust committed to them and of a misapplication of the bounty of the Founder.' This minute too was transmitted to the bishop.

A lengthy correspondence now took place between Skinner and the Earl. Skinner noted that his 'intimation to resign' had been 'refused by the Trustees' and continued, 'As long as I am able to take a fair share and to provide for and to superintend the whole of the work of my office, I am advised by my Bishop . . . that it is my duty to God and the Church to abide where I am, and that it is not my duty to resign my position as a Parish Priest.' Since he was now forbidden by the Trustees 'to go abroad for warmth' he asked permission to rearrange the rooms at the lodge at his own expense 'to bring me the most warmth at home.' The Earl, however, rejected the suggestion that the Trustees had refused his intimation to resign the wardenship. What they had objected too was his apparent intention to retain the vicarage and thus to separate the two offices. Skinner now tried the Turkish baths at Bristol with such beneficial effect that he returned to his duties at Newland for Advent and Christmas, but he found these difficult, and 'those who watched the struggle often felt as though he must faint and die at the very foot of the altar.'

In his report to the Trustees AGM in January 1877 Skinner requested leave of absence for eight weeks to pursue a course of medical treatment. The Trustees agreed to this (with Lord Beauchamp's dissent being minuted) on the clear understanding that he must thereafter reside throughout the year at Newland or 'be subject to Rule 40', and that in the meantime he must provide an acceptable substitute to reside in the lodge during his absence. Rule forty read,

> A majority, not being less than two-thirds, of the Trustees for the time being may, at a Special Meeting, of which the Warden and Chaplain shall have at least a month's notice, and at which he may attend and be heard for himself, remove the Warden and Chaplain from his office for misconduct, neglect of or incapacity to perform properly the duties of his office, and appoint another in his place. This, however, referred only to the warden and chaplain and could have no legal force with regard to his incumbency.

Skinner spent his leave with further treatment at Bristol and returned to Newland in April. His friend Pusey wrote that since the bishop thought that his parishioners 'would lose more by his resignation than by his absence during winter, there was no reasonable cause to deprive him of his post for the sake of the small number in the parish who inhabited the almshouses.' But finding that the Trustees would not withdraw their ultimatum he offered him the post of chaplain to the convalescent hospital at Ascot, run by the Sisters of the Priory there. His doctor thought that the climate of Ascot might be more congenial, and he therefore accepted the post. On 3 July 1877 he wrote to the Trustees announcing his intention 'being alive on the 29th September [Michaelmas Day] of the present year, to retire on that day from his office of Warden of the Charity.' He went on to acknowledge the general kindness with which the Trustees had met his 'manifold shortcomings and failures' and 'the repeated indulgence with which they have treated his very weak and failing health.'

This letter was read to the Trustees at their meeting on 16 August, and Sir Edmund Lechmere then stated that 'Mr Skinner had authorised him to say that it was his intention to resign the Vicarage of Newland into the Bishop's hands on Sept. 29, and that the Bishop was willing to accept the resignation.' The use of Sir Edmund as an intermediary is interesting, and it may be that, although the Trustees were patrons of the living, Skinner did not wish to appear to be formally accepting their contention that the two offices were inseparable. Be that as it may, the news cannot have come as a surprise for, after various complimentary remarks, Colonel Scott proposed that the Reverend George Cosby White, vicar of St Matthias, Malvern Link, be Skinner's successor both as warden and vicar.[1]

But even now in the summer Skinner's health was not good. On 30 August he wrote, 'I have not preached or celebrated or even occupied my stall for five weeks; I am such a wreck.' He preached for

---

[1] A special meeting was held in October at which White's appointment as Warden was confirmed and it was resolved that he be presented to the vicarage.

the last time on Sunday 23 September, celebrated on Michaelmas Day with seventy-seven communicants, and left for London on the same day. His wife wrote of his farewell,

> Yesterday, after Litany, to which all the pensioners came except Barnes, who is dying, the dear Warden gave them a parting address. Everyone was weeping, some of them sobbing, and he with much difficulty from emotion was hardly able to articulate. Then when he had given them his blessing, he stood on the doorstep and shook hands with each one as they came out. I don't think the first Warden will ever be forgotten.

As for his remaining years, he spent four of these at Ascot—where he enjoyed the company and correspondence of Pusey who spent most of his vacations there—but still felt obliged to go abroad or to Bath each winter. In October 1881 he moved permanently to Bath, and Pusey wrote, 'My dearest Friend, It is very, very sad, as all partings are. I had so hoped that this [Ascot] would have been your home until God should call you to your everlasting home. I had such bright dreams of your future usefulness here.' But the move was of no avail. His health continued to decline, and he died peacefully on 29 December, aged sixty-three. His body was received into Newland church on the evening of 4 January 1882, an all-night vigil of prayer was held, and there was a choral communion next morning before his burial in the churchyard next to the grave of his beloved daughter.

We have noted Skinner's weaknesses, but perhaps the last words should be those of Pusey in a letter to a friend, 'What a store there must be of love for him in heaven—of those whom by God's grace, he won to God, or to whom he was the channel of God's love, and loved in him.'

The Consolidation and Continuation

Chapter Ten
The Second Vicar-Warden
George Cosby White, 1877–1897

George Cosby White[1] was born in 1825 and graduated at Trinity College, Cambridge. After a curacy at Wantage, under W. J. Butler who later became Dean of Lincoln, he was appointed warden of the House of Charity in Soho. There, in 1851, he preached on Good Friday what he believed was the first three-hour devotion in the Church of England. Three years later he became Provost of Cumbrae in Scotland, but poor health led him to return to parochial work at Chislehurst where he married Harriette and had two children—Bernard who was killed in the 1880 Basuto war, and Mary who in 1878 married his curate, E. J. Eyre, who had followed him from Malvern Link to Newland.

In 1857 White succeeded Skinner as priest-in-charge of St Barnabas, Pimlico, and in 1866 became its first vicar. Initially riots and persecution continued, but at Easter 1868 there were 483 communicants, and most of his years there were 'of comparative peace

---

[1] The archives contain a small typed volume, *Notes on the Life of the Reverend George Cosby White 1825–1918, by a Priest of The St Barnabas' Hostel, Newland, 1921;* the priest in question was Canon Griffin.

and of great progress. But he remained a staunch anglo-catholic. In 1862 he was a founder of the Confraternity of the Blessed Sacrament, in 1873 he was one of twenty-eight leading anglo-catholic priests (Skinner was another) who signed a Declaration on Confession and Absolution, as set forth in the Church of England, and it was said of him that 'At one period in his life he heard more confessions than any priest of the Church of England.' In 1880 he was one of the pall-bearers at the funeral of Father Lowder.

White also had an abiding interest in church music, and at Chislehurst he compiled a small book, *Introits and Hymns, with Some Anthems, Adapted to the Seasons of the Christian Year* which went into three editions and was used in the famous London church of All Saints, Margaret Street. In 1858 he was one of five clergy who met at St Barnabas vicarage to plan a new hymn book. The result, *Hymns Ancient and Modern,* was an immediate success and there was serious discussion of its becoming the Church of England's official hymn book.[2] White continued his involvement with it, quickly introduced it into Newland, and from 1889 till 1904 was chairman of its Compilers.

In 1876 White resigned from Pimlico and—at the invitation of Lord Beauchamp, the patron—became vicar of St Matthias, Malvern Link. But, as we have seen, a year later he was appointed vicar of Newland and warden of the almshouses. Hunt describes him as,

> A chubby, wiry man—grave and dignified, very reserved, but with a shy gentle humour . . . He could listen patiently to everyone as though he had all the time in the world, allowing them to speak freely and giving answer with a grave courtesy . . . He thus brought a balm of peace to the parish . . . It was a quality needed by Newland after the whirling prophetic ministry of Skinner.

The 'balm of peace' involved the avoidance of controversy unless it was absolutely necessary, and for a short time, at the command of

---

[2] *Historical Companion to Hymns Ancient and Modern,* ed. Maurice Frost, 1962.

the Bishop of Worcester, he gave up the use of eucharistic vestments, though he was later able to resume them. But this incurred the wrath of Skinner who wrote on 24 November 1877,

> I have been shocked this morning by a report . . . that you have changed the dear Ritual of so many years standing, and abolished the use of the Eucharistic Vestments, which have been worn without intermission of a single day for ten years! I am unwilling to believe this report on any authority less certain than your own. Kindly therefore tell me how it is—that I may know what step to take (if any) for asserting God's Honour and vindicating the Catholic Worship of the Church.

On 25 January 1888 Skinner wrote again,

> I would never be at one with my sense of duty until I have had your innovation in the matter of the Vestments thoroughly sorted out with the Bishop, and this I mean to have. As things stand at present, you have taken away the Vestments at the insistence of the Bishop. Your act makes my use of the Vestments, for ten years, to appear a continuous act of defiance of the Bishop.

On 25 February he wrote further,

> I would not wound your dear sensitive heart any more by the sad Vestment question, after this, believe me, I have no wish to draw you into a word of controversy with me. Indeed, I do not see how we could, being what we are to each other not to carry on any more together upon it. But you are too good to fail to be able to enter into my deep and sore disappointment, and to see that there are points in which your abrupt and sudden change, at the Bp's request, has compromised my practice and teaching and my credit as a loyal Priest in the Diocese, for so many years, and that I must have that out with the Bishop and get his Lordship's explanation of pressure upon you,

as against Absolute toleration of me. Having elicited that, I will do no more but will leave the issue in God's Hands.

Later he wrote, 'I have now had the whole of the Vestment matter out with the Bishop, as I promised you I should; and our correspondence . . . will be printed in a few days, for the information of all concerned.' It duly appeared under the title *Changes and Chances: A correspondence with Bishop Philpott.*

In his 25 January letter Skinner also objected that White had replaced the *Daily Service Hymnal* by *Hymns Ancient and Modern.* (HAM) It had been decided at the beginnings of the community that the latter was not suited to the peculiar requirements of Newland, and 'with all deference to you, Newland is the 'home and birthplace' of *The Daily Service Hymnal* and,

> It would be easy to show every reason why the use of the Book should not have been disturbed. Forgive me if I say that it will be difficult to give me one good reason why it should have been sacrificed to the HAM. But perhaps I have been misinformed, and you may have but added on HAM as an appended use.

On 25 February he wrote further,

> I have relieved my mind by saying what troubled me about the Hymn Book the speciality of which was that it was, deliberately, drawn up for the peculiar needs of Newland with HAM before us, at the time—and the notion of 'uniformity' distinctly rejected, so far as N was concerned. And now—for no valid reason (because the speciality of N still takes it out of the category of 'uniform' parishes) all this provision—and its labour and cost—is lost. . . . But I will not refer to the subject any more.

Skinner cannot really have expected that his successor, even a longstanding friend like White, would make no changes. Happily he seems to have realised that, having voiced his complaints, he could not pursue them indefinitely. Happily again, there is no indication that White with his gentle disposition took any offence.

White normally restricted his absences from Newland to six weeks of the year, not usually consecutive, and his absences were briefer than Skinner's. For most of the twenty years of his ministry he enjoyed the assistance of a curate, and the church, community and parish progressed quietly and happily, while his house was a centre of hospitality and welcome.

Shortly after his institution there was a special service in the church on Founder's Day, followed by a dinner given by the Trustees. Invitations were sent to local farmers, pensioners and their wives, and a few others; fifty-four sat down to dinner. In January 1878 he reported that the health of the pensioners had been 'unusually good', and his only anxiety concerned 'some very aged single men.' In May the Trustees were informed of West's impending resignation as clerk/organist. They seem to have assumed that his successor would be non-resident and decided that the school premises should be used for 'the very aged single men', that the clerk's house be handed over to the matron and that the matron's house should be used for infirm women pensioners. They also authorised White to enquire whether W. F. Cox would be willing to become clerk. Whether they also expected him to be organist as well, and whether they eventually appointed him, is not clear, but it seems that from 1878 to 1897 the clerk/organist was probably non-resident.

In August 1878 White asked the Trustees to consider reviving the choir school, possibly with the boys attending a local school, and suggested that with only minimal alterations they could be accommodated in the original choir school building with parts of it still being used by the aged single men. The Trustees' readiness to consider reviving the school is evidence that the financial reasons given for its closure in 1869 were largely a pretext for removing a constant source of friction between themselves and Skinner. White was authorised to prepare a scheme for maintaining eight choir boys, orphans of parents employed in agriculture, to be educated at some neighbouring schools, at a cost as near £200 per annum as possible, and a sub-committee was set up to work on this. The sub-committee acted speedily, and on 7 January 1879 they reported that they had placed advertisements in various papers announcing the Trustees' intention to elect eight boys, as described by White, to serve as choristers in the church. They would be boarded, clothed and educated free of charge. Candidates must be not less than eight years old, and give proof of having a good voice and being able to read fluently. Nine applications had been received, of whom three had been rejected by the organist as not having good enough voices; one remained to be examined, and five had been accepted as probationers for an initial period of three months.

In October 1879 White reported that eight choirboys were now in residence and that they had all passed their three-months probation. They were being educated at Malvern Link and Madresfield schools, and he recommended their formal admission to the foundation. The cost would be well within the £200 allowed In January 1881 he reported that, as far as church services were concerned, 'a simple dignity, such as befits a village church, has been imparted to them'; they were well respected by their teachers and their conduct in the almshouses was satisfactory. In 1882 and 1883 he again reported that the school was proving satisfactory, and in October 1884, he asked for the appointment of two supernumerary choristers to be in training ready to fill vacancies; he would arrange for them to sleep at the schoolmistress's house in the village at his own expense. This was approved.

In his January 1888 report he appended details of the choristers' diet:

Breakfast: half of the boys to have porridge and milk, with bread and butter; the other half to have coffee and bacon, turn and turn about. The whole to have bread and butter always

Dinner: meat and vegetables; a pudding every other day

Tea: tea, bread and butter, jam or treacle

Before going to bed, a cup of cocoa from October to March inclusive, a cup of milk from April to September inclusive.

In 1890 White reported that the number of boys was down to five, and that the answers to three or four advertisements had been 'few and unsatisfactory.' We have no further knowledge of the school in White's years. We have no names of organists or choirmasters, which we would have had they later become famous; we can only surmise that it was adequate but not distinguished.

The next major item was the tower. Hardwick had reduced its proposed size as early as 1860 when it was clear that economies were needed, and the earliest photograph shows it as little more than a 'lofty arched gateway' as it was described at the dedication. But the vision of something grander with a 'middle floor' had not been lost, and its completion was one of the improvements suggested by the Earl in 1868. At last, in January 1881, a sub-committee was appointed to take 'the necessary steps for completing the tower' and to 'review the financial position of the Charity.' They contacted Hardwick, and in January 1882 the Trustees authorised them to sign a contract with him for a sum not exceeding £1,500. In October they reported that the tower would be completed in a month's time at a cost of £1,350. The contractors were W. Collins of Tewkesbury, while,

> Messrs Gillet and Bland have also contracted to supply a clock of first-rate quality for £127. This is considerably in excess of the sum usually paid for ordinary Turret Clocks. But in this case it was necessary to have machinery of sufficient power to strike the hours on a bell of 7 cwt and chime the quarters on four other bells of proportionate weights—which bells the Warden has kindly undertaken to provide.[3]

---

[3] The register gives the cost of the tower as £1,634.

The tower, which is accessed from the porter's lodge, is undoubtedly impressive and, as well as the clock mechanism, the new floor had water tanks with coal fires for heating the water which could be used for laundry purposes or pumped to the Quadrangle. Nonetheless the tower as a whole appears somewhat squat or ill-proportioned. Hobhouse, reviewing Hardwick's work at Newland as a whole, considered that 'the most unsuccessful element is the gateway tower, which is large and square with, rising from it, not a mere spire, but one of Hardwick's favourite North French roofs, complete with lanterns in the sides, and a line of ironwork on the crest.'

As for the almshouses, at their annual meeting in January each year the Trustees met the pensioners in the boardroom and asked if they had any complaints. In 1879 the first-ever complaint was made—that they disliked the use of the mortuary chapel. The Trustees resolved 'that the Treasurer and Warden take steps to have the Lich House put in such decent and seemly order that all reasonable objections to the use of it by the Pensioners may be removed'; the cost was not to exceed £25. White reported in January 1880 that this had duly been done. He emphasised the utility of the chapel and added, 'It is quite understood among the Pensioners that it is a rule of the Charity that their bodies shall be placed there immediately after death.'

In January 1880 White reported that the Community of St Peter, Kilburn, had agreed to provide two nursing sisters and a sewing sister in place of the East Grinstead sisters. In January 1881 he mentioned five cases of severe illness or infirmity and stated that the pensions, especially of married couples, were not adequate to meet the cost of the 'beef tea and mutton broth' which were necessary. He suggested that the sisters should be empowered to give such necessities at their discretion and to charge them to the nursing account. The Trustees authorised the beef tea, but said nothing about mutton broth! In March, however, they agreed that any pensioners unable to cook for themselves should be provided with a 'school dinner' and that 3s. per week should be deducted from their pensions to pay for this.[4]

The 1881 census showed that White and his wife had three servants living with them. There were two Sisters of Mercy, also with a servant, and thirty-one pensioners—including three males over ninety—along with a grandson and an adult daughter. But strangely, although the choir school had now been revived and in 1879 had eight boys in residence, no choristers are recorded at Newland in this census and, although two might have been living with their parents two or three miles away, there is no hint of any kind of corporate lodgings—though there is a tradition that at some point the boys were boarded out. Similarly there is no reference to a master or matron, though someone must have been in charge of them whether resident or not.

Almost every year new pensioners were elected to fill the vacancies caused by those who had died. One elected in March 1881 was Miles Tugwell Chandler, aged seventy-one, from Malvern Link. He had been born in 1809 at Randwick in Gloucestershire, and on 19 February 1844 at Hempstead in Gloucestershire had married Eliza Jenkins, who had been born *c.*1818 at Upton-upon-Severn and who, now aged sixty-four, was admitted to the almshouses along with her husband. Miles died the same year as his admission—on 14 December—and was buried in the churchyard on 17 December. White reported that his widow was 'worthy to succeed her husband as pensioner' and proposed that she move to the clerk's house. Eliza remained in the almshouses until her death on 18 October 1896, and she was buried in the churchyard on 23 October. At the time there was nothing to distinguish Miles and Eliza from any other pensioners, but in 2011 a phone call from a family genealogist to the chaplain confirmed that they were great-great-great-grandparents of the present Duchess of Cambridge.[5]

---

[4] This was approved by the Charity Commissioner in June 1882.

[5] The line of descent from Miles and Eliza is:
Theophilus Benjamin Chandler, born 1848, Malvern; married 22 November 1868,

[See p.126 for n.5 cont.]

One wonders how many other distinguished people have been descended from Beauchamp residents.

In January 1883 Dr Weir reported that in the past year the health of the pensioners had been generally good, but nine of the 28 were suffering from 'disease of the brain or general nervous system' and required great care and attention from the sisters. He suggested that no pensioner be admitted without a medical certificate stating that he or she was not suffering from 'brain disease or any other disease which renders them totally dependent.' In January 1884 White reported nine deaths in 1883 as against an average of three per year from 1864 to 1882, and that 'in fact throughout the year the Almshouses were practically a hospital . . . and the able-bodied in a very small minority.' It was agreed that the clerk's house be used as an infirmary for single patients, with a living-in servant, and perhaps it was now that the sisters' house ceased to be used as an infirmary.

In October White reported that the use of the clerk's house for three chronic cases had greatly eased the nursing situation. But in April 1885 he reported that 'there are 14 persons living alone, most of them of great age, many very infirm and requiring to have their fires lighted and constant attention.' There were similar problems with some of the married residents. In 1887 he was able to report that there had been no deaths and scarcely any serious illness, though in 1891 he reported much sickness and five deaths, four of which has taken place in the infirmary. In 1894 a link with the early days was lost when Dr

---

Stoke Poges parish church, Bucks, Amelia White, born 13 February 1846, Ivor, Bucks.; died 22 November 1927, Norwood. Edith Eliza Chandler, born 21 January 1889 New Denham, Bucks; married 27 March 1909, Uxbridge Register Office, Stephen Charles Goldsmith, born 6 November 1886, Acton Green; died 5 January 1938. Ronald John James Goldsmith, born 25 April 1931, Norwood; married 8 August 1953, Holy Trinity, Southall, Dorothy Harrison, born 26 June 1935, East Sunderland; died ? 21 July 2006. Carole Elizabeth Goldsmith, born 31 January 1955, Perivale; married 21 June 1980, Dorney parish church, Bucks, Michael Frances Middleton, born 23 June 1949, Leeds. Catherine Elizabeth Middleton, born 9 June 1982, Reading; married 29 April 2011, Westminster Abbey, HRH Prince William Arthur Philip Louis, Duke of Cambridge, born 21 June 1982.

Weir resigned as medical officer; his son, Dr Archibald Weir, jnr., was appointed in his stead.

Of the sixty-nine pensioners admitted under White, only a third survived for ten or more years, a smaller proportion than in Skinner's day, though three men and two women lived into their nineties, the oldest being Harriet Hyde at ninety-six and Thomas Gittins at ninety-four. But despite the devoted care of the sick it was not possible to retain all of them in the almshouses, and two or three ended their days at the Powick Asylum.

In January 1888 a sub-committee was set up to consider a suggestion by Lord Beauchamp for the erection of additional almshouses, the inmates of which should be nominated and maintained by him irrespective of previous employment, and in January 1889 it was resolved,

> That the Trustees are willing to sell to Lord Beauchamp as much of the Charity land as is coloured green on the plan now produced, with a view to the erection thereon by him of four almshouses, the inmates of which are to be subject in all respects to the discipline and authority of the Trustees, but to be nominated and maintained by Lord Beauchamp, his heirs and assignees, a proper fund for repairs being provided by him.

The flats were duly erected in 1889 and are now known as Lygon Lodge.

In 1890 White's wife died aged only sixty-nine, and in the 1891 census he was alone at the vicarage apart from two servants. In the community as a whole there were now three nursing sisters, the porter and his wife, and thirty-two pensioners; there were two grandchildren, a son and daughter-in-law, and three adult daughters. There were also six choristers and a matron. In 1893 White reported that 'any breach of discipline is most exceptional', but in 1896 he had to report his first case of drunkenness. He was sorry for the offender since 'it is difficult for men who are past work, and indifferent readers, to know how to spend their time', but he thought that 'married couples, widows or single women are likely to prove the most satisfactory recipients of the benefits of the Charity.' Six months later he warned again against the election of single men unless, as in one case, they brought a daughter to live with them. Of the last three widowers elected, one was about to marry a fellow-pensioner, 'and I thought it better to allow this, lest scandal should arise', and another was 'hunting about the village to find someone to take care of him.' There had in fact been an earlier pensioner's marriage in White's day, though the one he referred to, between Thomas Greenhill and Elizabeth Drew, was the first case of two pensioners marrying each other.

In 1893 White started what may have been the first Newland parish magazine—a hand-written duplicated production of four sides, selling at ½d. a month. The volume for that year, the only one which survives, gives the hymns for each Sunday and the subjects for afternoon catechizing and also contains brief articles with a church relevance on historical matters or current affairs. More important it affords an insight into the everyday life of a small rural parish. There was indeed something distinctive, if not exotic, about Newland, but that was far from being the whole story.

In January he warned against a Mormon preacher who had recently been holding meetings in the parish, and also gave notice that on the first Sunday of each month there would be additional celebration at 7 a.m. for those who found 8 a.m. too late. In February he pleaded for more support for the Working Men's Society whose meetings were few, irregular and badly attended. In March he mentioned that lectures were also poorly attended, though concerts had proved more popular. In April he referred to a missionary working party, and in June to a Bloemfontein working party. In July he reported on an outing of the 'Guild of St Leonard'—a young men's group which met every Tuesday evening and was then just a year old. Eleven members and five friends had joined an Oddfellows' Excursion. They left just after 3 a.m. and reached Portsmouth at 10 a.m. where some saw the sea for the first time. Their return train left shortly after 8 p.m. and reached Malvern Link about 3.20 a.m. He also mentioned in July a diocesan inspection of religious education at Newland school. This was deemed 'excellent' in all five categories, and the inspector reported, 'This school if smaller is as good as ever—I know no children better taught, or who take more pleasure in learning.'

In August he gave a fascinating history of 'Wedding Breakfasts', and also reported on a choir outing to London on the day of the wedding of the Duke of York, later King George V, to Princess Mary of Teck. They left at an early hour and reached London shortly before 8am; thereafter 'Some went off at once to secure good places for seeing the Royal Procession, while others went to Matins at St Paul's Cathedral to see whether Londoners could come up to Newland in the matter of singing.' In September he referred to 'the coming of age of our popular young landlord, Earl Beauchamp' and expressed the hope that he would dine with the residents on Founders Day. In November he apologised for his writing which some people could not read and announced that in 1894 the Chronicle would be printed, though at an increased cost of 1*d.* per month. He also mentioned the establishment of a free night school, initially for men and boys, meeting weekly. In December he referred to a magic lantern entertainment for sunday school children and also a sale of work from 2 p.m. till 7 p.m.

In the church, White completed—as quickly as he could—the frescoes 'in the chapel and cloisters',[6] i.e. those on the south of the chancel and around the sacristy, and to his credit he consulted Skinner on their designs. On 25 February 1878 Skinner wrote,

> I truly appreciate your kindness in asking for any ideas I may have had about the Chancel aisle. I have always had a clear idea of what I should like there, and if I had been spared I should have carried it out. I should have dealt with the space above the arches and columns in the simplest way—carrying on a dado or wall, similar to the

---

[6] The 'chapel' here refers not to the mortuary chapel, but to that part of the south chapel where the female pensioners sat and which was sometimes known as their 'chapel'.

N. Wall (eating with Jesus) with grass below and flowering shrubs or trees in the spaces beneath the Arches. In like manner, I should have dealt with Western (upper stage) wall, some simple tracery around the Rose Window, and the mullions (just to keep it altogether) and probably a brick pattern on the wall. But, within the Chapel itself, I should have carried an arcade, all around (I mean in S and W) and placed niches and low pedestals with an Apostolic woman on each—that the dear old women might realise their companionship in Christ with those whose names are in the book of Life.

In the autumn White sent Skinner some drawings on which he made helpful comments and the work duly proceeded, and result was,

> Above the arches on the aisle side of the south arcade is a figure of Our Lord holding the vine which extends on either side.
>
> On the south wall of the chancel aisle are the Virgin and Child surrounded by adoring angels; below her are women of the OT—Sarah, Rebekah, Rachel and Ruth -and of the gospel story—Mary Cleopas, Joanna and Susanna.
>
> On the west wall of the aisle are women from the Acts—Dorcas, Priscilla, Phoebe, Lois and Lydia.
>
> In the vestibule outside the sacristy, on the west wall are Eli, Samuel and Hannah.
>
> On the east, and above the organ, Asaph, Ethan and Heman (Asaph was David's choirmaster, and Ethan and Heman musicians, cf. 1 Kings 4:31 and 1 Chronicles 15:19).
>
> High up on the left is St Christopher with the Christ child.
>
> The organ pipes are decorated and include verses from Psalm 150 and a threefold Alleluia

It was also in his period that, after Skinner's death, Mrs Skinner donated the ornate sedalia 'in memory of thirty-three years spent together in great happiness and also of the scholarship and example from which benefitted.' The sedalia, with its seven angels and their trumpets (which have a habit of being broken off when cleaners are over-enthusiastic) is a prominent feature of the sanctuary, though the memorial tablet is hidden away in the organist's area.

In March 1881 a sub-committee proposed that application be made to the Charity Commissioners to increase the warden's stipend to £300 p.a. since he was bound to employ a curate on account of the daily services required. The commissioners authorised the Trustees to pay a sum not exceeding £100 as the stipend of a curate, and White expressed his pleasure at this.

Combined with his quiet and saintly character, White also had business-like qualities and a sound grasp of practical affairs, and—with his share of the royalties from *Hymns Ancient and Modern*—he acquired substantial private means. Like Skinner he was also exceedingly generous. He donated, and later repaired, the Lych Gate. From 1880 to 1896 he was also Chaplain-General to the Convent of the Holy Name in Malvern Link, to which he was a generous benefactor, and from 1896 to 1897 he was their warden.

In January 1889 he submitted a memorandum to the Trustees to the effect that he was 'ready to provide an endowment which would in part support the Organist':

1. The salary of the present Organist is £8 a month, and it is unlikely that an efficient man could be found for less.

2. The offertory contributes £15 to £20 towards his salary, and ought not to contribute more.

3. From £75 to £80 must be forthcoming if the daily choral service is maintained.

4. The Warden is ready to hand over to the Trustees £1,000 G.E.R. 4 per cent stock, which would provide £40 a year for this purpose.

5. He would wish it to be held by them in Trust and paid to the Warden as long as the daily choral service is kept up.

6. If at any time the Choir School should be given up or the Warden should drop the daily choral service his desire would be that it should revert to the Trustees and be used for the Infirmary of the Almshouses.

The Trustees accepted this offer with gratitude.

In tribute to the sixth Earl who died in 1891, at his own expense he put two three-light dormer windows high up in the south wall above 'women's chapel.' The one on the left shows three angels of the Sanctus', while the right one depicts the archangels Gabriel, Michael and Raphael. Later, in 1895, he offered the Trustees his extensive, scholarly and valuable collection of books on theology, liturgiology, church history and the like to form the nucleus of a library, and this again was gladly accepted. He then left money to build, furnish and endow a library 'for the use of priests here, for diocesan clergy, for scholars engaged in study and research, and also for priests making retreats at Newland, and for lectures for the clergy.' The library building, probably designed by C. F. Whitcombe, and its attendant cloakroom (also a gift from White) was ultimately erected in 1910. Hunt comments,

> Everything connected with it is of the best and in the Newland tradition: the handsome embossed Italian ceiling, glass book cases, a spacious fireplace, alcoves for private study, the parquet floor, and concealed central heating; all are tastefully designed for convenience and comfort.

In May 1897 he gave notice that he would be retiring at Michaelmas at the age of seventy-two. But this was not the end of his work for the community. In August 1899 the Trustees accepted with gratitude his offer to build and endow (with a sum of about £1,600) two semi-detached houses for the benefit of clergy 'obliged by failing health or length of years to resign their benefices.' They should be in 'poor or straitened circumstances', aged sixty-five or over, and the nominations were to be by the trustees and the warden. Wives or children could live with them but must vacate the house within three months of their death. The houses were duly built as 'The Hostel of St Barnabas.' Basic furniture was provided, and each had a small garden. No duties were expected of the occupants, who lived free of rent and rates, but the warden at his discretion might allow them a share in the ministry and sacramental life of the church, and they were encouraged to give assistance in the diocese.

After his retirement from Newland, White acted for a while as domestic chaplain to the Bishop of Truro. He then made his home with his daughter Mary and her husband at Clevedon in Somerset, where he became a much-loved assistant priest at St John's church. He died in 1918, aged ninety-three, and was buried, by his own wish, in the churchyard of All Saints, East Clevedon, though Harriette had been buried at Newland.

Chapter Eleven
The Third Vicar-Warden Robert Wylde, 1897–1926

On Cosby White's resignation, the Reverend Robert Wylde was appointed to succeed him at the invitation of his friend Lord Beauchamp. Born in 1843, he was ordained in 1867 to a title at Northfield (then in the diocese of Worcester). He was rector of Northfield from 1880 to 1891, then rector of St Martin's Worcester from 1891 to 1897. While at Newland he was elected a proctor in convocation from 1908 to 1918, and appointed an honorary canon in 1910. His wife had died in 1885, and his only son died at the age of eleven though his daughter survived him.

One of his choristers, T. F. Bye who later became organist, recalled,

> His manner was so genial and completely free from any sort of pomposity, that one felt at ease immediately. We in the choir were always so conscious of his friendliness. He frequently joined in our games on the Common and in the Board Room. In fact, while retaining the respect due to his position, he was very much one of us, and we all felt for him the deepest affection. He was full of

fun and loved his jokes. On the whole I think he was the happiest person I can remember, or that I have ever known.

Wylde had hardly arrived when in December 1897 he had to report that the sisters from St Peter's Kilburn had withdrawn their nursing services and that he had replaced them with sisters from St Mary the Virgin's Wantage. There was further change in 1910 when Dr Weir resigned as medical officer. A little later, in 1913, the Trustees expressed their dissatisfaction with the nursing arrangements and their willingness to engage a nurse directly at a salary of not less than £60 a year in addition to lodging, while the sister would receive £40. Whether this was done is not clear, for the following year they were glad that the present arrangements should continue. But in 1926 the Wantage sisters withdrew their services and were replaced by the Sisters of the Epiphany at Truro.

Initially there seems to have been some confusion about the position of Lygon Lodge residents. Wylde consulted Lord Beauchamp about this, and he in turn consulted his mother and sister on what they knew of his father's wishes. He then wrote,

> Certainly the Lygon pensioners were to be subject to the same authority and rule as the Beauchamp pensioners. Thus I should be very much surprised to hear that they did not attend service, ask permission before absenting themselves or assume in any way a position apart from the others. On the matter of cloaks (not I suppose a matter of discipline) I would be glad to know what you think. I am not indisposed to make the cloak optional and the badge compulsory. But once and for all may I say it is my wish as it was my father's intention that you should be warden to the Lygon pensioners also, and with that authority also the responsibility.

As far as the Beauchamp pensioners were concerned, in January 1900 Wylde pointed out the undesirability of admitting those too old and ill to benefit from the place,

If Pensioners are for the most part elected who by reason of their great age and chronic complaints are barely ever able to leave their rooms until they are carried to their graves, the Charity assumes the character of a hospital for the dying rather than a home for the living where they have the privilege of spending the last fifteen or twenty years of their life in quiet and peaceful preparation. I have noticed that when Pensioners are admitted so late in life they do not value the advantages of the place. They are too old to bear the strain of leaving their old house and surroundings—also the great increase in the number of chronic invalids places a strain upon the nursing strength of the charity which it is hardly capable of bearing.'

In 1901, however, there were only two pensioners over ninety, and the full community consisted of Wylde, his sister and daughter and three servants; the porter and his wife; two Sisters of Mercy, one with a servant; a curate with a servant; thirty-six pensioners (including those at Lygon who were not differentiated in the census), a daughter and a grandson, and the matron and eight boarders in the choir school; there were also three visitors. There were thus sixty members of the community in the broadest sense, with ages ranging from the youngest choirboy at ten to the oldest pensioner at ninety-four.

In January 1902 Wylde was still eager for the appointment of younger pensioners who would be 'able to help in any light work in the grounds.' The last younger pensioner to be admitted had arrived 'in a very feeble state of health' and died shortly afterwards, and he recommended strongly,

> That the candidates for admission should pass our own medical man, instead of, or as well as, the Doctor in whose parish they reside. Experience seems to show that there is a tendency to give a too sanguine report of those chronic invalids, whom parish doctors would naturally be glad to see transferred from their own parish.

On a happier note he expressed the pensioners' thanks to the Trustees for the dinner they had been given in the board room to commemorate the King's coronation.

In January 1907 White in retirement offered to build two more St Barnabas houses, this time for ex-missionaries, and this too was gratefully accepted. Although those nearest the almshouses were the first to be built, the numbering was in reverse: the new ones were numbers one and two, and the older ones numbers three and four. This was because, although it was possible to walk from the almshouses to St Barnabas, the latter had a separate entrance from the road, from which numbers one and two were the first to be approached.

In 1911, with thirteen residents in St Barnabas, we would have expected the community to be larger than in 1901, but in fact it had dropped by one to fifty-nine. It now consisted of Wylde, his sister, daughter and two servants; the porter (a different one) and his wife; three pensioners and a daughter in the Lygon Houses; twenty-one pensioners and the daughter of two deceased ones in the original almshouses, along with a sister in charge of the infirmary and a sister in charge of the almshouses (presumably these were still nuns, though this is not explicitly stated); the matron (a new one) and nine boarders in the choir school; four clergy, three wives, three daughters and four servants in St Barnabas. The number of pensioners had dropped from thirty-six to twenty-four, and they occupied only eighteen of the almshouses as against twenty-six in 1901. Presumably this was one of the occasional periods when there was a large number of unfilled vacancies. The oldest inhabitant, aged ninety-two, was the only nonagenarian.

The Trustees met on 11 April 1912 and their minutes state that 'His Grace the Archbishop of Canterbury who was visiting the Almshouses entered the Boardroom and conversed with the Trustees.' The archbishop, Dr Randall Davidson, was spending the week with the bishop of Worcester at Hartlebury. His main public function was to open a new diocesan registry, but otherwise his stay seems to have been primarily for holiday. His visit to the almshouses, an indication of their high profile, was not reported in the local papers and seems to have been semi-private. One would love to know more of it.

Prior to receiving the archbishop, the Trustees resolved that 'future elections of Pensioners should be contingent upon the State Pension of 5s. a week' and the treasurer 'was asked to arrange for the reduction which would therefore be possible in the amount allowed by the Charity.' Pensions were mentioned again in 1915 when the Trustees agreed that 'Employers of labour should be paid a pension equivalent to the Old Age Pension allowance until they reach the age at which they would naturally receive it.' It seems that during the war pensioners were granted 'the privilege' of doing work outside the almshouses, and in 1919 the question was raised as to whether they might still do this. The Trustees decided to leave this to the discretion of the warden. In 1920 it was agreed that the house committee 'should decide as to the adjustment of pensions, so that those entitled to the Old Age Pension should be able to get it.' In 1925 Wylde referred to 'there being three helpless pensioners needing a great deal of attention', and again urged 'that very old and infirm people should not be appointed.' It was decided to keep the two houses next to the infirmary vacant, so that these cases could be moved there to be nearer the nursing sisters.

The 1921 census is not yet in the public domain but, while censuses have their value in giving facts and figures, these are only the bare bones and happily these bones were 'clothed' in some reminiscences by A. T. (Bertie) Shaw who wrote,

> When I went to live in the organist's house in the quadrangle in 1922 all the almshouses were inhabited by pensioners, many of whom were extremely interesting characters. To see the old men playing bowls on a summer evening was to see a picture of autumn in Arcadia. But there was another side to the picture. One old man living on an upper floor was so firmly convinced that the old dame beneath was a witch that he was afraid to come downstairs. Sometimes he would be imprisoned all day and as the 'usual offices' are all outside his

fears presented Canon Wylde and the nursing sisters with a difficult problem. My two aged house keepers (pensioners), neither of whom could read or write, also believed in the baleful influence of the so-called witch and would never stir outside my door if she was within sight.

The late Lady Beauchamp took a personal interest in the problem when the Warden mentioned it to her. She made enquiries among her friends and presently gave Canon Wylde a peculiar stone which had been sent to her by a person who assured her that it was an infallible charm against bewitchment.

Not caring very much to associate himself with a belief in magic—black or white—the Warden asked me to fetch the old pensioner to his study. After some words of encouragement he (the Warden) prayed that the old man's fears might be removed. He then gave him the stone 'in memory of the occasion' without saying anything about its magical properties. Nevertheless the purpose of the interview was achieved: That chapter of trouble was closed.

But there were now some financial difficulties, and by January 1920 there was a 'considerable overdraft at the Bank.' In January 1921 it was reported that the bank had refused a further overdraft, but that crisis had been averted by a £300 loan from Lord Beauchamp. Three economies were proposed: the choir school allowance be cut to £150 a year, the pensioners' coal allowance to revert to two tons, and the gas lights to be turned off entirely in summer, and in autumn and winter when there was moonlight, and the pensioners' gas be limited to four hours per night. By 1923 the position was beginning to improve. In 1924 the treasurer hoped that the charity would be out of debt by the end of the year, but recommended that no elections be held to fill the four vacant almshouses until this was the case. It was suggested that suitable applicants might be allowed to occupy the vacant rooms at their own expense since three houses were already occupied in this way, but this suggestion was not pursued, and in February 1925 the treasurer reported that after several years in debt the charity was now solvent again. In February 1926 it was agreed that a new gas system was required and also that electric light should be installed; this latter cost £253.

In 1917 a married couple was asked to leave shortly after their admission, in 1921 Wylde reported a case of insubordination, and in 1922 a complaint was made at the Trustees' annual enquiry. Pensioner Barnes claimed that the porter had 'wantonly attacked him and injured his back', and produced several witnesses to support him. The porter was 'severely reprimanded.' The Trustees hoped that he would 'forthwith apologise', but agreed that 'on account of his war service the breach of discipline would be overlooked.' There was another complaint in 1923 about 'the bad quality of the coal.' A third complaint followed in 1926 when pensioner Church said that there was unrest because of the fear that 'when very infirm they should be sent to the Workhouse [at Upton].' The chairman replied that they should have no fear of this, but if they were too infirm to look after themselves and had no friends who could nurse them, some had been sent to the infirmary, 'not as paupers but as guests from the Beauchamp Charity who paid for them.' But not all was gloom. Of the eighty-eight pensioners admitted under Wylde, about half remained for ten years or more. Seven of them, six women and one man, attained their nineties and Emma Symes after at least thirty-four years in Lygon lived on till 1935 when she died at ninety-eight, the oldest resident to date.

There is no suggestion that Wylde was in any sense neglectful of his duty towards the pensioners. Yet one wonders if, in his later years, he was losing his grip on the almshouses. Had he retained this, he might have sensed the pensioners' dissatisfactions and dealt with them before they were brought to the Trustees. One wonders too whether at heart he was more interested in the church and the choir school than in the almshouses.

Wylde quickly introduced a sung celebration of the eucharist on Sundays at 9.30 a.m. as well as the traditional said one at 8 a.m.; this was soon changed to 10am for those who wished to stay on for matins and sermon at 11 a.m. By 1904 a short sermon was added, but the service still lasted under an hour, and it may be that, although the eucharist itself was sung, there were no hymns. On Advent Sunday 1910 he took the momentous step of abolishing choral matins and introducing a sung eucharist, initially at 10.30 a.m. This has persisted ever since (though the hour was later changed to 11 a.m.), but for many years, because of the contemporary discipline of fasting, there was a significant congregation but rarely more than one lay communicant.

Wylde wrote simple articles in the parish magazine on things like the sign of the cross and bowing to the altar, but, like Cosby White, he believed in obedience, and the parish magazine for January 1906 records,

> A very beautiful Censer has been presented to the Church, which will be used for the present, in accordance with the wishes of the Bishops, before not during the service of the Holy Eucharist. The use of Incense in the worship of Almighty God is one of the most beautiful and scriptural ceremonies (see Mal 1:11), which is ordered by our Prayer Book in the Ornaments Rubric, but the Bishops have the power of directing when and where Incense shall be used—we shall therefore use it only according to the regulations laid down by them.

His pattern of Sunday morning services for 1919–20 was,

7 a.m.	Holy Communion (first Sunday).
8 a.m.	Holy Communion.
10 a.m.	Matins.
10.30 a.m.	Holy Communion.

On weekdays, Holy Communion was at 8 a.m., Matins at 10 a.m. and Evensong at 6 p.m.

In Lent 1922 he urged the importance of attendance at the daily eucharist, and suggested that 'If the circumstances of your daily life make it impossible . . . you should listen for the Sacring bell (which rings at the time of the Consecration in order that those who are within hearing outside may be abler to unite themselves with those who are pleading the Holy Sacrifice in the Church).' In 1926 he advertised 'Sung Mass' on Ash Wednesday, and this is the first known public use of 'Mass' at Newland. From now on 'communion', 'eucharist' and 'mass' were all in common use.

It was possibly in Wylde's time that the normal rite for the eucharist became what was known as 'the interim rite.' This was a basically prayer-book service, but with the kyries instead of the ten commandments, and with the prayer of oblation and the Lord's Prayer following the prayer of consecration. Lay people were able to follow the service with a little green booklet, *At the Holy Communion,* published by the Cowley Fathers.

Wylde was above all an enthusiastic musician and was involved in 'every local movement which had as its object the encouragement of interest in the art of music.' Who he inherited as organist we do not know, but he must have resigned—possibly when White did—and now, if not before, the posts of clerk and organist were separated. From 1904 to 1924 the clerk was Miss A. W. Crompton. She was succeeded in 1925 by Mr B. Amphlett who died shortly afterwards, and he was succeeded by his widow. As for organists, Wylde clearly had the contacts to obtain a distinguished succession,[1] all of whom resided in what now became known as the Organist's house:

Dr Edgar T. Cook (1897–1908) was an articled pupil of Sir Ivor Atkins at Worcester Cathedral. He left to become organist and choirmaster of Southwark Cathedral.

T. F. Bye (1908–11 and again 1919–20) was a former member of the choir school who as an undergraduate became president of the Oxford University Music Club. One time organist at St Matthew's

---

[1] Three of these—Cook, C. Biggs and Shaw—were invited to contribute organ accompaniments to hymn melodies to the *Plainsong Hymn Book,* published by the compilers of *Hymns Ancient and Modern* in 1932.

Westminster, then concurrently a music teacher at Malvern College. He later joined the music staff at Uppingham.

Claude Joseph Biggs (1911–19) combined the post with a Professorship at the Royal College of Music, London. He later became director of music at Radley College and a professor at the Royal College of Music at Manchester. He died on 22nd August 1971 at Ledbury, aged 88.

Ronald Biggs (1920–21), the brother of Claude, was concurrently a teacher at Malvern College and subsequently joined the BBC.

Albert Thompson (Bertie) Shaw (October 1921–81) was initially an assistant music master at Malvern College, but in 1928 (when he married at Newland) he became director of music and art master at the Royal Grammar School, Worcester. He was also at various times chairman of the Worcester Concert Club, Elgar Festivals Ltd, and the Elgar Society. In 1930 he moved from the Organist's house to Worcester.

Wylde sought to make the music of the church as perfect as possible and he quickly introduced congregational music practices on Friday evenings. But he was particularly dedicated to the use of plainsong which had been used at Newland before, though to what extent we do not know. He regarded plainsong as the church's 'natural folk-song' and he followed the principles of the first *Book of Common Prayer,* viz. 'priest and people combining to sing the Mass and the Office in a plain tune.' It is ironical that he should have succeeded someone so closely linked with *Hymns Ancient and Modern,* for by now those who looked for excellence both in words and music were increasingly dissatisfied with that book, and the result was *The English Hymnal,* published in 1906. This latter was used for many years at Newland, and it may well have been introduced by Wylde.

At Sunday mass a group of men joined the boys. The kyries, creed and gloria were normally sung to an invariable setting so that the congregation could join in. This setting may have been *A Plainsong Mass* published by the Faith Press and sometimes called the 'Leighton

Mass';[2] it was deemed in the 1980s to have been of very long standing at St Leonard's, and it certainly dated back to the days of Bertie Shaw. Alongside this, there were the variable introits, sequences and propers sung by the choir alone. Several different settings were used for the sanctus, while on great festivals a more elaborate setting was used for the gloria. Office-hymns apart, there was only a small repertoire of hymns 'selected for their musical and literary merit.'[3]

Bertie Shaw recalls,

> The singing of the psalms was never considered to be a congregational privilege. Whenever someone in the congregation began to mar the perfection of verbal rhythm and musical cadence the Warden used to signal to me to transpose the tone up out of the offenders range.
>
> In this connection I well remember an occasion early in my times when someone, singing very badly out of tune, attempted to join in the Introit. The old Canon turned round in his stall and said in a loud voice, 'Shut up, you're spoiling the music.'
>
> Newland , musically speaking, was run very much on collegiate lines. It was the business of the choir to sing to the glory of God; not merely to edify the congregation or to please the grumblers by singing juicy hymn-tunes or showy anthems which have nothing but their entertainment value to commend them.

To his credit Wylde realised that his high standards might be too much for some people. Sometimes he used *The Durham Mission Hymn-Book*,[4] and in 1904 he experimented with moving the fully choral Sunday evensong to 4 p.m. (without a sermon) and making

---

[2] The Faith Press had offices at Leighton Buzzard, and the Leighton Mass had been 'sung unaccompanied on Saints Days by the men of the Faith Press since 1907'.

[3] The plainsong books used in his time included *Hymn-Melodies . . . from the Sarum Antiphonal . . . together with Sequences; Offices or Introits . . . from the Sarum Gradual; The Plainchant of the Ordinary of the Mass*. St Leonard's also had its own book of carols.

[4] At some later point *The Mirfield Mission Hymn-Book* was used.

the 6.30 p.m. service a plainer one with the psalms said, no anthem, and a sermon. But this plainer service proved unpopular, and he quickly reverted to the previous arrangement.

On his arrival Wylde found the choir boys 'somewhat indisciplined' and he attributed this to the age of the matron, Mrs Jenkins, who had done excellent work in the past but had been in office for eighteen or nineteen years and was now aged seventy-five. He quickly replaced her with a younger woman, Miss Salter, and reported that 'the boys are much improved already in every way.' But he was soon obliged to send two of them away for 'serious misconduct', and in January 1899 there were only six left. The following year he was able to report that there were eight in the school and in that year the choir won five prizes at the musical competition at Worcester. From 1902 they gave an annual concert in the community, and at Christmas they sang carols at Madresfield Court and were then entertained royally.

The boys sang evensong every day to plainsong, including the psalms to the Sarum Psalter and office-hymns to the proper melodies, and Hunt comments, 'The boys became highly skilled in the beauty of this difficult and intricate branch of church music, and the singing of the psalms and canticles at the daily Evensong—frequently without organ—was a joy to hear, and greatly valued.' Many experts in plainsong used to visit Newland to hear the choir, among them G. H. Palmer, Dom Anselm Hughes, Sir Richard Terry and Sir Sydney Nicholson, and 'in public competitions the Newland choir was invariably the winning plainsong choir.'

By 1911 Miss Salter had been replaced as matron by Miss Ray, and in November of that year Wylde gave an interview to George Treadaway, the Duke of Newcastle's organist and choirmaster, who was anxious to seek advice as to the Duke's proposed choir school at Clumber Park. He stated that the school had a wide reputation, that boys were obtained without advertisement, that there were usually more applications than could be entertained and that they were drawn from various classes, with no distinction made in their treatment. There was no written agreement with parents, but they were required to pay £5 a year though occasionally this was waived. Parents met all other expenses including travelling, though Wylde provided caps, sweaters etc. at the expense of the Trustees.

Boys were usually admitted at the age of nine and generally remained till their voices broke. There was no promise of help thereafter, though of his own initiative he helped where he could. The boys sang at Newland church on all Sundays and holy days and at the daily evensong. They were educated at the local council school, there being no church school, though three boys went daily to King's School, Worcester at their parents' expense. They had no fixed holidays except for a month in the summer. For recreation they had the times set apart for such at their respective schools, and on Saturdays they were encouraged to play football, cricket etc.

The matron was appointed by, and responsible to, the warden and was assisted by a cleaning woman two or three days a week. She had entire charge of the school under the warden, and in a sense everything depended on her, hence the importance of the right matron, who to avoid friction must be responsible to the warden and no one else. It was also 'absolutely indispensible' that 'if there be two dormitories for the boys, the matron's bedroom should be placed between the two, and that there should be a curtained window in the walls of the her room adjoining the boys' rooms, so that at any time—without leaving her own room—she would be able to see everything that was going on in the dormitories.'[5]

In time there were so many applications for boys from educated families that Wylde withdrew the boys from the local schools and gave them full-time education under the supervision of himself and his sister. There were lessons in the morning (including Latin and Greek), 'prep' in the afternoon, and choir practice after tea (with the men singers joining them on Fridays). Hunt writes, 'The life was strenuous in term-time, but interspersed with many festivities . . . Plays and concerts were given in the Board Room, and the boys had their

---

[5] For this paragraph I am again indebted to Colin R. Brownlee.

part in the general community life.' There was also a scout troop under Canon Griffen who acted as chaplain to the boys. On Sunday afternoons the boys were entertained in the Warden's Lodge, and then allowed to play bowls in the Quadrangle. Alternatively they had tea in the school, with some of the clergy and the organist as visitors. On Sunday evenings they would ramble across the fields to Old Hills with the Matron. They also enjoyed a firework display, but on 6 November, St Leonard's Day, rather than on the fifth.

But although the musical standard was so high, the financial situation remained insecure. In 1900 expenditure on the school increased from £170 to £240, and a report by Munn and the treasurer criticised the extravagant food provided such as tinned salmon and fancy biscuits. Wylde was asked to consider carefully 'how the expense of the school may be kept as low as possible', bearing in mind that, although it was 'most desirable that the choir school should continue', if the income of the charity continued to diminish it would be necessary to seek authority to discontinue the school. In 1902 he reported that the expenses had been reduced by more than £70. In 1909 £217 was spent on the choir school. By 1914 expenses had been reduced and the Trustees authorised the purchase of a new piano, but they rose again in 1916, and it was resolved that Wylde 'should keep them down to £200 a year in addition to what he received from the boys' parents.' In January 1920 up to £250 p.a. was allowed, but later that year it was proposed that the warden should form a committee to share the responsibility of the school and its finances, and that after six months the Trustees' contribution should be limited to £150 per annum. At this time the full fees, for those whose parents could afford them, were £50 a year, though these in no way met the true costs. Around 1925 further economies were made by withdrawing of boys from the King's School and sending them instead to the Royal Grammar School, which did not charge fees.

The Trustees continued their annual grant, and there were modest fees for parents who could afford them, but for the most part it was Wylde himself, with the help of some friends, who carried most of the burden. A national appeal was launched, supported by Sir Edward Elgar, Sir Ivor Atkins and Bishop Gore, but the response was limited.

In the church, in 1905 Wylde welcomed the gift from Lady Beauchamp of three sanctuary lamps made the previous year. In general there was little need now to add to the church, though after the First World War a memorial tablet was erected to the south of the Chancel Gates 'in grateful memory' of nine young men 'who served in this choir and sanctuary'; unusually the inscription here was in English.

Wylde encouraged the religious life of the parish by lectures, missionary talks and retreats, and its social life by plays, concerts and garden parties. Around 1909 he established a branch of the Church of England Men's Society, though this probably lapsed *c.*1916 as a result of the war. From 1910 he was allowed to use the library for specific church purposes, especially on Sundays, and for meetings, conferences and the like. He raised a fund to buy the village school which had closed around 1921 and to convert it for use as a parish hall.[6] It also fell to him on 27 May 1920 to chair the first meeting of the Parochial Church Council, a body which had been brought into being in parishes throughout the country by the 1919 Enabling Act. Its minutes do not make inspiring reading, and it was primarily concerned with everyday financial matters, though these included the allocation of the offertories and of missionary giving. The minutes for October 1926 also record that volunteers had cleaned the mortuary chapel, and 'it was hoped that occasional celebrations might take place there.'

Wylde revived the idea of a retreat house, made preparations for a public appeal and printed copies of a proposed design, but all these were put into abeyance when war broke out. But from 1901 to 1922 onwards twice-yearly retreats flourished even in the absence of a retreat house, and in 1908 there was even a bishops' retreat attended by six overseas bishops. The clergy, sometimes as

---

[6] Now a private house.

many as fifteen to thirty-five, were housed in the warden's lodge and elsewhere in the community and the village. Meals were held in the boardroom and served from the warden's lodge, while 'the chapel and library provided places of quiet for study and meditation, and the grounds for silent walks.' The conductors were often monks from Mirfield or Cowley but there were also leading Anglo-Catholics such as V. S. S. Coles, Darwell Stone and W. H. Frere, who later became Bishop of Truro.

In 1898 Wylde had a curate whom he accommodated in the schoolmaster's house, and he moved the infirmary to one of the 'archway' houses. He had several subsequent curates and was also assisted (like his successors) by the clergy of St Barnabas and occasionally by other retired clergy living nearby. But his final years were beset by infirmity of body, though not of mind and there was probably a slight decline in church life.

In July 1926, 'having a long time been incapacitated', he announced his intention to resign at Michaelmas, and it was agreed that he be allowed to move into a St Barnabas house. In fact he was too ill to move and he remained in the warden's lodge where he died in March 1927. Hunt describes his solemn requiem as a 'memorable' occasion: the boys were joined in rendering the plainchant by the sisters of the Convent of the Holy Name, and forty robed clergy attended. 'Would, could Newland ever be the same? . . . As they laid his tired body to rest many of those present felt that they would never see his like again.'

They were probably right.

Chapter Twelve
The Years to the Centenary, 1927–1964

The first three vicar-wardens were forty-three, fifty-two and fifty-four when appointed, and they served an average of just over twenty years each. Skinner was a national figure who appeared both in the *Dictionary of National Biography* and its Oxford successor. White was another national figure and Wylde was a distinguished local one. All three in their different ways could be described as giants. But for the next thirty-seven years there were six vicar-wardens, five of whom were in their sixties when appointed, and they served an average of only six years each. They were faithful and dedicated but, although one stayed for sixteen years and clearly had a long-term influence, none could be deemed giants.

Maurice Frederick Bell, September 1927 to May 1929, was born in London in 1862. He graduated from Oxford, trained further at Cuddesdon and was ordained in Liverpool in 1885. In 1904 he became vicar of St Mark's, Regents Park, and later moved to the diocese of Oxford. He was another accomplished musician. He made several contributions to *The English Hymnal,* including the famous translation, 'Hail Thee, Festival Day,' contributed to the *Oxford Book of Carols* and wrote a book *Church Music*. He was familiar with Newland's musical tradition and came with his wife with the intention of doing all he could to preserve it. Sadly in 1929 he resigned—officially on account of ill-health. One source suggests that he retired to Italy and another that he died in 1931, but it seems fairly clear that he died in 1947 aged eighty-four in the Chanctonbury district of Sussex. There is general agreement that he ultimately converted to Roman Catholicism.[1]

Francis Wilfred Osborn, August 1929 to January 1938, was born *c.*1862. Like Bell he was an Oxford man and had also trained at Cuddesdon. Ordained at Worcester in 1895, after his curacies he became vicar first of St Michael, Camden Town, and later of St James, Plymouth. He was then vice-principal of St Mary's College, Edinburgh. His family had lived in Malvern Link for some years, so he knew of Newland and its traditions. He was sixty-seven, and had been retired for two years, when he moved with his wife into the warden's lodge. In January 1930 he revived the parish magazine, which had come 'to an untimely end' as a result of the war, and he was the first vicar to be referred to as 'Father' in the PCC minutes. He resigned in January 1938 on health grounds. Two years later his house and library were destroyed by enemy action, and thereafter he spent part of each year at Malvern Link, joining in the worship at Newland and giving unobtrusive but valued guidance to his successors. He died in Scotland in 1952 at the age of ninety and was buried in Dundee.

Arthur Wilfrid Hatherly, 1937–1941. On Osborn's retirement, J. W. Greaves, rector of Madresfield, expressed to his fellow-trustees his concern about the difficulty of finding a replacement of suitable churchmanship, with a good knowledge of plainsong 'for which Newland and its choir school had become famous', and also with sufficient private means; they agreed to raise the stipend to £275 a year. He then suggested Hatherly, vicar of Milton Abbas, Dorset, whom he knew personally, and this was agreed. Hatherly, born in 1872, was another Oxford man and he was ordained there in 1895, but he had

---

[1] His name does not appear in the 1938 edition of *Crockford's Clerical Directory*, or thereafter.

spent much of his early ministry at Birmingham and Smethwick and when he and his wife arrived at Newland he was already a tired man. He announced his resignation in 1941 owing to ill health and died later that year, aged 69; he was the first vicar to be referred as 'Father' in the Trustees' minutes as well as those of the PCC.

Canon John Hunt, 1942–1958. Newland PCC hoped for a vicar-warden 'who will carry on the traditions of Newland', ideally 'a younger and more vigorous priest.' Hunt, a Worcestershire man born in 1886, was a Durham graduate and, after further training at Lichfield, was ordained in Worcester in 1914. Apart from a year in London, he had spent the whole of his ministry in Worcester, and was currently vicar of Wichenford and rural dean of Martley, and also an honorary canon. Now in his mid-fifties, he moved into the community with his wife Mary, proved a diligent pastor and was rural dean of Powick from 1943 to 1951. The books he bequeathed to the library confirm that he was a scholarly man, and on retirement he wrote the first history of the church and community. This hugely valuable source acknowledges the failure of the retreat house to materialise and the eventual closure of the choir school, but in general it depicts church and community almost as 'the new Jerusalem' and is wholly uncritical. Yet Hunt knew that both had their problems, and in a private letter he wrote scathingly about the shortcomings of a brother-priest in a tone that is wholly different from that of his public history. There is a contradiction here which we cannot resolve. He retired in 1958, moved to 1 St Barnabas, and continued to assist as required. He died on 6 July 1974, aged eighty-seven.

Francis Benjamin Darke, June 1958 to March 1963. Another Worcestershire man, born in 1896, he was previously vicar of St Paul, Worcester, where 'Woodbine Willie' had once been incumbent. He exercised a quiet ministry and was looking forward to celebrating the centenary of the community, but he and his wife retired to Worcester on account of his ill-health. He died shortly afterwards in London, aged sixty-eight, and was buried at Newland on 5 September.

Frederick Trevor Bott, instituted in July 1963, was born in

Leicestershire in 1903 but was trained and—in 1929—ordained in Trinidad where he served a curacy at St Paul, San Fernando. Immediately before to coming to Newland he was vicar of Norton and Lenchwick, near Evesham. He revived the parish magazine in 1964 and it was he who presided over the centenary celebrations.

Pensioners and Almshouses

In 1928, twenty-five years after Wylde had proposed it, the Trustees decided that 'in future the Medical Officer should see and approve of all new pensioners before they took up their residence.' In 1932 Osborn referred to difficulties with regard to the pensioners' use of lighting, in getting them to fulfil their obligation to give useful work in the almshouses, and in the matter of leave of absence. In the light of these difficulties the Trustees issued a new set of rules. Some of these go back to the original foundation. Others must have been issued subsequently, though there is no record of their promulgation. The new set were allegedly 'Issued by Resolution of the Trustees, January 18th, 1932.' But the Trustees minutes of that date include only a response to the specific items raised by the warden. Presumably these were now added to an existing set of rules.

> No Trade or Calling whatsoever shall be exercised within the Almshouses by any person for his or her own gain without the permission of the Warden.
>
> All able-bodied pensioners according to their ability, shall be ready to employ themselves usefully according to the Rules and Regulations of the Almshouses.
>
> (Constitution Statutes, Paragraph 37).
>
> Pensioners are required to keep their stairs, archways, passage to yard and yard clean.
>
> Those living upstairs to scrub the landing and stairs in turn.
>
> Those living downstairs to clean the Archway stones in turn to the other side of the staircase.
>
> The Passage to the Yard to be done by all the inmates in turn

The Yard to be kept clean by the men in each Archway.

No lines may be put up in the passages to dry clothes and the Landings and Passages to be kept as clear as possible.

Any Pensioner unable to do the required cleaning must get someone to do it for him or her for a small payment.

All lights must be out by 10 o'clock pm.

Except in cases of illness or in special circumstances approved by the Warden, no Pensioner may be absent from the Almshouses for more than a fortnight at a time, without written leave from the Warden or two of the Trustees.

No Pensioner is allowed in the Allotments on Sundays after 10.00 a.m.

Pensioners desiring to be absent from the Morning Service should obtain leave from the Warden the day before.

The way in and out of the Quadrangle is by the main porch only and by no other way.

Note. At the request of the Trustees the Warden will put up in the Porter's Lodge entrance a Roster of Pensioners responsible for such duties as he may assign to them in accordance with paragraph 37 of the Almshouses Constitution. The Warden relies on the Pensioners to carry out the duties so assigned.

In 1929 J. W. Greaves was appointed clerk, and in 1941 he was succeeded by J. G. R. Blackwall, his successor as rector of Madresfield though not apparently a trustee. Both these were obviously non-resident, but from 1949 to 1960 H. P. Pembridge was clerk; he resided in one of the Lygon Lodges, and 'almost all their technical work of the Trust was delegated' to him. From 1961 to 1963 he was succeeded by G. L. E. Longman and then from 1963 to 1970 by E. A. Beale. It is not clear if Longman was resident, but Beale was not.

For many years the Trustees had assumed that the St Barnabas houses were their responsibility. In 1932, however, the treasurer discovered that the deed under which St Barnabas was constituted required 'an entirely different body from the Beauchamp Charity

Trustees, though appointed from the latter.' The only survivor of the original trustees was Lord Beauchamp who now appointed eight of the Beauchamp Trustees to join him as trustees of the Hostel. From then till 1960 the Hostel Trustees met as a separate body.

In 1932 again the question of widows was raised: 'The custom had been to continue the pensions to them, but there was no authority for this in the Statutes.' Under clause thirty-one, however, the Trustees could make a rule to deal with this matter, and it was formally approved that on the death of a male pensioner 'the name of his widow, if there be one, shall be submitted to the Trustees, and if approved by them she shall become the pensioner of the Charity.' This, however, referred only to the almshouses and not to St Barnabas.

Later in 1932 there were more financial problems. The Trustees' income was to be reduced by nearly £188, and they saw no alternative but to reduce the amounts paid to pensioners. They therefore resolved that from 1 January 1933:

> Pensioners receiving the Old Age Pension should be paid 5s. a week, those not in receipt of Old Age Pension should receive 7s. 6d. a week, and that in the case of Pensioners who . . . might as having been employers of agricultural labour receive a higher pension, no payment should exceed 12s. 6d. a week.[2]

In 1934 a pensioner complained that they 'were not allowed the medicines which they had formerly been accustomed to have.' The treasurer explained that the pensioners 'had got into the habit of going to the chemists without authority and ordering the things they wanted.' As a result the chemist's bill had become excessive and he had ruled that drugs etc. were to be provided only on the

---

[2] In the light of this it is strange that in January 1935 the Treasurer reported 'that there was some hardship in the case of pensioners who were not in receipt of Old Age Pensions, and that unless their friends were able to help, the normal pension of 5s. a week was inadequate'. It was agreed then the Treasurer and the Warden could augment the pension in these cases where they deemed it necessary.

orders of the doctor or sister in charge. This was approved by the Trustees. Another complaint was made in 1936 that pensioners were not allowed to see the doctor when they wished and were made to wait until his next visiting day. It was explained that 'it was in the discretion of the sister-in-charge, and the nurse, to send for the doctor specially when required,' but the case that led to the complaint had not been an urgent one, and this had been confirmed by the doctor.

In 1937 the Warden reported the repeated insobriety of a pensioner who had left voluntarily prior to being required to leave, and also 'the disinclination of some' to help in the maintenance of the grounds. He was instructed to send a circular letter to the pensioners reminding them of their obligations here. It was also agreed that the pensions of those not receiving the Old Age Pension should be increased from 7s. 6d. to 10s. a week.

At a practical level, in 1931 the Trustees decided to deepen the well and install an electric motor for pumping; this was cheaper than getting water from Malvern UDC. In 1933 they were concerned about the use of oil lamps and stoves, and they decreed that these could be used only by the special permission of the warden. It was also agreed that two additional fire extinguishers should be provided, so that there be three in all the buildings. In 1937 a scheme was approved for heating the pensioners' bedrooms with radiators and a boiler for each set of four flats.

In 1938 the nurses who had been provided by various religious communities were finally withdrawn by the last of these communities and replaced by a paid lay nurse with a free house. It was also in 1938 that the eighth Earl invited to Madresfield some of the considerable number of Ligons (note the variant spelling) from the United States. They paid a further visit in 1963 and it is highly likely that they visited Newland on these occasions. Another eminent visitor—'to Lord Beauchamp's Home for Impoverished Clergymen'—in the 1930s was Evelyn Waugh.

After the outbreak of the Second World War in 1939, one Trustee became a prisoner of war, and others found it difficult to get to meetings. The porter was required to register for National Service, and iron railings in the grounds were requisitioned for scrap iron. But on the whole the community was remarkably unaffected, and the residents' complaints were very domestic. In January 1942 one pensioner asked that they might be excused church one morning a week to facilitate shopping, also whether she could sit with her husband in church in the evening. The Trustees decided to leave the first question to the new warden, Canon Hunt, though they themselves were quite agreeable 'provided that all Pensioners took the same morning.' To her second request they saw no objection. A second pensioner complained of 'a certain amount of bullying'; this apparently referred to the nurse, and later the treasurer expressed his view that she 'had had too much authority outside her own specialised work', but things would be adjusted when Canon Hunt took over. This pensioner also asked permission to attend Malvern Link church on alternate Sunday mornings: 'to this the Trustees did not agree.'

In his first report in July 1942 Hunt referred to three pensioners who were 'entirely out of sympathy with the Traditions of Newland and a disturbing element to the Community.' He urged stricter enquiry with regard to future applications, and to this 'the Trustees entirely agreed.' At the end of 1942 the Trustees' general account was overdrawn by about £300. The following year, in an attempt to rectify this and in accordance with wartime regulations, they let three flats to tenants for the duration of the war and agreed that a fourth flat should be similarly let. One tenant, however, proved unsatisfactory and was given immediate notice. In 1946 Hunt urged that for the good of the community 'those flats now let should be filled with pensioners as they became vacant.' The Trustees 'thoroughly agreed . . . so far as the Community's good was involved but considered that the financial position was not yet sound enough to forego this source of income' and it was resolved that tenancies should be continued 'for the time being.' There was still an overdraft of £388 and it was not till 1948 that the treasurer could report that this had been cleared. Meanwhile in 1947 it was suggested that vacancies might be advertised 'further afield and possibly in the *Church Times.*'

From 1944 it was felt that—despite the 1932 revision—there were many anomalies in the rules, and in 1950 attendance at daily morning service was mentioned specifically. In 1949 there was correspondence with the Charity Commissioners about a revision of the scheme, and in 1950 formal application was made for amendments, but there were the usual legal delays and the scheme remained unchanged for many years. Despite this, in May 1961 the Trustees dropped the wearing of cloaks by the pensioners, and the rules on compulsory churchgoing were eased, though it is not clear to what extent.

Up to June 1948 all pensioners still received a pension from the charity, but thereafter pensions seem gradually to have been restricted to those already in receipt of one and there is no record of their being paid after November 1962. In 1949 it was reported that the Charity Commissioners had stated that, in view of the new national health service, it was no longer necessary for the Trustees to pay a retaining fee to a doctor, and the services of the medical officer were now dispensed with.[3]

In 1953 there were great celebrations for the Queen's coronation. On 31 May there was a service of preparation at 6.30 p.m. Then on the day itself, 2 June, there were eucharists at 7.30 a.m. and 9 a.m. These were followed by the ceremonial dedication of a memorial plot on the Common at 2 p.m., children's sports at 2.30 p.m., coronation teas for all parishioners at 4 p.m., 5 p.m. (children) and 6 p.m., a grand concert in the Quadrangle grounds at 7 p.m. followed by a short service of thanksgiving, and finally a bonfire and fireworks display at 10 p.m. On Saturday 6 June there was a fête in the Quadrangle, and on Saturday 20 June all residents were invited to tea at Madresfield Court.

---

[3] Dr Stevens had resigned in 1932 on his emigration to New Zealand. He had been succeeded by his partner, Dr Jamison, who in turn was succeeded by Dr G. Waugh Scott in 1943.

As the 1964 centenary drew near the PCC discussed how best it might be commemorated, and in September 1959 Hunt offered to compile a history in twenty-seven monthly instalments. This offer was gratefully accepted and these instalments, later retyped on quarto, became his book, *A History of St Leonards Church Newland*. Meanwhile the Trustees made plans for major works, the most ambitious since the community was founded. Several pensioners had left the community after only a short time. In some cases this may have been because of illness, but perhaps some did not warm to the community's religious foundation while others deemed the housing inadequate. Godfrey Russell, one of the Trustees, explained that 'The main structure of the Almshouses was reasonable but the facilities heatwise and as regards sanitary and washing facilities were almost completely absent, almspeople having to go into their back yards for the use of perhaps one toilet to two almshouses and no bathrooms.' The electric wiring was also unsafe. He inspected the almshouses with the local authority, and it was agreed that 'they were unfit to live in.'

In 1963–64, with Mr Bellamy of Worcester as architect, £32,000 was spent on modernising the almshouses—bathrooms, oil-fired central heating, new sanitary arrangements, redecoration etc.—and, for Russell, 'the Almshouses once more became a great credit to the Trustees and a great comfort to their occupants.' The addition of bathrooms slightly spoiled the view of the north front of the almshouses, but there was no way of avoiding this. At the same time the choir school was converted into two self-contained flats, plans were agreed for three flats in the warden's lodge,[4] and the sisters' house was renovated. The Beauchamp family gave £4,000, and another trustee gave a generous donation. There was also work on the parish room or pantry where the boardroom kitchen now stands. But although concern had been expressed in 1959 about the condition

---

[4] Specifications and plans for all these works still exist in the Beauchamp archives, but only two were created at this stage. The architect was a Mr Walker from Birmingham.

of the old vicarage coach house, now for the first time was recorded as 'St Christopher's', nothing was done about this—or about the St Barnabas houses which happily were in good condition

In July 1964 the *Worcester Diocesan Messenger* referred to the centenary and reported that,

> Looking ahead, the Earl sees a continuing need—indeed, a growing need for this much sought after accommodation, but there may be a shift, he says, in the type of occupant. More homes may be found for retired clergy and perhaps something will be done for clergy widows. Under the present constitution, the almshouses are available only for needy folk with an agricultural background; if a clergyman dies in one of the four adjoining clergy houses of St Barnabas, his widow must, after a decent interval, move out. These are matters for the trustees, who undoubtedly have the vision and practical good sense to do whatever is best for the unique community at Newland.

The week of the centenary saw great celebrations. On Saturday 18 July there was a quiet afternoon, conducted by Father Russell, chaplain-general of the Convent of the Holy Name. On Monday evening there was the first evensong of the festival, and then on 21 July there was holy communion at 7 a.m. and 8 a.m., a sung eucharist at 10.30 a.m. and a festival service in the evening, with singing led by the Worcester Cathedral voluntary choir. After an introduction, giving thanks 'for the great tradition of Catholic worship and teaching which has persisted by the providence of Almighty God from its first days to this present time', there followed evensong, at which Lord Beauchamp read the first lesson and the sermon was preached by C. E. Stuart, Assistant Bishop of Worcester. There was then a procession of crucifer, choir, clergy, pensioners, trustees and general congregation to the Quadrangle for the rehallowing of the newly-modernised almshouses and the unveiling by William, eighth Earl Beauchamp of a memorial plaque.

This was not all. On Thursday 23 July there was a parish supper and entertainment, on Friday 24 July a requiem for departed benefactors, former wardens, members of the community etc, on Saturday afternoon a programme for children, and on Sunday 26 July celebrations of holy communion at 7 a.m. and 8 a.m., matins (said), a procession and sung eucharist, and finally solemn evensong and sermon.

Meanwhile throughout this period the parish, which of course included the community, continued like any other with a servers' guild, Mothers Union, rummage sales, and collections and sales for missions Organisations included a coal and clothing club, and talents club. The annual fair was important—later there was both a summer fête and an autumn fayre—and there were occasional whist drives, film shows, concerts, tea parties, coach trips and barbecues.

The Choir School

Bell took the choir school very seriously, kept careful records and had the brook drained to create a swimming pool for the boys at the bottom of the warden's garden. In 1928 he noted that numbers had dwindled and appealed to *Church Times* readers to assist in obtaining recruits. In January 1929 he informed the Trustees that the school's position was precarious, and asked for an increase on their present grant of £150. The Trustees increased this to £200, but with the boys' fees amounting to £300 there was still a shortfall of £100. Osborn also took the school seriously and appealed for help to meet this. But he saw the boys as his responsibility rather than the organist's, he acted as their confessor and was more of a disciplinarian than Wylde. This led to problems, and Shaw states that after Osborne's appointment he 'never entered the school buildings' and that the school 'lost its family atmosphere and became more institutional.' He also complained that the swimming pool was filled up and that the boys were confined to their own quarters.

But the Trustees had ongoing financial problems with regard to the charity as a whole and in 1933 they found it necessary to reduce the grant to £150. In 1936, however, the school's financial position was still grave, and they increased it by £25.

Few of the boys were now local, and with fees (though subsidised) of £12 a term the school was no longer wholly a charity. The boys were normally aged between eight and eleven when they arrived, and they usually remained until their voices broke. Some, however, left earlier: they were academically or musically incompetent, their behaviour was bad, their parent or parents had financial problems or wanted them at home, or their health could not cope with the daily journey to Worcester. In 1936 there were ten boys in the school; they went by bus to Worcester Royal Grammar School and returned in time for tea at 5 p.m. and evensong at 6 p.m.; six of the boys came from Kenton, near Harrow, whose vicar had guaranteed a supply of boys, but by 1938 the number was down to three. Hatherly explained that,

> The school had no great advantages to offer which would compensate for the demands made upon the boys, and their journeys to Worcester Grammar School deprived them of the amenities of a Boarding School, their residence at Newland cut them out of the games and social life of the school, while the fees paid (£36 a year) were not greatly less than those of the cheaper boarding schools.'

The treasurer now proposed the introduction of boys sent by the Church of England Waifs and Strays Society[5] who agreed to send eight boys to form the nucleus of the school and to pay a grant of 8*s*. a week for each boy. But in 1941 Hatherly reported that the school was ceasing to pay its way, and that the Society had been asked to increase their contribution. Various trustees organised fund-raising events and there were a number of donations, so at the AGM in 1943 Hunt was able to report that the deficit had been wiped out and there was a small balance in hand.

There was still a small balance in 1945, but after a long report from Hunt on 18 May 1945 the Trustees decided on its closure 'pro tem.' This saved them £175 a year, the current amount of their grant, and

---

[5] Now the Church of England Children's Society.

the closure took effect on Whitsunday. Hunt immediately informed the PCC and discussed the implications. They could continue as they did when the choristers were on long vacation, or they could attempt to form a choir of ladies, with men if possible, but 'processions would have to be dropped, and most likely the weekday Mass.'[6]

He made various enquiries in the hope of saving it, while the Trustees considered the redecorating and 'temporary' letting of the school and the master's house, but sadly 'pro tem' and 'temporary' proved to be permanent. Nonetheless the possibility of its revival was not wholly ruled out, and in March 1949 the clerk wrote, 'Whilst it is always hoped that in the not too distant future it may be possible to re-establish this special part of the original Scheme, should circumstances permit, it is not proposed to do so at present'

The Church and its Services

Bell quickly noticed that the frescos had become dirty, and that an accumulation of dust and grime, smoke, and the fumes of candles, gas and incense had dimmed the colours on the roof and walls. In January 1928 he asked the Trustees for 'help in the cleaning and re-brightening of the chancel.' The Trustees pointed out that 'the congregation and not the Trustees were responsible for the decoration of their parish church', but they made a grant of £100 'without prejudice' on condition that an expert was consulted before it was spent. An Oxford architect then visited the church and stated that it would be a misfortune if any decorations were erased.

This work was undertaken by Clayton and Bell, and an inscription on the chancel arch states in Latin of course—'These paintings were restored in pious memory of the second warden, George Cosby-White.'[7] But Bell instructed Clayton and Bell to paint out (with blue-green oil colour) all the lower frescoes of virgin martyrs on the

---

[6] The reference to the weekday mass is puzzling, but perhaps there were occasions when the celebrant and a boy server were the only people present.

[7] The hyphenated form is strictly incorrect. Although he was generally known as Cosby White, Cosby was in fact his second Christian name.

north wall and the decoration beneath them. It was probably at this time that the sanctuary frescoes of St Stephen and St Laurence and those on the jambs of the chancel windows were painted out, though happily not in the same colour, and that colouring was added to the reredos. At the same time Bell had gilded riddle-posts made for the altar.

The cleaning and restoration were successful, but the painting out of so many figures upset the balance of the decorative scheme in the chancel. Bell reported in January 1929 that he had been able to add £150 to the Trustees' £100, and that he had spent £233. He asked the Trustees to view the work done and to make a further grant 'so that he could continue the work', and they donated a further £10. Bell realised—too late—that the obliteration of so much decoration was a mistake, but his successor discovered the original cartoons in Clayton and Bell's archives, and in 1937 the frescoes of the virgin martyrs were repainted. The parish magazine reported,

> Some of the figures on the walls of the chancel were badly damaged a year ago by wet coming from a defective gutter in the roof. Messrs Clayton and Bell, who originally decorated the whole church, were consulted and their estimate accepted for repairing the damage and restoring the figures. This has now been done. At the same time advantage was taken of this opportunity to restore the six figures of saints which had been painted out with a great patch of blue in years gone by. The patch has ever since been an eyesore along the whole North wall of the chancel. . . . It is a great satisfaction to see [the figures] again . . . The work was executed most skilfully by Mr Orridge, the representative of Clayton and Bell, and took three weeks to do.'[8]

Clayton and Bell estimated £100 for cleaning the paintings on the nave walls 'sadly injured by the gas formerly used.' Funds were not

---

[8] This work was paid for from the legacy of a Miss Gillham.

available at the time, but a subsequent gift of £200 enabled the work to proceed though unfortunately in some areas the ugly paint remains to this day.

The parish population was now increasing slightly and some of the newcomers, unlike the older residents who had been brought up in it, found the anglo-catholic ethos uncongenial. In July 1928 Bell reported to the PCC that 'he had received a donation towards furnishing a statue of the Madonna and child to be placed in the church.'[9] Consideration was deferred till September when he explained that 'Such a statue would add to the adornment of our Church because of its artistic beauty; but more than that it would illustrate the doctrine of the perfection of the Divinity and Humanity of our dear Lord, and emphasize the importance of the Incarnation which is being called into question at the present time.' A resolution to accept the offer was passed by eight votes to six, but 'The Warden not being satisfied with such a small majority proposed . . . "that the gift be accepted and placed for the time being in the Chapel of All Souls, and that they should apply for a Faculty to place the statue in the church."' This was carried unanimously.

A faculty was duly applied for, with the statue to be sited in the southeast corner of the nave; it would be placed on a pedestal, and there would be a canopy above it with the text, 'The Word was made flesh.' Fifty parishioners (none of whom were almshouse residents) now petitioned against it as 'inconsistent with the Teachings of the Church of England.' Bell broke the objectors down into four nonconformists, thirteen communicants (most of them only Easter communicants) and thirty-three non-communicants, and he assured the registrar that 'We should never dream of carrying such a Figure in procession, and we have no intention of setting up a stand for votive candles.' But the bishop was also unhappy and had written to the registrar, 'This is, perhaps of all the churches in the diocese,

---

[9] NADFAS describe this as 'painted cast-metal statue of Madonna and child. Madonna wears painted gold crown and cape, blue coat and gold dress with red belt. Child has gold robe'.

the one where I should regret to see any more statues introduced.' Whether Bell sensed that there was opposition from above and feared that the faculty might be refused, or whether he thought it unwise to proceed with what was parochially so controversial, we do not know, but in December he reported to the PCC that he and the wardens had withdrawn their application; the statue remains in the All Souls (Cloister) Chapel to this day. At the next PCC meeting, in March 1929, Bell announced his resignation on grounds of 'ill-health'—but that was probably a euphemism for disappointment and frustration, and he lived for another eighteen years.

Despite this furore Bell's successor, Osborn, consolidated the anglo-catholic tradition. He also used the title 'Father' of his brother-clergy from time to time, and from now on this became more general. Hunt states that he showed great patience and tact in dealing with the unhappy newcomers and that with assiduous visiting and individual teaching he was able to win over most of them. He also re-established Newland as a centre for retreats; in June 1931 a retreat was held for the first time for nine years and these continued throughout his incumbency each June or July. But he had problems with the organist as well as with the newcomers. He disliked plainsong and, while he bowed to strong opposition in agreeing to continue this, he sympathised with those who wanted a 'popular service' and, according to Shaw, 'he changed the unique character of the service by introducing subjective hymns.'

The gifts continued. In 1932 a humeral veil was given by Miss Tait, one of Osborn's former parishioners from London.' A small paten and chalice were given by Father and Mrs Worster in commemoration of the golden jubilee of his priesthood, twenty years of which had been spent at St Barnabas. In July 1936 there was mention of a silver wafer box given by his widow in memory of Father McLoughlin, also of St Barnabas, and of a silver censer—smaller and easier to handle then the original one which would now be used only on great festivals—given by Mrs Bagnall in memory of her husband. A carpet for the sanctuary was given by Father and Mrs Osborn who also gave the best white cope, the clasp of which contains the jewels given to him by his former parishioners in Camden Town; this cope was also the work of Miss Tait.

It was also at this time that the wire gates were attached to the church porch to keep out 'stray animals and birds.' The outdoor processional lights were given by a Miss Bright, and the Lectern Bibles (King James Version), hand-bound and tooled, the work of Mr Garrett of Malvern Art School, were given in memory of the parents of a member of the congregation. The Mothers' Union banner was added during Hatherly's ministry and was the work of one of his friends. Oak seats for churchwardens were given by Basil Strannack in thanksgiving for special mercies and in memory of his parents. An illuminated vellum recording the names of the vicar-wardens was the work and gift of Mr C. J. Brooks. The oak vestment chest in the sacristy was a gift of Osborn after his retirement.

In 1942 it was decided to install an aumbry in memory of Hatherly, and this was duly installed in the north wall of the sanctuary.[10] The tabernacle within it is that previously used from 1897 in the sisters' chapel beyond the oriel window. Its decorated front was designed by the Warham Guild and its silver light (recently electrified) was given by members of the Guild of St Barnabas who for many years met in the church for their monthly office. In 1959 two aluminium candlesticks to replace the existing and original brass ones were a memorial gift for O. W. Stokes, a former churchwarden. The original brass altar cross, not matching the new candlesticks, was put into storage together with the brass candlesticks.

In July 1944 the PCC considered 'the desirability of changing from Plainsong to Anglican chants for the Psalms and Canticles at the Sunday evening services.'

Discussion continued in September, and there were strong arguments on both sides. No vote was taken, but Hunt said he

---

[10] The faculty was granted, as was usual at that time, on condition that 'both kinds' were to be reserved, and that there should be 'no service or ceremony connected with the sacred elements so reserved'.

had obtained the sense of the meeting and proposed a six-month experiment whereby anglican chant (without the choristers) should be used every Sunday except on great festivals. It is interesting that this discussion took place when Bertie Shaw was on a year's absence, and that it was ultimately deemed a failure. After the closure of the choir school Shaw said that there was 'no possibility' of forming a choir of local boys and, although 'a voluntary Choir of Ladies' sang at some of the services, the musical tradition gradually faded. It is difficult to conceive how the use of plainsong survived; perhaps the clergy at St Barnabas were able to help. But in April 1951, as a diocesan mission drew near, the question was raised again, and Hunt proposed that until the mission anglican chants should be used for the psalms while plainsong should continue for the canticles.

Still on the subject of music, it was noted in 1961 that the hymnbooks were very worn, and that an anonymous donor had offered to replace them. The donor had no strong views as to what the new ones should be, but in 1951 *Hymns Ancient and Modern Revised* had been issued and he/she hoped that this would be considered alongside the existing *English Hymnal*. The PCC decided to seek congregational comments, but Darke pre-empted these by ordering copies of *Hymns Ancient and Modern Revised* and was severely criticised for this at the next PCC meeting. For a while both books were used, black numbers on the hymn board indicating *The English Hymnal* and red numbers *Hymns Ancient and Modern Revised*. In the event, the copies of *Hymns Ancient and Modern Revised* were disposed of and the donor duly presented new copies of *The English Hymnal*. Less controversially, new bookcases for the storage of hymn books and prayer books were presented in 1961 by Dorothy Pembridge in memory of her parents.

In 1945 the possibility of amplifiers was raised at the PCC, but it was felt that these would be too expensive. In 1949 a new notice board outside the church was provided as a war memorial; this was the anonymous gift of John Valentine Hewer, landlord of the Newland Swan, one of whose sons had been lost at sea in the war. Later, In 1953 a 'Bishop's Chair of the time of Charles II' was found among some 'discarded furniture' and when Hewer heard of this 'he obtained expert antique restorers' help and had it beautifully restored and given back to the church' where it is now used by priests hearing confessions. Then in 1957 the PCC decided that the riddle posts and wings should be removed—they had had a life of only thirty years, but were too fine to be burnt and are currently stored rather inconveniently in the Library. A new boiler was installed, and in July 1969 there was major rewiring in the church and cloister buildings.

Thanks to the revived parish magazine we have a clear idea of the service pattern in Osborn's day. It is probably what he inherited, for (with one exception) he gives no hint that any of it was new. Thus in 1930 the Sunday services were:

7 a.m.	Holy Communion (first Sunday only)
8 a.m.	Holy Communion
10.15 a.m.	Matins
10.45 a.m.	Litany or Processsion
11 a.m.	Holy Communion (sung)
3 p.m.	Catechism
3.45 p.m.	Holy Baptism
6.30 p.m.	Evensong

There was holy communion, matins and evensong on each weekday, and confessions were heard 'according to the Time-Table in the Church Porch.'

Under Bott the pattern was much the same, except that afternoon catechising was replaced by the St Leonard's Guild for children which met on Sunday mornings under the leadership of a sister from the Community of the Holy Name. Confessions were heard on Friday afternoons or later Saturday evenings. Under Darke, in November 1960 it was agreed that on the first Sunday of the month, when there was a Eucharist at 7 a.m., the 8 a.m. celebration should be replaced by a Family Mass at 9 a.m., but this was abandoned after a year.

As for the chapel, in 1928 Bell noted that 'the stone slab in the

Mortuary was a welcome addition and more decent for carrying out the burial rites, and in 1930 it was described as 'the Chapel of All Souls.' In 1945 a credence table was provided for 'the All Souls Chapel' in memory of a Miss Clarke. In 1949 it was claimed dubiously that, 'Although belonging to the Charity the cost of upkeep does not fall on the Charity, but on the church congregation. But any substantial repairs would be the responsibility of the Warden.' In 1959 there were small repairs to what was still called the All Souls Chapel.

The Library

In 1934 Osborn completed the cataloguing of the library at his own expense. The library building was also completely renovated in his time and the roof repaired, the cost being met partly by balances from the endowment and partly by the Trustees. As well as being used for study, it was also used for PCC meetings, and sometimes for the Mothers' Union and the Sunday kindergarten. In 1960 there were further repairs to the library roof, and in May 1961 the Trustees decided to open up the library to the whole community and to enlarge the scope of its books though nothing materialised of this.

The Last Fifty Years

Chapter Thirteen
The Last Vicar-Wardens, 1965–1979

The years immediately after the centenary were not happy ones. In 1965 Bott wrote that there was too much looking back, 'Love for Newland, an understandable and praiseworthy thing, can (and I fear has in some) become a selfish indulgence in nostalgia, holding them and Newland in a stranglehold.' The centenary should have involved both thanksgiving for the past and 'dedication to the tasks of the future', but 'in the unhappy atmosphere of the past few months' this vision had been lost. In the same year a new pensioner asked why pensioners were made to sit apart from the rest of the congregation, and also why they were not deemed eligible for election to the PCC. But the 'unhappy atmosphere' went much deeper, and Bott expressed to the bishop his own unhappiness. Subsequently the archdeacon met the clerk and one of the Trustees. In December Bott suggested to the Trustees that almost everyone in the community was against him. The Trustees, for their part, were aware of the general unhappiness, which they ascribed to the warden's personality, and felt that there should be a change of warden; they communicated their views to the bishop and the archdeacon. In January 1966 one resident left because of 'the Warden's continued unfriendly attitude to her', while at the same time Bott reported to the Trustees that 'Some agitation by a tiny minority has forced me to make attendance at prayers VOLUNTARY, and to permit Pensioners to occupy seats in the Nave of the Church at 11 a.m. IF THEY WISH TO DO SO,' but only one Pensioner had failed to attend prayers and only two had moved to the nave on Sundays.[1]

Part of Bott's problem may have been that he misjudged the nature of the community. Many of the pensioners no longer thought of themselves as 'inmates.' Gradually, and without any formal resolutions, the composition of the community had begun to change. There were fewer 'decayed agricultural labourers' and fewer former employees of the Madresfield estate. Most new residents came from the Malvern area where the community was best known, but some came because they had visited, or had a relation in, the Community of the Holy Name, while others were recommended by one of the missionary societies. But though unhappy in the community, Bott was happy in the parish where he introduced a harvest service at the Swan after Sunday evensong, In 1966, announcing that he and his wife would be leaving, he was sure that 'the overwhelming majority of the Community, congregation, and parishioners will regret our departure' and asked for prayer 'that (this time) you may be given the right man as your new Vicar.' This regret was not felt by most in the community, though it may have been felt by the wider congregation—there was no criticism of him in the PCC minutes, and the churchwardens wrote warmly of him. In October he became vicar of Stoulton with Drakes Broughton, and he died in Horsham in 1987 aged eighty-four.

On Bott's resignation the PCC expressed their wish for 'a married man in good health who had a sympathetic and understanding wife', and the Trustees eventually chose Richard Arthur Charles Brodribb who was vicar-warden from January 1967 to October 1979. Brodribb,

---

[1] It is difficult to reconcile these comments with the Trustees' 1961 relaxation of the rules on churchgoing.

born in Cheshire in 1918, had previously been vicar of St Anne, Wrenthorpe, Wakefield, and he came with his wife, Nancie, and daughter, Dorothy. He was certainly active in the parish, but it may be that, like some of his predecessors, he was more concerned with the parish than the pensioners. In 1976 the Trustees asked him 'if he would be willing to make more frequent visits and to take a more active part in the Community' and in 1977 they discussed his lack of pastoral visiting and decided that Lady Beauchamp should talk to him about this. His wife died on 21 April, 1979, aged sixty-three, and he himself died in office—the first vicar-warden to do so—on 22 October the same year, aged sixty-one.

Brodribb continued the anglo-catholic tradition. In 1968 he preached a Lent course to assist with discussions on the recently issued Series 2 service for holy communion, but Newland decided not to adopt this, and in 1974 he described Newland as 'a spiritual home for refugees from Series 2 and Series 3.' His conservatism is further illustrated by his refusal to introduce the occasional evening eucharists which had now become common in anglo-catholic churches.

For some years there had been a monthly 10.15 a.m. communion on Wednesdays, but from 1968 this was increased to twice a month in the winter. In 1972, however, the monthly 7 a.m. Sunday communion was dropped, and in the same year the sisters withdrew from their oversight of the St Leonards Guild which may have lapsed. Brodribb now held four Sunday services—low mass, matins and litany (said), sung mass and evensong and sermon (which was usually solemn on festivals)—and he continued the Newland tradition of daily matins, eucharist and evensong. But the musical tradition had been lost, and there was now no choir at all even though Bertie Shaw continued as organist.

In the church building, in 1973 (under Farrar Bell, grandson of Alfred Bell who had overseen the original work) the frescoes were restored again at a cost of *c*. £1,000. As for the chapel, a photograph *c*. 1974 shows it simply furnished with two chairs on each side of the aisle, a space for the catafalque and a tabernacle on the altar. In 1976 the secretary, Mrs Meriel Serjeant, who had replaced Beale as clerk and who lived in Malvern Wells, asked the PCC whether, to avoid the expense of heating the church everyday, they would be willing for weekday services to be held in the chapel. In 1974 Godfrey Russell stated that the Trustees 'certainly own the Old Chapel', but in 1979, as it was becoming clear that repairs were needed, Mrs Serjeant asked Jeremy Russell, the Trustees' solicitor, for advice as to whose responsibility these were. He replied that 'although at the outset the Trustees may have had to restore the old Chapel, this responsibility may now have passed to the Church of England.' But this was incorrect and when the time came it was the Trustees who took responsibility.

Pensioners and Almshouses

What was deemed acceptable for married couples in 1864 was not deemed so now. All Quadrangle flats were now regarded as 'single flats', and in 1970 the Trustees decided that 'married couples should not normally be considered in future and that preference should be given to men rather than women.' They also agreed that where pensioners in an upstairs flat needed to move downstairs on health grounds they should be given priority when the next vacancy occurred. It was also in 1970 that the Trustees obtained permission from the Charity Commissioners to levy contributions from the alms people (as opposed to the rents they were already receiving from tenants). This was a momentous move. Originally the charity gave pensions; now it required contributions—though these were, and are, much less than what would be required by a commercial concern, and the pensioners continued to enjoy many benefits such as free heating and the services of the porter, warden and nurse. There were social benefits too. From 1969 there was sherry and dinner on Christmas Day for the 20 or so who had not gone to their families, and often Lord and Lady Beauchamp joined them for sherry. There were also visits to Madresfield and Hanley Castle.

As early as 1966 there had been discussion about the conversion of the original St Barnabas houses, numbers 3 and 4, into four flats.

This was agreed, and the work was completed in 1968; the flats were known as numbers 5–8, probably in anticipation of the ultimate conversion of the other two houses. There were a good number of clerical enquiries for these, though while some welcomed the reduction in size others felt that the lack of a study rendered them too small. Brodribb reported to the Trustees that the question has been raised as to whether their tenancy should be extended to other than retired clergy. He hoped they would consider making them available to clergy widows who at present had to vacate their flats three months after their husbands' death, but 'to extend the scope of the tenancy beyond clergy widows would perhaps be too much of a departure from the purpose of these homes, and might even amount to a breach of contract with the present residents who have expected to come into homes for retired clergymen and their wives.' In 1970 the Trustees obtained the permission of the Charity Commissioners to allow the widow of a deceased priest to continue in residence.

Presumably the question of allowing other than clergy into St Barnabas had been raised by the Trustees' restriction of the Quadrangle to single residents. The new flats in the warden's lodge and in the choir school were suitable for couples, but these were currently let to tenants. Another possibility for a couple might have been St Christopher's, the old coach house. There were discussions about its modernisation in 1968 but nothing was done. A new single tenant was appointed in September 1969, but in 1970 the secretary wondered if it had any future. In a letter to the solicitor, she explained that the tenant was just about to redecorate inside, but 'when I looked at the stairs and some of the woodwork I was worried to find active woodworm. If the stairs were to collapse I suppose we could be in trouble.' She had given the tenant a large can of Rentokil so that the wood could be treated before painting, 'but I do not feel that this is the ultimate answer, as, for instance, the outside WC used by this tenant has a pretty leaky roof which is basically part of the main roof structure of the Warden's and Deaconess's apartments; also the outside drain piping is rusting away' She expressed her anxiety again in 1973, and in 1974 some of the Trustees looked at it with a view to deciding on its future, but nothing was decided.

In 1972 Mrs Serjeant thought that the almshouses should be better known, and it was arranged that a journalist should be invited to the next Trustees' tea party. As a result, in June 1972 the *Malvern Gazette* reported that,

> The inhabitants come from all walks of life, from places far away and near at hand. Some, for instance, are retired missionaries, home again after a lifetime in Africa or India, while others are footmen, porters, butlers: people who have spent their lives in service at Madresfield Court.
>
> For there are really only two demands made of entrants to the almshouses: They must have given service to others and still be able to fend for themselves; though a resident nurse, a porter, and a warden are always on hand.

Strangely, despite the recent modernisation of the almshouses, in 1973 the Trustees were experiencing difficulty in finding suitable residents. They later discussed how applicants' finances should affect their eligibility. A draft on admission policies, perhaps drawn up in preparation for this, noted that there were currently four requirements: 'They must have very limited financial means; they must be C of E, preferably practising; they must have been of some service to the community before; they should have some local connections.' But the first of these was a problem, for what were 'limited financial means'? At this time anyone with a very small pension of, say, £50 a year over and above the OAP, or with capital of £1,000, was considered suitable financially. Anyone who had more, but was suitable under the other qualifications and was a possible benefit to the community, was put on the waiting list for a tenant's flat. But this had resulted in a number of people waiting for tenants' accommodation, whereas when an almshouse was vacant there was no one to fill it immediately.

There were three possible solutions: to 'equate the finances of an applicant with need', to 'ignore the financial aspect of an applicant to the extent of, say, £5,000 capital', or to 'amalgamate all the vacancies, almshouses and tenancies together, reverting to the original foundation (except of course the converted school), charging higher contributions for the larger flats (which could become married accommodation, as opposed to single people).' Since the rise in contributions from 1 July pensioners were paying £208 per annum, while tenants' rents varied from £104 to £200. The tenants had formerly subsidised the almshouses by their higher rents, but this was no longer the case (though tenants had had no claim on the services of the sister or the porter). If the third of the possible solutions were favoured, in time the amounts paid would be based entirely on the size of the accommodation offered.

The Trustees agreed that no definite figure for capital should be fixed as a maximum but, other things being equal, those 'with the most straitened finances' should have preference. They also felt that many people disliked words like 'almshouses' and 'charity', and they decided informally to change the name to 'The Beauchamp Community at Newland.' They further decided, in line with the Charity Commissioners' recommendations, 'that the tenants' flats should revert to almshouses as they became vacant', that 'there would only be one list' and that 'the larger flats would if possible be allocated to married people.' This was a reversal of their 1970 policy, but it made for a more integrated community. Distinctions between pensioners and tenants and between contributions and rents were abolished, and residents would now be on a more equal footing. The 'larger flats' referred to comprised the two new wardens lodge flats and the two new choir school flats. Lygon Lodge could also accommodate couples, although the flats here were probably still restricted to retired Madresfield employees nominated by Lord Beauchamp.

In 1974 there was more discussion about the creation of four further flats in 1 and 2 St Barnabas, and also about the possibility of handing over the St Barnabas Charity to the Church of England

Pensions Board, but the Trustees decided not to pursue these options. To the west of these flats, however, was a paddock belonging to the Madresfield estate and for which planning permission had been refused. In 1975 the Trustees were told that 'there was a good chance that it might be handed over to the Community and that at a later date the land might be used in some profitable way'; in October 1977 it was duly leased to them. Then, in 1979 they obtained planning permission for 1 and 2 St Barnabas to be let as a rest home. The lease was fixed for twenty-one years at £1,000 for the first year and £1,500 for the second and third year; thereafter it was to be reviewed every three years.[2] The Charity Commissioners agreed to this.

In 1977 for the first and only time the Trustees felt that the behaviour of one Quadrangle resident was so unacceptable that they must take legal action for his removal. They were successful in this, but there were clearly lessons to be learned and Mrs Serjeant wrote to Brodribb about applicants:

> They must all have two references from people who really know them, and the applicants must know what they are applying for: I have just received the revised 'licence' which now takes the form of rules and an acceptance document and has been concocted by the Charity Commission, the National Association of Almshouses and Jeremy Russell. I think you will agree that it is much clearer than the old forms, and in fact reverts to much earlier practice.

Much energy was now devoted to ensuring that the rules and the licences should be as foolproof as possible. In 1974 Godfrey Russell in a memorandum on the history of the charities, had written,

> The Rules of the Charity were very strict and no useful purpose it is thought will be served by going further into them in detail insofar as

---

[2] This was later amended to £1,500 for the first six years, with a review to follow thereafter.

over the many years of its existence a large proportion of these Rules have doubtless quite improperly been honoured more in the breach than the observance, and it is the wish of the Trustees that when at long last the Scheme is drawn up and approved it will be modified to accord with modern practice in the times in which we live. If it were strictly adhered to today there would in all probability be no persons willing to accept residence in the Almshouses.

The rules subsequently agreed in 1977 were:

1. All residences and premises shall be kept clean and tidy and be open to inspection by the Warden or the Trustees at all reasonable times.

2. Care shall be taken to see that no nuisance or annoyance is caused to the Trustees or any other occupier. In particular no playing of musical instruments, radio or TV in such a way as to be audible from outside or from an adjoining flat after 10.00 p.m. and before 9.00 a.m.

3. All refuse shall be deposited in the proper receptacles.

4. No domestic pets shall be allowed except with the express permission of the Trustees.

5. No other persons shall be allowed to stay overnight in the residence except with the permission of the Warden.

6. The use of paraffin oil heaters is strictly prohibited.

7. Occupiers are not allowed to make any structural alteration to the fabric, nor to alter the plumbing or electrical installation without the prior consent of the Trustees.

8. The occupier shall notify the Warden or the Secretary when going away or leaving the accommodation empty overnight. The occupier shall not vacate the residence for more than 28 days in any 12 months without the consent of the Trustees.

9. No washing shall be hung from any window and clothes shall be dried only in such place or places as the Warden or Trustees shall approve.

10. Nothing shall be done to cause any obstruction around the Community such as parking or allowing bicycles or vehicles to be parked in the Quadrangle or in any place not approved by the Trustees.

11. No business or trade is to be carried on on the premises.

12. Each occupier will be required to contribute towards the cost of management, maintenance, heating and lighting in the Community's residences. Such contribution will be fixed by the Trustees. Where there is a separate meter installed for any particular premises the occupier shall pay for such gas water and electricity as he or she shall use. It is therefore imperative that care should be taken not to waste water or electricity.

13. All occupiers shall conform to and obey the Rules of the Constitution of the Charities forming the Beauchamp Community and any further Rules which may from time to time be made, and the lawful requests of the Warden or Secretary.

14. The Trustees reserve the right to terminate the licence of any occupier at any time, whereupon the occupier shall then vacate the accommodation forthwith.

It is interesting to compare these rules with those of 1932 ones.

There is now no reference to the able-bodied being ready to employ themselves usefully or to clean and scrub the common areas. Nor is there any reference to church attendance even on Sundays, though possibly this was taken for granted.

The year 1977 saw the retirement of the lay nurse. The Trustees decided not to replace her, and Mrs Doris Bullock, the porter's wife, was asked to take over the general care of the residents' health which she duly did until she and her husband retired in November 1978 and moved to the Choir School. Brodribb reported to the Trustees in 1979 that 'Newland owes a debt to Mr and Mrs Bullock which it can never repay, for they have done so much out of the kindness of their hearts in addition to their official duties, and they have made an incalculable contribution to the comfort and happiness of countless people during the years that they have been here.' The Bullocks were replaced by Mr and Mrs Beaumont, and Brodribb reported that 'they have applied themselves to their tasks with great resolution and have gained the confidence of everyone in the community.' But from now on there was no longer any formal medical or nursing care. The officers of the community and their assistants gave such devoted care as they could, but inevitably there were limits to this. District nurses and social service staff visited those residents who needed them. But with people living longer it became increasingly common for those who became very frail mentally or physically to move to a local care or nursing home, and burial in the churchyard became increasingly rare.

Meanwhile, on the death of the Honourable Richard Lygon in 1970 the American Ligons proposed as a memorial to him an electric winder for the clock in the community tower, and the Trustees entrusted this to the original makers, Gillett and Johnston of Croydon. On 27 June 1973 many of the Ligons were present when a commemorative plaque was unveiled by the Gatehouse.

Later, in January 1975, Mrs Serjeant was asked to obtain planning permission for the derelict walled garden site on what had previously been the kitchen garden, just under an acre in extent, which formed the west boundary of the site between the road and the stream, and later that year outline planning permission was given for building of dwellings 'for occupation of elderly residents', but nothing was done at the time and the outline planning permission lapsed.

The Library

As early as 1966 it was suggested that the books should be valued, and in 1975 Dr Benediks of Birmingham University valued them at £3,000–£3,500. The Trustees now envisaged selling them, but the Charity Commissioners refused permission and required that they be transferred to the diocesan library. If this library did not want them, they could indeed be sold but the proceeds should be given to the diocese. The Trustees objected strongly to this, and in October 1979 the diocesan library reported that there were only 'a few rare books' and 'a handful of more recent books' that they would like. The Trustees decided to inform the Charity Commissioners of this and to await their reactions. Meanwhile Mrs Serjeant fulminated and wrote to the solicitor,

> I am incensed by the Charity Commissioners attitude about the Library, for had it been Cosby White's intention that the Diocese should have full use of the books he would certainly have given over the books direct to the Cathedral library in his will. As it is he left them to the Community and we have looked after them for all these years, and now they expect us to sit back and watch the Diocese gather in thousands of pounds at Christies etc. At the very least we should have a proportion of the proceeds for the maintenance of the building in which they were housed, or alternatively a handsome donation. I hope you will point out that the original intentions were for the use of the clergy residing in the Beauchamp Charity, and since we have to maintain a proportion of retired clergy at the Community the books or proceeds should not go only to the Diocese. I do not consider that the Charity Commissioners have made a correct interpretation of the original bequest.

A New Scheme

The revision of the official scheme, first mooted *c.*1949, had long been dormant but in 1974 discussions began again and on 14 December 1979 a new scheme was finally sealed. This brought together the original almshouses, the Lygon almshouses and St Barnabas. The number of Trustees was now not less than seven and not more than twelve, and they were to meet not less than twice a year. They were to appoint a chairman for the year, a Church of England chaplain, who might or might not be the vicar of Newland, and they were to appoint a member of the Church of England as warden, who might or might not be a clergyman. They might also appoint a nurse and a porter, and they might let 1 and 2 St Barnabas. Residents were to be poor members of the Church of England and 'so far as practicable not less than one eighth nor more than one quarter' should be retired clergymen. All this brought the legal scheme more into line with what had developed. New residents whatever their background now tended to move in to whatever appropriate flat or house was vacant (and in 1980 the first lay resident moved into St Barnabas), while clergy might be found in St Barnabas, Lygon Lodge, the wardens lodge or the Quadrangle.

Pastoral Reorganisation

The ministry of St Leonard's had always covered both almshouses and parish, and it had also reached further. The list of officers in 1974 showed the vicar-warden and five honorary assistant priests living in the community, along with one churchwarden and the PCC secretary and treasurer. But the Mothers Union secretary and the magazine secretary lived elsewhere in the parish, while the other churchwarden, the electoral roll officer, the organist and the master of ceremonies lived outside the parish. But Newland had a population of only 250 (although it boasted four thousand communions a year, a remarkable number for a country church) and, with the number of available clergy declining, the diocesan synod was now considering merging the parish with that of Malvern Link, and leaving St Leonard's for the almshouses only, to be served by the clergy at St Barnabas. In 1975 an alternative suggestion was made that Newland should be divided between Malvern Link and Powick, but again that its church should become simply the chapel of the almshouses.

By the time of Brodribb's death, there was a new scheme and the diocese was proposing to unite the benefice of Newland (including the almshouses) with that of Guarlford and Madresfield, with an incumbent living in Madresfield. But the Trustees felt that there should continue to be a resident chaplain for the community and that its distinctive tradition should be maintained. They therefore appointed as chaplain Hartley Brown, the vicar of Guarlford who was aged sixty-five and about to retire to the community. At the same time they appointed Mrs Beaumont, the Porter's wife, as a lay female warden to work alongside him, and she and her husband moved into the warden's lodge. But one trustee pointed out that, under the old constitution which was still in force at that point, the warden must be ordained, and eventually it was agreed that there should be a 'Chaplain-Warden' and a 'Lay-Warden.'

Chapter Fourteen
The Administrator
Mrs Vera Rowberry, 1980–1999

The year 1980 saw more changes in the life of the community both in structure and personnel than any previous year since its foundation. We have noted the appointment of Father Brown as chaplain and Mrs Beaumont as lay warden, but Mrs Serjeant now resigned as secretary, and in May 1980 the Trustees appointed Mrs Vera Rowberry to succeed her from the end of June. Meanwhile it was decided that Mr Beaumont would continue as gardener, porter and handyman until a married couple could be found to assist and to live in the Porter's Lodge. In March 1980 Eric Oseman was appointed gardener and handyman, and he and his wife, Mary, also acted as stand-in wardens every other weekend while Mr Beaumont continued to do general maintenance on a casual basis. When the Beaumonts resigned in October, it was decided not to appoint another warden at this stage, and Mrs Oseman was promoted to 'Community Assistant.'

Chaplains

There were seven resident chaplains during this period. But theirs was a less exalted office than that of the vicar-wardens who preceded them. Their ages on appointment ranged from fifty-nine to seventy-eight, and on average they served only three years.

July 1980 to May 1982. Hartley Brown, though appointed in 1979, began his ministry only in July 1980. Surprisingly, in view of the celibacy of many anglo-catholic clergy, all the vicar-wardens had been married, and Father Brown, an oblate of Nashdom Abbey, was the first celibate to hold office in the community. He lived, with his housekeeper Kathleen Frith, in the former Sisters' House, now renamed the Chaplain's House. He died in May 1982, and there is a simple memorial tablet to him in the Cloister Chapel.

July 1982 to December 1984. Matthew William Hardwicke Nichols, born 1904, aged seventy-eight, and a second celibate. The last of his previous posts was chaplain of St Margaret's convent, Aberdeen. On retiring from this, he moved in 1978 to twenty-two The Quadrangle, and accepted the Trustees' invitation to succeed Father Brown. On ceasing to be chaplain he moved to St Christopher's, and he died in September 1985.[1]

December 1984 to September 1988. John Arthur Arrowsmith Maund, Bp, aged seventy-five, born 1909. After two curacies he began work in South Africa, and for his work as an army chaplain was awarded the MC. He was bishop of Basutoland from 1950 to 1956 and of Lesotho (where his wife died) from 1955 to 1976. He was awarded the CBE for services to the church overseas and, before coming to Beauchamp, lived in the ecumenical community at Hengrave Hall in Suffolk. On retirement he moved to flat one in the warden's lodge. He died in July 1998, aged eighty-eight, and was buried at Newland.

September 1988 to June 1990. Clarence Simpson, aged seventy-five, born 1913. Previously 1977–80 honorary curate of Welsh Newton with Llanrothal before his retirement to Gloucestershire. On his retirement as chaplain he and his wife, Norma, moved to Malvern

---

[1] In 1982 he published his memoirs under the title, *Dry Breasts*, which was Cardinal Newman's description of the Church of England. The memoirs, which do not include any reference to his time at Beauchamp, illustrate both his strengths and his weaknesses.

Link and then to St Barnabas, Lingfield. He died in 1997.

May 1991 to December 1996. Brian Gilbert Burr, aged sixty-eight, born 1923. Previously team rector of Torre in the diocese of Exeter. On retirement he moved to 5 St Barnabas. He died on 25 December 2004, and was buried at Madresfield. His widow, Ruth, remained at St Barnabas until 2010 when she moved to a care home near Kidderminster where she died the following year.

January to September 1997. Geoffrey John Marsh, aged fifty-nine, born 1938. Previously chaplain and head of religious studies at Hereford Cathedral School. He died suddenly *en route* to Assisi, after a ministry here of less than a year, and was buried at Newland.

July 1998 to April 1999. Walter James Jennings, aged sixty-one, born 1937. Previously vicar of All Saints Pittsville, Cheltenham. On leaving the community, where most residents wished him to remain, he and his wife, Linda, moved to their own house in Malvern Wells, and he still assists at Old St Martin's in Worcester.

Mrs Rowberry

Increasingly the key person and the pillar of continuity was Mrs Rowberry. She had been born in Durham in 1923, but moved to Worcestershire and married Albert William (Bob) Rowberry in the Droitwich area in 1947. She had held a number of secretarial posts, and had also worked for the Conservative Party and the WRVS. Although appointed initially to Beauchamp as part-time secretary/treasurer and clerk to the Trustees, in 1985 she was formally appointed warden (though this title was later used for her resident assistants), and in 1988 her title was changed to secretary/administrator. By now she was working full-time for the community and was already its *de facto* 'chief executive.' She never resided in the community, living variously in Collets Green and Worcester, but she loved it with all her heart and she served it with passion and competence.

Every weekday Mrs Rowberry was in the office, and every Sunday she was in church: she noted which residents were absent and would subsequently question them about the reasons for this. She ruled the community firmly but lovingly, and she tended to regard the chaplains as answerable to the Trustees through her rather than directly. On the one hand she believed in keeping her distance. She would never visit residents socially and would never accept gifts from them except, as she put it, their love. On the other hand she would care for them devotedly when they were ill, and she provided a legendary Christmas dinner for those who would otherwise have been alone. She was usually assisted by a married couple in the porter's lodge with the husband as porter and the wife now styled warden. If there was any emergency at night she expected them to contact her, and if necessary she would always return immediately to the community. Bishop Pickard wrote of her,

> Often she not only acts for the Trustees but has to advise them and direct their thinking in the right way. Apart from a load of office work she does a round of the sick people every day, she is at hand to see people at any time and deals with the small as well as the more weightier [sic] problems, from bandaging a cut finger to dealing with people's financial problems, and making arrangements for house repairs and such like. She knows everyone in the Community and makes a point of giving them time to talk so that they feel at home and are being cared.

She also coped valiantly with the tensions and the sometimes tortuous negotiations arising from the separation of the office of warden from that of incumbent, the pastoral future of St Leonard's, the development of Pyndar Court and the sale of further land in the early 1990s.

Mrs Rowberry's contribution to the community for nearly two difficult decades cannot be exaggerated, though she had critics who thought her snobbish (her copy of *Who's Who* was usually prominent) and felt that she had favourites. But eventually the gradual failure of her sight and her consequent inability to drive, her increasing suspicion of others in positions of responsibility in the community, the decline of her general health, the death of her husband and her reluctance to 'let go' made life difficult both for her and for the community. It was suggested in November 1999 that she retire at the end of the year, but she left immediately and never returned. Soon after her retirement she suffered a severe stroke, but eventually she was able to return to her home where several members of the community continued to visit her. She died on 22 November 2004, aged eighty-one, and she is rightly commemorated in a plaque outside the guest flat.

Parish and Community

In April 1981 the united benefice of Newland, Guarlford and Madresfield was formally created, and on 27 November the Reverend David H. Martin was instituted as incumbent. This was two years after Father Brodribb's death, and during the interregnum the services were maintained largely by the clergy of the community. Increasingly the community, and not least perhaps Mrs Rowberry, had begun to regard St Leonard's as 'theirs.' But now St Leonard's was clearly both the parish church of Newland, served by an incumbent living in Madresfield, and the chapel of the Beauchamp Community, served by a resident chaplain. Mr Martin worked hard to draw his three parishes closer together and to reach out into the wider community.

In August 1982 he launched a combined monthly parish magazine, *Grapevine,* which was distributed free of charge to all homes and which still continues, though reduced from 1996 to five or six issues a year. But, with differences of churchmanship, competing demands for the use of the church, ambiguity about many matters of detail and a Skinner-like inflexibility in Father Nichols, there was much scope for misunderstanding. Relationships between chaplain and incumbent deteriorated, and there was much 'unhappiness and division.' Soon both the archdeacon and the bishop were involved. There were also practical problems about parish fêtes in the community's grounds and social gatherings in its buildings.

In November 1984 the bishop of Worcester convened a meeting of all parties, and in January 1985 he circulated some rulings which he hoped would be acceptable to all, though much would depend on their goodwill:

1. Existing Sunday arrangements at 8 a.m., 11 a.m. and 6.30 p.m. were confirmed. On any holy day when both parish and community wished to use the church, the community would use it in the morning and the parish in the evening, unless chaplain and incumbent agreed on a joint service. The community would have the use of the church for daily morning and evening prayer.

2. The community would normally use the small chapel on holy days, but would hold traditional Holy Week services in the church.

3. The parish could use the church on other appropriate occasions but should consult well in advance with the chaplain. Incumbent and chaplain should be in full consultation for weddings and funerals.

4. Collections should go to the parish when the incumbent officiates and to the community when the chaplain officiates.

5. The PCC would order the affairs of the parish, but the community could have its own Community Church Committee, chaired by the chaplain.

6. The upkeep and insurance of the church was the responsibility of the incumbent in co-operation with the PCC. But the community should pay for its own altar supplies and should also pay an annual contribution towards heat, light, maintenance and insurance. This contribution should be decided by the archdeacon after consultation with interested parties.

Following these rulings (which the Trustees deemed 'acceptable for the time being'), relations became much happier. Nonetheless, in August 1995 the editor of *Grapevine* reported complaints that it contained little news of Newland. This was certainly true as far as the community was concerned, and Mrs Rowberry would not have wished it otherwise. For her, the community was one thing but the benefice was quite another, and the less they had to do with each other, the better.

Meanwhile there had been rumblings about further pastoral reorganisation. As early as 1982 it was suggested that St Leonard's should have been declared redundant as a parish church and returned to the Trustees as a chapel for the community, and this was apparently now favoured by the diocese. In June 1983 the Trustees supported it, and pointed out the 'indisputable' lack of parish support for the church with parish Sunday attendance ranging from two to a maximum of seven. But after a meeting with Newland PCC they changed their opinion, and thought it would be better for Newland to be separated from the benefice and to have its own vicar/chaplain as before. In May 1984 a scheme was put forward that Newland should become a new parish and benefice, with patronage shared between the bishop and the Trustees, and that Guarlford and Madresfield should form a new benefice with Powick. As far as Newland was concerned, the Trustees accepted this scheme and confirmed that the church would be maintained by them as in the past, that the parish share would be payable by the parish and by them as in the past, and that the appointment of a new chaplain would be made jointly by the bishop and them. But Guarlford and Madresfield voted unanimously against the scheme, and Newland also rejected it by nine votes to seven.

On Founders Day 1989 a special service, very much a community occasion, was held to celebrate the one hundred and twenty-fifth anniversary of the foundation. Thanks were offered—as at the centenary—'for the great tradition of Catholic worship and teaching which has persisted by the providence of Almighty God from its first days to this present time, when it still pertains in accordance with the Founder's wishes.' The following Sunday a special sermon was preached by Robert Milburn, a former dean of Worcester and one of the community's most distinguished residents at the time.

In 1991 Mr Martin moved to Alvechurch and the Trustees resolved unanimously that they be allowed to revert to the pre-1980 position, but Newland PCC resolved, also unanimously, that they did not want the status of the church to be changed. In 1992 the Reverend (from 1994 Canon) John Green, vicar of St John-in-Bedwardine, was appointed priest-in-charge of the benefice as well as Diocesan Director of Ordinands and Director of Post-Ordination Training; approximately a third of his time was be given to the parishes and two-thirds to his diocesan work. He and the chaplain worked amicably on the 1985 basis, but in 1994 there were further discussions about the future of St Leonard's, and in 1995 proposals were made for it to be declared redundant as a parish church and leased to the Trustees as 'the Chapel of the Beauchamp Community.' In 1996 a draft pastoral scheme was produced, and the area occupied by the community was to be declared extra-parochial. In May 1997 it was finally agreed that the parishes of Madresfield and Newland be united to form the parish of Madresfield with Newland, and that the benefice be renamed 'Guarlford and Madresfield with Newland.' At the same time the parish church of Newland was declared redundant, and an extra-parochial place was constituted to be known as 'The Beauchamp Community with Saint Leonard's Chapelry, Newland.'[2] This part of the scheme was activated on 20 June 1998[3] when there was a special service of thanksgiving and rededication as the church became 'The Private Chapel of the Beauchamp Community.' The bishop of Worcester preached at this, and the archdeacon received the keys from the priest-in-charge and

---

[2] In November, in a letter to clergy who enquired about the vacant chaplaincy, Mrs Rowberry wrote, 'This year The Queen designated Beauchamp Community and St Leonard's Church a "peculiar", and so we are not of the Diocese, as such and are not liable to pay quota'. Except for the reference to the quota, this was a misleading statement. All pastoral schemes need the assent of the Queen in Council, and the implication that the Queen had taken a special interest in Beauchamp was not true. Again, although the community and church were now extra-parochial, they were not a 'peculiar' which is a highly technical term. They remained part 'of the Diocese', and the bishop was not pleased when he heard that Mrs Rowberry was claiming otherwise.

[3] Although the lease dates from this date, it was not officially signed till 1999.

passed them into the safe keeping of the chairman of the Trustees. After the service there was a pig-roast.

When Canon Green moved in July 1999 to devote himself full-time to diocesan work, the benefice was placed under the care of the Reverend David Nichol who was already priest-in-charge of the neighbouring Powick. He stayed there until July 2005 when he became vicar of Holy Trinity and St James', West Malvern.

The Almshouses

In 1981 the *Malvern Gazette* wrote of the community, 'Residents come from all walks of life, and the qualifications for entry to Newland are that people must be over fifty-five and must have given years of community service in some form or another.' In fact since the community was primarily for retired people admissions under sixty or sixty-five were uncommon, and the requirement of 'years of community service' was probably more an ideal than a strict requirement.

At a practical level, despite the modernisation and refurbishment of the almshouses for the 1964 centenary, little had been done subsequently and, whereas there was a statutory quinquennial inspection of the church, there was no such provision for the almshouses. The vicar-wardens had been diligent pastors but they were not trained in building-management, and in September 1980 several major items of repair and restoration were identified:

> Central heating in warden's lodge flats facing east
> Changing central heating valves to self-control to save oil costs
> Re-pointing fifty barley stick chimneys—some in dangerous condition
> Repairs to roof of boardroom
> Re-plastering library wall to eradicate damp
> Replacing gutters and downpipes
> Restoration and repair of chapel.

Mrs Rowberry quickly involved herself with these and with the raising of the necessary money. In October she wrote to Lady Beauchamp, now chairman of the Trustees, and commented, 'Newland is so beautiful, and the residents both so appreciative and happy, from somewhere we have to find the money to carry on, or else, hand it over in its entirety to the State—what a sad and sobering thought . . . Where can we look for help?'

The Trustees relied for their income on interest from investments, on nominal contributions from the residents and on donations. They spent £12,000 in repairs in 1980, but they could not spend more and in 1981 they launched an 'appeal for the survival of the Beauchamp Community, Newland.' In a letter to prospective donors Lady Beauchamp explained,

> Through the years the Trustees have completely modernised the houses and converted them into forty-four self-contained flats, each comprising a sitting room, bedroom, bathroom and kitchen all centrally heated. Our residents, from all walks of life, are still pensioners of limited means and each one makes a weekly contribution toward the cost of maintenance. I use the word 'toward' advisedly because, as you will readily appreciate, as costs soar it becomes increasingly difficult to carry on. Our fifty-six barley stick chimneys urgently need £30,000 to repair them, many being in a dangerous condition: the fourteenth century chapel has been temporarily closed until £7,000 is found to restore it; the central heating boilers are wearing out and will need replacing ere long. The list is endless, and our task seemingly impossible.
>
> To this end we are launching a public appeal for £50,000 to help the community survive—will you help us, please?

Amazingly within twelve months almost £50,000 had been raised. Further, as it was clear that there would no more resident incumbents, plans were made for the creation of two more flats in the warden's lodge—number one on the ground floor, and number two upstairs—and in 1983 St Christopher's was at last modernised.

Pyndar Court

From 1980 the Trustees had regular discussions about the old kitchen garden and Mrs Rowberry immediately sought to regain the planning permission which had lapsed. She was in touch with a variety of charities: first Friends of Harding Housing Association and then the Artee Housing Society Ltd of Ledbury, both of which envisaged erecting 26 one-bedroom flats. In November 1982 the parish council opposed the application: it was a serious over-development, not in keeping with the area, not 'infill' but an extension into a rural area, a most unsuitable design, it was a private development and it would spoil the amenity of views across the common. The council organised a petition against the development and this attracted seventy-five signatories, but the Trustees argued that the council did not have the facts before them when they made their objections.

Mrs Rowberry put the Trustees' case before a public meeting convened by the council and the council received twenty letters supporting the plan. The Area Planning Officer recommended approval, but in January 1983, by eleven votes to three, Malvern Hills District Council refused Artee's application on three grounds—the Beauchamp Almshouses were within a rural area which was not allocated for development of any sort, the development would be likely to affect the general character and appearance of this very attractive area, and Artee was not a 'registered charity' as such.

In May 1983 Artee appealed against the council's ruling, and in September the appeal was allowed, but Artee was then taken over by another association and dropped out of the picture. In 1984 tenders were invited 'for licence to Build Beauchamp Community Extension at Newland', and it was still envisaged that there should be twenty-six units 'for persons of not less than retirement age.' Each unit would have an alarm system connected to the flat of the Beauchamp warden, and residents would have the use of the communal areas at Beauchamp but would contribute to their maintenance by a service charge. Tenders were submitted by Village Green Ltd, who offered £160,000 and proposed to build twenty-one units consisting of nine two-bedroom cottages and twelve one-bedroom flats which they would sell from £33,500 to £46,000, and by Lansdown Homes in association with Walkham Homes, who offered £140,000 (later increased to £180,000) and proposed to build twenty-six units which they would sell from £51,000 to £56,000.

The Lansdown tender was accepted and they employed the Mason Richards Partnership as their architects. A Lansdown publicity sheet spoke of 'a unique courtyard development' and explained,

> Each property has been specifically designed to provide retirement accommodation for people who are seeking a comfortable alternative to their existing home, without the need to worry about the up-keep of a garden, which is perhaps too large or a house that requires constant attention. Exclusively for people over sixty, Pyndar Court offers the perfect solution, where you can maintain your independence, whilst enjoying a relaxing and carefree lifestyle.

Building was scheduled to start on 5 May 1986, and in July 1986 *Grapevine* commented,

> Few can have failed to see the new building works taking place at Newland on land adjoining Newland Churchyard. This development, which is being undertaken by the local building firm of Wilesmith, is for Lansdown Homes Ltd of Worle, Weston-super-Mare. The project is to provide twenty-four two-storey and two one-storey dwellings built in the shape of a letter E. It is anticipated that the houses will be ready for occupation by March of next year and will be sold from £50,000 each.

In 1987 a show-house was opened, and the development now consisted of twenty-two two-bedroom cottages and four two-bedroom bungalows. The name Pyndar Court was requested by

Lady Beauchamp in honour of her late husband, and each of the six differently designed homes were named from the Beauchamp family tree—Pindar, Elmley, Greville, Lygon, Lambert and Charlotte. Prices were from £63,750, and twenty-six parking spaces were allotted.

The Trustees discussed whether there should be an official opener for the new complex, and it was agreed that the Duchess of York should be approached, but nothing more was heard of this.

Management was vested, though not without reservations, in Retirement Care, and initially it was agreed that, for an appropriate contribution, the Trustees would provide a warden and an assistant warden to offer a twenty-four-hour emergency call service and that accommodation would be found for a warden in the Beauchamp Community. But this arrangement proved only temporary. The last warden, Mrs Pat James, appointed in September 1988, resigned in October 1989 and the newly-formed Pyndar Residents Association then decided unanimously that they did not require a resident warden.

Initially it seems to have been envisaged that the properties would be leased, but in the event they were owner-occupied. Their residents were not bound by any Beauchamp rules and, while they were regarded as honorary members of the community and welcomed to join in any community services or activities, they were not under the slightest obligation to do so. In 1996 there was discussion as to whether the extra-parochial area of the Beauchamp community should include Pyndar as its residents wished, but the diocese rejected this on the ground that Pyndar was not part of the original Beauchamp charity. Nonetheless a good number of Pyndar residents involved themselves in the life of the church or community and made a major contribution to it.

Woodlands

On 13 March 1980, 1–2 St Barnabas was leased by Mrs D. Margaret Saunder and her sister Mrs E. M. May, though latterly only by Mrs Saunder aided by her husband Ted, and they established a 'rest and retirement home' known as Woodlands. It survived as such for twelve years.

In March 1990 a set of proposals entitled 'Malvern—the Future 1989 to 2001+' was published for public information and comment after six months discussion by a group of councillors and council officers. Among the options listed was the creation of a Malvern retail park close to the community, and especially to Woodlands, on land owned largely by the Madresfield estate. But land at the western end of the community, leased from the Madresfield estate by the Trustees, part of which they had subsequently leased to Woodlands, was also needed to secure access from the A449 Worcester Road to the proposed development. There were a number of other interested parties and for several months there was almost daily correspondence until in 1991 the Trustees surrendered the lease of the paddock to the Madresfield Estate for a million pounds.

Meanwhile, in October 1990 the Trustees were informed that the tenants of Woodlands might be willing to consider the surrender of their lease, and at this stage the Trustees envisaged acquiring Woodlands themselves and running it as an adjunct to the community. They believed that a rest home 'would form a natural and desirable addition to the Community to permit those residents no longer able to look after themselves in their own accommodation within the Community to remain amongst their friends and in surroundings that they know until such time as they may need a permanent nursing home.' The Charity Commissioners were in principle not unsympathetic, and on 17 October 1992 a revised scheme was sealed giving the Trustees legal authority to create a rest home. In April 1993 Mr and Mrs Saunder decided that it was now time for them to retire. They wrote in *Grapevine*,

> One and 2 St Barnabas was built for retired clergy, and stood empty for several years. Thanks to keen interest and moral support from the late Countess Beauchamp, and much hard work and help from family and friends, we opened as a rest home August 1980, taking in three residents:- the late Mrs L. Cockerill of the quadrangle, Father Davies

of St Barnabas, who went into care in North Wales and returned to end his days at Newland with us, and Mrs Nora Gould, mother of the Rector of Bromyard.

The opening of the ground floor now means we are able to register for five, but we are still working on the first floor, which when completed will provide in all accommodation for twelve residents.

Owning and working in the Home proved very rewarding tinged with sadness at the passing of so many friends, with their differing ways. Now in view of all the changes so close to the Home, we feel this is a suitable time to retire.

Meanwhile the Trustees had been advised that 'extensive and expensive structural modernisations' would be required, and in the event they purchased Woodlands on 31 March 1993 for £187,500 with the intention of closing it on 31 July. At this stage they were uncertain whether to create four flats in it, or two flats and a frailty unit for the community, but the idea of four flats proved most popular. A flat in the warden's lodge was briefly considered for conversion to a frailty care unit, but it was not deemed suitable.

At that time road access to Woodlands was by its own wrought-iron gate, but this was too close to the proposed new roundabout for continued use by traffic, and as part of the various 'deals' the developers built a new access road from the Beauchamp car park, where the cherry trees are now, and also erected some additional railings, did some shrub and tree planting and double glazing which cost them in the region of £50,000. Henceforth the wrought-iron gate was used only by pedestrians. The conversion of Woodlands into four flats was achieved in October 1994. Thus instead of the previous four St Barnabas houses there are now eight flats. Numbers 5–8 are still known as St Barnabas, though in defiance of history numbers 1–4 retain the name Woodlands. This is sad in that they were equally part of the St Barnabas charity, and it was as St Barnabas that they were known for their first seventy years. It would be good if they could revert to that name.

General

The American Ligons paid further visits in 1983 and 1993 and proved generous supporters. In 1993 the Trustees established a management committee which would meet monthly, and they clarified the duties of the administrator, solicitor and accountant One of their first acts was to update the community rules yet again, and to advertise for new residents but, although they spent £200 on this they met with little success. It may be that both almshouses and grounds were now looking slightly weary, and the Trustees were determined to press ahead with improvements to both. More work was possible after the sale of the kitchen garden site, and this included in August 1993 the erection of a store shed, the building of carports and the extension of the emergency system to nine flats which had no bell. In 1994 the Trustees decided that kitchens should be refitted when flats became vacant. In 1997 the boardroom kitchen was enlarged and modernised, and subsequently work began on the conversion of flat one in the warden's lodge into a guest room to replace the smaller one at 19 Quadrangle.

The Church and its Services

In October 1981 Bertie Shaw died at the age of eighty-four, having just celebrated his diamond jubilee as organist of St Leonard's. In later years his tenure may have been somewhat nominal as he was frequently away, not least overseas where he had a son in Hong Kong, and he was reliant on deputies among whom were Dorothy Pembridge, Gordon Barnes and Father Nichols. But he had stuck with Newland through thick and thin, from the heyday of the choir school to its ultimate demise and beyond, and it was at Newland that his funeral was held.

In the building, further work on the frescoes was done from 1986 to 1988. This was enabled by Gordon Barnes who left his residuary estate (amounting to £49,430) to the community with his first charge being to conserve the frescoes. His executor, the

Reverend John Guise, obtained estimates from Clayton and Bell and from Gartner, Petzold and Smith. He referred these to the Council for the Care of Churches and was strongly advised to accept the latter which he duly did. The ceilings were cleaned at a cost of £5,763 plus VAT, but no attempt was made to remove the overpainting from the reredos or the blue paint on the north chancel wall, though both were considered as were improvements to the lighting.

In November 1988, to celebrate the completion of the work (which also included work on the organ) there was a week of festivities. This began with a Friday evening organ recital by Andrew Millington, then organist of Guildford Cathedral and now of Exeter Cathedral. He had been brought up in Stocks Lane where his parents lived, and had used Newland as his 'practice' organ. His father was a regular worshipper at Newland (though he later joined the Priory choir), and his mother was a pillar of the Newland Mothers Union and remained a faithful 8 a.m. communicant at St Leonards until they moved to a care home. After the recital there was a cheese and wine party in the boardroom, on the Saturday there was an open day, and on the Sunday (which fortuitously was St Leonard's Day) as well as the usual eucharists there was a festal evensong with the Venerable Frank Bentley, archdeacon of Worcester, as the preacher.

In January 1988, Bishop Maund proposed that a small portable altar be placed in the chancel or at the head of the nave, and moved when not in use; such an altar was actually made but as it proved insubstantial it was not used. Father Marsh also gave a sacristy bell on permanent loan.

In April 1996 Father Burr noted that the altar candlesticks, donated in 1959, were both badly worn, one being bent, and that their aluminium finish did not fit in with the reredos. It was proposed to put back the original brass candlesticks and altar cross, only to discover that in 1965 Father Bott had sold them to a church in Africa. Father Burr then proposed that two new candlesticks be purchased at a cost of £230 'made of fibreglass of Florentine style and with a golden finish which would be compatible with the altar and its surrounds.' Some years later, he expressed his regret that he had not ordered six rather than two, stating, 'I really love "the big six", and when I saw Newland Church for the first time I was surprised that it didn't have them.'

After Father Brodribb's death, matins and litany on Sunday were dropped, as eventually were daily matins and evensong though not the daily eucharist. There was now an 8 a.m. Sunday eucharist primarily for the parish celebrated by the incumbent and an 11 a.m. eucharist primarily for the community celebrated by the chaplain. This arrangement suited the incumbent as it enabled him to conduct regular services at Guarlford at 10 a.m. and at Madresfield at 11.15 a.m., but it did not suit everyone in the community. At this stage the 8 a.m. service had a congregation not greatly below the later one,[4] but an analysis by Father Nichols for ten random Sundays from August to December 1982 showed total communicants as 194, of whom ninety-four were from the community, fifty-one from the parish and forty-seven from outside the parish—though conversely the 11 a.m. community congregation was boosted both by parishioners and by others beyond it. Beauchamp chaplains also conducted evensong on Sundays at 6.30 p.m. (or from 1984 to 1988 vespers at 4 p.m.), but congregations were small, and for some periods the sermon was abandoned. They also celebrated the daily eucharists. In 1987 the incumbent officiated at evening worship on Whit Sunday, and in September 1987 he started evensong on the first Sunday of most months. With a congregation often of over twenty this continued till 1997, but increasingly evensong was conducted by the community chaplain, though sometimes it was a 'benefice evensong' conducted by the incumbent.

On Maundy Thursday 1980 there was Newland's first evening mass,

---

[4] On the three Sundays after Easter, in 1979 there was a total of fifty-five communicants at 8 a.m. and eighty-two at 11 a.m.; in 1985 the figures were fifty-seven at 8 a.m. and eighty-seven at 11 a.m.

with a second following on Corpus Christi. Evening celebrations now increased, and from Lent 1983 there were 8 a.m. celebrations on Tuesdays, Thursdays and Saturdays, and 7 p.m. ones on Mondays, Wednesdays and Fridays (though from 1985 the Wednesday one was moved to 10 a.m., and later the evening ones were moved to 6.30 p.m. and then to 6 p.m.). As for other services, advent and Christmas carol services were not uncommon. Father Brown held afternoon mothering sunday services, an afternoon service on Whit Sunday in 1981 and a 10 a.m. family service on Easter Sunday in 1982, but none of these continued after his death.

In April 1985 a Beauchamp Community Church Committee was established, open not only to community members but also to others who attended when the chaplain was officiating, and it met regularly until July 1997 when it was overtaken by events. Their minutes, covering both the routine and the controversial, were similar to those of an ordinary PCC. But a recurring concern was the music which seems to have reached an all-time low. One problem was that Beauchamp's *Leighton Mass* setting was virtually unknown elsewhere and, while it had 'worked' when there was a professional organist and a trained choir, it proved difficult without these, and for many people the Sunday Eucharist was decidedly lugubrious.

In October 1988 the chaplain proposed that the better known Merbecke setting be used in place of the present one, or at least that the gloria and creed should be said. There was vigorous opposition to this, and in January he withdrew his proposal, 'He now realised how much this music meant to the members of the Community, assured them that no change would be made, and apologised for any unintentional hurt to their feelings.' In the same month the Trustees resolved, 'It is the unanimous decision of the Trustees after consulting their Constitution that there shall be no change in the unique form of service or music of the Beauchamp Community Services.' But a year later, in January 1990, the annual general meeting passed by a large majority a motion that for six months an experiment be made of 'said mass with hymns.' The chairman said that he would report this to the Trustees, and in July he stated that the Trustees desired that the tradition of a *sung* eucharist be maintained, though otherwise the chaplain was responsible for the form of the service. It was agreed however that the creed could be said, except on the first Sunday of the month. But discontent continued, and in 1995 the church committee, noting that the setting of the mass currently in use was to be discussed by the Trustees, passed unanimously a motion 'that the traditional setting of the Mass be adhered to.' This was accepted by the Trustees, except that they agreed to the use of Merbecke for the kyries and to the *saying* of the creed on every Sunday. But not all was negative, and in 1992 *The New English Hymnal* was introduced, copies being paid for by Mary Overton in memory of her late husband, Father John Overton, a retired priest who though not living in the community had given much help to St Leonard's in the 1980s.

In 1981 the Trustees agreed to restore the chapel at a cost of around £5,000. As a result in 1982 the catafalque was removed to the archway beside the porter's lodge, and the chapel restored and refitted, and in future the daily eucharists were celebrated here rather than in the church. Father Nichols once referred to the chapel as 'St Michael's Chapel', perhaps recalling the original dedication of the old church, but this never caught on and it quickly became known as the Cloister Chapel. On 27 August 1986 Bishop Maund consecrated a new altar for it—a simple but pleasing table made by Alan Gray—a retired priest. He felt that it needed no frontal, not least since he celebrated facing the people. Bishop Maund, however, was a small man and his successors found this mode of celebration difficult, so the altar-table was moved back to the east wall. In 1993 new heaters were installed, in 1994 the sanctuary lamp was re-instated and an all-seasons frontal provided for the altar, and in 1995 a simple desk lectern replaced an old brass one.

Chapter Fifteen
The New Millenium: 2000–2014

After Mrs Rowberry's resignation Peter Hughes, the Madresfield Estate agent, became clerk to the Trustees. No new administrator as such was appointed, and instead the post of warden was upgraded. There was now a succession of wardens:

November 1999 to December 2003. Mrs Johanna Flint, who had been warden under Mrs Rowberry and lived in the porter's lodge, took over the administration of the community and the day to day responsibility while her husband John continued as maintenance supervisor and caretaker. Both worked in close partnership with the chaplain. Johanna, a German by birth, was dearly loved and she brought a new stability to the community; residents were desperately sad when she was diagnosed with cancer and subsequently died.

February 2004 to February 2007. Mrs Jean Wild had worked at Madresfield Court before joining the community in 1996. On appointment as warden she moved from the Quadrangle to St Christopher's, and as she was a 'people person' the administration was undertaken by the chaplain. Sadly she too was diagnosed with cancer, so she resigned as warden and moved back to the Quadrangle. She died in 2010.

December 2007 to September 2008. Mrs Megan Burnett had been brought up in Malvern, had close associations with St Matthias church and trained as a nurse. After 32 years in Zimbabwe, she returned to England in 1995. She lived in the Quadrangle, and was just getting into her stride as warden when ill-health forced her to resign. Happily she was able to remain in her flat (where she still lives as a valued member of the community) and her health has significantly improved.

February 2009 onwards. Mrs Lesley Lewis, the present warden, was born in Lancashire, trained as a radiographer and married Ken by whom she had two children. In 1972 they emigrated to South Africa where Ken was ordained in 1998 shortly before retiring. In 2001 they moved to Ireland where she worked in a hospital while Ken assisted in local parishes till his death in 2007. Lesley lives in one of the Lygon Lodge flats.

All the wardens have been ably assisted by one or two deputies (including Delia Bryans, Diana Crews, Eileen Samuels, Ronnie Whitford, and latterly Paula Brady, Sylvia Mair and Julie Allsopp), and the arrangement has worked well. On the buildings side, John Flint resigned in 2004 and moved to Woodlands. He was succeeded by Roger Hodkinson who lived with his wife Jenny in the porters lodge. Sadly Roger became ill and died in 2012, and John Flint took over again for a year; Jenny moved to the Quadrangle.

There have been two chaplains during this period:

April 2000 to November 2007. John Mark Meredith Dalby. Born in 1938 and aged sixty-two on appointment. He was ordained in Oxford in 1963 and served in Buckinghamshire, Birmingham, London and Manchester before becoming archdeacon of Rochdale. On his retirement as chaplain he moved to St Christopher's where he still lives.

December 2007 onwards. Hartley Roger Watson. Born in 1940

and aged sixty-seven on appointment. He was ordained in London in 1964 and served thereafter as an RAF chaplain, in Truro and as rector of Brigstock with Stanion, Lowick and Sudborough, Peterborough. He was accompanied by his wife Jane who quickly became a pillar of the choir.

Today the almshouses and other buildings are well-maintained, and flats are usually refurbished when a long-standing resident dies or moves. There is normally an upper age-limit of seventy-five for new residents while the minimum age is sixty; this ensures a constant supply of younger residents as existing ones get older. Such ageing is inevitable in a community like Beauchamp, and perhaps the only sad aspect of life here is seeing friends and fellow-residents getting older and more infirm—and realising that this is also true of oneself. It is made clear to all applicants that the community is in no sense a nursing home, and it is difficult to know how best to cope with the more infirm.

Until recently there were cords which residents could pull if they needed emergency contact with a warden, but these had their limitations—several residents had falls and, while they could see the cords, they could not reach them. The cords were replaced by phones which residents could carry on their persons or place by their bedside and which provided immediate access to a warden. But these proved complicated, and many residents declined to use them. They have now been abandoned and, while there is a warden on duty twenty-four hours a day, the only means of contacting her is by landline or mobile telephone. Yet not all residents have a landline phone by their bedside, and not all have a mobile phone. It is difficult to see the way forward here. Meanwhile the trend for residents to move to a care or nursing home for their last years has continued. There have been only two deaths in the community itself in this period, both of them unexpected, and there have been no Beauchamp burials in the churchyard, though in two or three cases ashes have been interred there.

There are some wonderful points of continuity. James Ruddock-Broyd, who formerly lived in Newland, has been associated with the community as trustee and then accountant for 40 years, while Mary Oseman, our oldest resident, has lived here since 1980. But some eventual deaths represent a major break with the past and this is particularly true of three in this period.

Dorothy Pembridge, named after Dorothy Lygon (later Lady Dorothy Heber-Percy), whose mother had been head nurse to the family from 1906 to 1914 and whose father later became clerk to the Trustees, worked as a Land Girl at Madresfield Court in the Second World War and used to attend Evensong at Newland. In 1942 she wrote a simple poem, 'Newland Quadrangle', which many years later was published in *Grapevine*:

> This place has cast its spell on me,
> Within its walls—tranquillity—
> Has made the world's mad clamour cease.
>
> The Pensioners with Staff and Cloak,
> The Choir-boys' voices—both invoke
> A blessing and make strain decrease.
>
> The velvet lawns, the flowers and trees;
> The organ's mellow tones—all these
> My pent-up spirit will release.
>
> 'I lift up my eyes unto the hills',
> And their quiet benediction stills
> All restlessness—I am at peace.

Dorothy came to live in the Quadrangle in 1948 and remained there till 1965, acting at times as churchwarden and as a relief organist. After a break when she lived in Leigh Sinton, she returned to the community and lived at Woodlands from 1994 to 2001. She died in a nursing home in 2004, and her many mementos and photographs were passed to the community archives.

Ted Bullock whom we have already mentioned was educated at Madresfield school, and joined Newland Sunday school on the first Sunday after his fifth birthday; thereafter he 'graduated to blowing the organ, singing in the choir, bell ringing.' After his marriage to Doris, he lived in the Old Vicarage. He was appointed porter in 1964 and was churchwarden for many years from 1967 as well as being server, crucifer and thurifer; he also looked after the graveyard and mowed the Quadrangle lawns, originally by donkey. In 1995 the *Worcester Evening News* reported, 'Ted Bullock used to play football on the small road in the middle of Newland. There were few cars when he kicked a ball about as a youngster in the village. "When the cars came down the road they were only going at about 20 m.p.h. as well," says Ted, eighty.' He and Doris remained in the community and were faithful communicants every Sunday at 8 a.m. till his death in 2006 and hers in 2007. We wish that we had been able to tape-record their many memories.

But happily the Madresfield links still continue. John and June Cowell moved to Madresfield in 1975, and June was caretaker of Madresfield school for twenty-six years; Guy Phillips ran the village post-office and for many years was chairman of the Madresfield club; Dot McCaig's son-in-law is agent for the Madresfield estate; Thelma Bailey's father-in-law was rector of Madresfield; Diana Crews' son-in-law worked for the estate as did Gerald Campbell; Norman Mills lived in the village.

Although Beauchamp is no longer part of the benefice, its links with the neighbourhood have actually grown stronger. In 2000 the millennium was celebrated by a pig roast in the Quadrangle organised by Newland parish council, and in 2002 the community acted as hosts for another pig roast to celebrate the Queen's Golden Jubilee. By now the Parish Council was holding its monthly meetings in the boardroom, as it still does; there is always a Beauchamp member on it, and there is always Beauchamp news in *Grapevine*.

In 2001 the community was featured briefly on an ITV programme, *Just a Moment,* and in the same year a social committee was formed; this arranged outings, 'under a tenner' pub lunches, and games afternoons. Other residents organised coffee mornings, occasional teas and suppers, barbecues and firework parties. All in all, social life is probably stronger than ever nowadays. For many years Pat Harrod (now left) and Eileen Samuels have hosted a monthly music evening.

The current rules are not greatly different from those of 1977, but rule twelve emphasises that 'Residents should be aware that the Beauchamp Community is not a Nursing Home and that they are expected to be self-sufficient', rule thirteen that 'It is expected that residents, as members of the Beauchamp Community, will attend the Community Church where services are held on Sundays and weekdays', and rule fourteen that 'Residents shall not be absent for more than fifty-six nights in any one year without the advance permission of the Trustees.' This last is more generous than an earlier limitation to twenty-eight nights and for a short time there was no limitation at all. One resident, however, abused this freedom and used her flat as a *pied-à-terre,* so a limitation was reinstated but, with a number of residents having children or other close relations in Africa, America or Australasia, it was felt that fifty-six was a more appropriate number than twenty-eight.

But there are other aspects of life not governed by rules. Prior to the opening of the retail park the nearest grocery store was the Co-op in Malvern Link, though a fishmonger and greengrocer made deliveries to the community. These deliveries eventually ceased, although newspapers and milk are still delivered daily to those who want them. After the opening of the park the roads adjacent to the community became much busier, and thanks largely to community agitation a pedestrian crossing was created in 2002 en route to the park. Most residents do their basic shopping there at Morrisons (formerly Safeways), though about half have cars and are able to venture further afield if they wish.

Close relations continue with the residents of Pyndar Court which is now managed by Peverel Retirement, and the visiting manager, Barry Argyle, is frequently to be seen there. Pyndar has had some distinguished residents, among them Sir Patrick Branigan and the Reverend Dr Robin Denniston

Church music began to improve beyond all recognition from 2001 when Charles Allsopp, previously organist at St Chad Stafford and Upton-upon-Severn, was appointed as organist and later came into residence with his wife Julie whose mother Pat Hipwell was already a resident. He quickly formed a residents' choir and was soon achieving high standards, so much so that even the traditional setting no longer sounded miserable. *New English Praise*, a supplement to its parent book, was introduced shortly after its publication, and in 2007 a setting of the modern liturgy by Dom Gregory Murray was introduced for midweek festivals when the service was sung. 2010 saw the introduction of the Communion Service in D major by L. J. White, with the old setting used in Advent and Lent, while Martin Shaw's 'Anglican Folk Mass' was introduced as an alternative in 2013.

In the chapel it had been agreed in 1996 that the rather cold blue carpet needed replacing, and in 2000 a warmer red one was laid in its place. In 2003 an all-seasons frontal was designed, made and presented by the sacristan, Eileen Samuels, a gifted embroidress, and in 2009 the sanctuary lamp was electrified. The organ was renovated again in 2008 thanks to a generous donation from the family of Pamela Bulmer, a former resident of Pyndar Court who died in 2006.

In the church a new illustrated guide-book by David Annett was produced in 2001, and this was followed by a new set of six postcards. A loop system was introduced in 2002, and in 2009 there was remedial work on a fresco at the southeast corner which had been damaged by the ingress of water.

In 2007–08 a group from NADFAS spent much time on conservation work in the library and on re-cataloguing its contents. This provided a valuable supplement to the 1934 card index. The library is now kept locked, and the most valuable items are stored elsewhere. In 2008 George Sharrock, then a resident of

Pyndar, was appointed honorary librarian, and he subsequently reported to the Trustees that the library currently contained 2,400 books, including 273 printed between 1500 and 1700. The rest were printed before 1900, except for a few added informally by later clergy residents. The total value is currently estimated as £130,000.

In 2009 again there was major rewiring at a cost of c. £32,000 and this greatly improved the lighting and enabled the roof designs to be clearly visible again. At the same time a new sanctuary carpet was purchased, largely from residents' donations, and a new green altar frontal and vestments were purchased from a donation by the American Ligons.[5] In 2010 a NADFAS group produced the most comprehensive listing ever made of the church and its furnishings, and this was beautifully illustrated.[6]

In 2011 a gospel book was donated by Jill Coleman in memory of her husband, Father Beverley Coleman, who had worshipped with the community for many years and given considerable help. Jill also donated the red service books which are used for the Sunday eucharist. Other recent donations to the church have been turned wooden bases for the acolytes torches and lace cottas for the servers, both given by Colin Brownlee and the restoration of the brass processional cross is a gift from Mrs Jenny Hodkinson, in memory of her husband Roger, a great stalwart of the church. Over the last two years, the altar serving team has been re-formed and the ritual is now that which befits anglo-catholic worship.[7]

More recently there has been a walking group, 'The Beauchamp Walkers', a monthly film show organised by Colin Brownlee who transforms the library into 'The Beauchamp Odeon' and regular concerts are organised by Charles Allsopp. The formation of the

---

[5] The American Ligons made further visits in 2001 (when they planted a tree) and in 2010, and on each occasion they held a service in church. They have made an annual donation.

[6] NADFAS strangely describes 'Blessed are the Meek' as 'The Flight into Egypt'.

[7] See Appendix II for further details on the ritual, liturgy and altar servers.

Garden Club has also been a great success and most residents attend the monthly meetings.[8]

The year 2013 saw the first ever Burns Night Supper in the boardroom, complete with piper and is already established in the calendar as a yearly event. The annual garden fête is one of the major events of the year, now being jointly managed by the community and the local branch of Save the Children.

As part of the one hundred and fiftieth anniversary celebrations the iron gates which lead into Chapel Meadow (the original name of the paddock) are being restored, as is the fountain in the centre of the Quadrangle. New heating will be installed in the Library (in memory of Father Mark Dalby) and the ugly over-painting in the church chancel, carried out in 1926, will be removed and the original design reinstated, thereby restoring the chancel to its former glory. Also, Diana Crews is generously donating a new Beauchamp flag, as the original is too delicate to fly from the tower.

However, the library raises problems. It was not part of the original foundation, and it has never fulfilled Cosby White's hopes. Mrs Rowberry described it as 'a white elephant' and it is hard to disagree with her. The community clergy make occasional use of it, but in the last twelve years only one visiting scholar has consulted it. One possibility for its future would be to preserve it 'as is' as an example of the library of a wealthy and scholarly Victorian clergyman. Another would be to dispose of the books *in toto,* even though the money would go to the diocese rather than to the Trustees, and to find an alternative use for the building. But perhaps the most creative possibility would be to retain those books (about a third) which are particularly relevant to Beauchamp, i.e. books relating to Tractarian history and liturgy, to sell the rest even if the proceeds went to the diocese, and to use the vacated shelves for archive material which is already being stored there.

There could also be a 'museum' for historical items from the

---

[8] See Appendix V for information on the gardens and grounds.

church which are no longer used but are still worth preserving and an exhibition centre—in 2013 there was an exhibition on the history of the Choir School[9] which aroused much interest, particularly as current residents had not fully realised its reputation and integral role in the daily life of the almshouses. Meanwhile, the Library has found a new lease of life as a venue for social functions and receptions and the installation of a new heating system will allow for all year round use.

---

[9] The exhibition was mounted by Colin R. Brownlee, as part of his researches into the Choir School.

Chapter Sixteen
Epilogue

We all tend to think that what we have we have grown up with or been introduced to in later life is what has always been. But this is not the case with Beauchamp. The church and the Quadrangle almshouses are constants even though there are no 'decayed agricultural labourers' now.

From 1864 to 1980 there was a vicar-warden living in the Warden's Lodge and with oversight of both the parish and the community.

From 1864 to 1939 there were uniformed nuns caring for the sick and living in what is now the Chaplain's House.

From 1878 to 1945 there were choirboys living in the School House and singing daily in the church.

From 1900 to 1980 there were only retired clergy living in the St Barnabas' houses.

The community was probably at its most diverse from 1900 to 1939 when it consisted of a resident priest-warden, the almshouse residents, the nuns, the choir boys, the St Barnabas clergy, and sometimes some other children and servants. Today, especially with the absence of the nuns and the choirboys as well as other children and servants, the community is much less varied. But, as a hymn puts it, 'time makes ancient good uncouth.'

Life moves on, society changes, and we can never recreate the past. As we celebrate, and give thanks for, our first 150 years, we can be sure that there will be further changes in the next 150 years.

Meanwhile we honour our founder and his first wife for their original vision, and we honour all who have gone before us. We thank the Trustees for their continuing oversight of the community, and in our different ways we all seek to make our own contribution to its ongoing life. All of us would say a hearty 'Amen' to the Beauchamp and community motto, 'My lot is cast in a fair ground.' And we hope and pray that the Trustees will be inspired to continue and to further this Christian and charitable foundation that it may be a blessing to future generations as it has been to past and present ones.

John Reginald Pindar, third Earl Beauchamp, 1855

Frederick Lygon, sixth Earl Beauchamp, 1867

Charlotte, Countess Beauchamp, 1845

James Skinner, first vicar-warden, 1861–77

The almshouses under construction, 1863

After the church was consecrated work continued on the frescos for a further twenty years. This photo shows the frescos by the altar awaiting completion.

Revd. Cosby White, second vicar-warden, with the residents and choristers, c.1880

Choir school choristers with their choirmaster Claude Biggs in the centre, the choir matron and Countess Beauchamp

The vicar-warden and his clergy, 1945

A group of female residents in Almshouse uniform of cloak with silver badge and bonnet, 1946

The altar boys of 1946

A watercolour of the original church,
demolished shortly after the completion of the current church

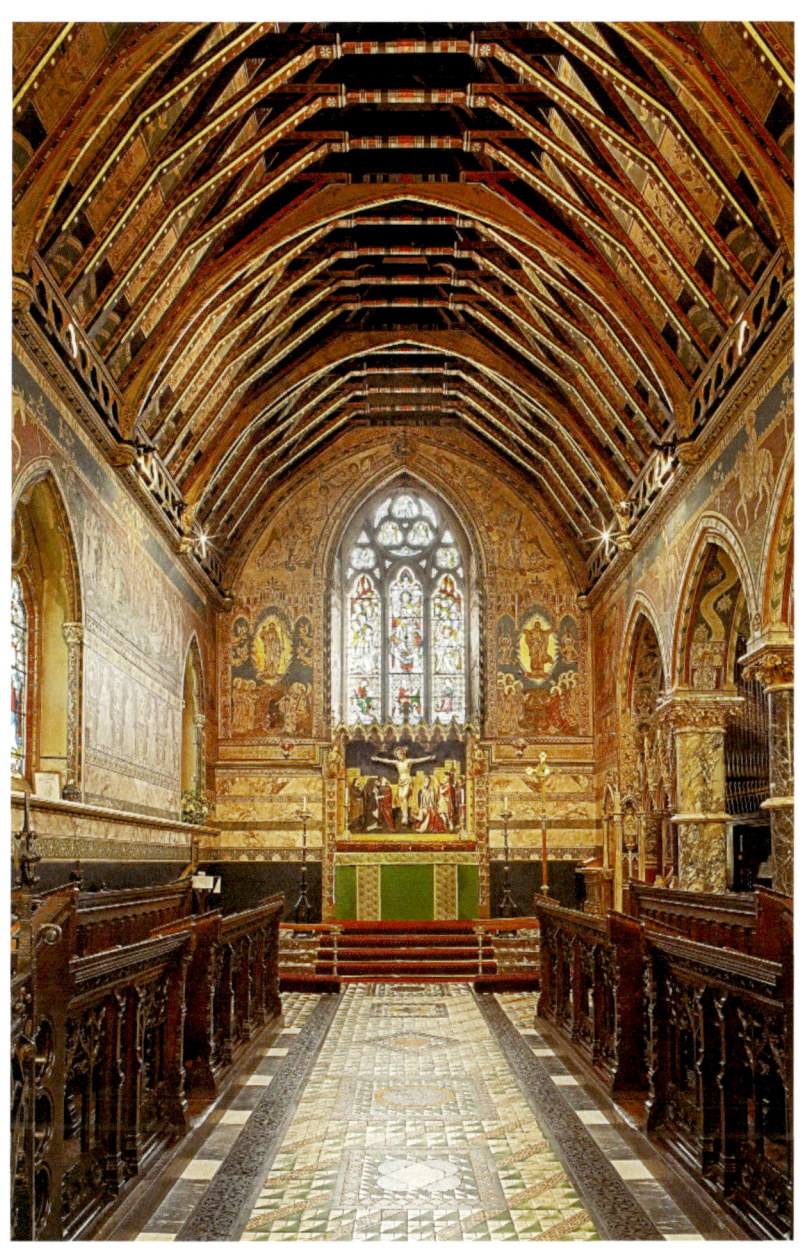

Interior of St Leonard's Church, 2013

A view of the Almshouses across the Quadrangle, 2013

Appendix I
People

Trustees

This list is drawn from the minutes of the Trustees and is probably accurate as far as names are concerned. But while the minutes records appointments, it often omits resignations, retirements or deaths.

1859, the Right Honourable George William, Lord Lyttelton, Hagley Hall, till 1876.

1859, the Right Honourable Henry Lygon, Viscount Elmley, Madresfield Court, (later fifth Earl), died 1856.

1859, the Right Honourable Charles, Earl Somers, Eastnor Castle, till 1875.

1859, Mr John Slaney Pakington of Kent's Green, Powick till 1875.

1859, Sir Edmund Anthony Harley Lechmere, Bart., Rhydd Court, Guarlford, till 1895?

1859, Mr William Edward Dowdeswell, Pull Court, Worcestershire, active 1875.

1859, the Reverend George Shaw Munn, Rector of Madresfield, died 1906.

1859, the Honourable Colonel Charles Grantham Scott, Baginton Hall, Warwickshire, active 1875.

1859, the Reverend Thomas Philpott, Belbroughton (vicar 1831–61), died 1878.

1859, the Right Honourable Henry, fourth Earl Beauchamp, Madresfield Court, died 1863.

1859, the Honourable Frederick Lygon, Madresfield Court (later sixth Earl), died 1891.

1859, the Right Honourable Sir John Somerset Pakington, Bart., (Lord Hampton of Westwood Park), till 1875.
1866, Sir Henry Edward Francis Lambert, Bart., died 1873.
1866, Major General Eardley Nicholas Willmot, died by 1879.
1875, Mr George Edward Martin, Ham Court, active 1895.
1875, Colonel Thomas Coningsby Norbury, Sherridge Court, active 1895.
1875, Captain William Charles Hill, Powick, active 1895.
1875, the Reverend Henry William Coventry, Severn Stoke, died 1920.
1879, Henry Foley Vernon, Hanbury Hall, active 1895.
1879, the Reverend William Willoughby Douglas, Rector of Salwarpe.
1879, William Corse Wells, MD, Yarnton Lodge, Great Malvern.
1895, William (seventh) Earl Beauchamp, died 1938.
1895, Viscount Cobham, resigned 1912.
1895, the Reverend Edward Dowdeswell, died c.1914.
1895, Colonel Parker.
1899, the Honourable Edward Lygon.
1903, the Bishop of Worcester.
1903, the Reverend Canon Pelly.
1903, the Reverend Sydney R. James, resigned 1910.
1909, Lettice Mary Elizabeth, Countess Beauchamp.
1909, Mr Eliot George Bromley Martin, St Cloud, Callow End.
1909, Mr Frederick Paget Norbury, Norrest, Malvern, died c.1939.
1909, the Reverend Hugh Howard Williams, Rector of Madresfield, resigned 1910.
1910, the Honourable Mrs Percy Allsopp, Battenhall Mount.
1910, the Honourable Reginald William Coventry, Croome Court, Severn Stoke.
1910, Mrs Norah Wilson, The Grange, Madresfield, resigned 1920.
1912, the Reverend Gabriel Gillett, Rector of Madresfield.
1914, Sir Henry Foley Grey, Bart., Enville Hall, Stourbridge, resigned or died 1917.
1914, the Right Honourable Herbert Stuart, Baron Hampton, Waresley Court, Kidderminster, resigned 1921.
1914, Colonel William Stallard, St John's House, Worcester, died 1933.
1914, the Reverend Hugh Howard Williams, Rector of Madresfield.
1914, Mrs Edith Emma Knight, Eastnor House, Malvern Link, resigned 1919.
1914, Miss Susan Bromley-Martin, Henwick Hall, Worcester, resigned 1924.
1915, the Reverend H. Linzee Giles, Vicar of Malvern, resigned 1924
1915, the Reverend Lancelot Andrews, resigned or died 1917.
1918, the Reverend Frederick George Copeland, Rector of Madresfield, resigned 1928.

1918, the Reverend Edgar Paul Amphlett, Vicar of Powick, died 1922.
1920, Lieut Commander Geoffrey Winsmore Hooper, RN, OBE, died 1922.
1920, the Honourable Mrs Britten, Kenswick Manor, resigned 1938.
1920, Colonel Shirley Arthur Stevenson Fetherstonhaugh, The Hermitage, Powick, died 1949.
1922, Wright Henderson, Abberley House, Malvern, died 1932.
1923, the Reverend Hubert Jones, Vicar of Hanley Castle.
1925, the Right Honourable Viscount Elmley, (later eighth Earl), Madresfield Court, died 1979.
1924, Mrs Eleanor Holland Martin, Overbury Court, Tewkesbury, active 1949.
1924, the Reverend Frederick Cecil Champion, Vicar of Powick, resigned 1939.
1929, the Reverend J. W. Greaves, Rector of Madresfield, died 1940.
1934, Commander F. J. Ratcliff, RN, Brocklewath, Colwall, resigned 1966.
1934, Mrs Winnmore Hooper, died 1951.
1939, Lady Constance Lechmere, Severn End, Hanley Castle, resigned 1976.
1939, Else, Countess Beauchamp, died 1989.
1939, Colonel Sir W. H. Wiggin, died 1951.
1941, the Reverend H. W. Hill, Vicar of Malvern Link, resigned 1945.
1941, the Honourable Richard Lygon, Pyndar House, Hanley Castle, died 1970.
1945, the Reverend Harry Hartley, Vicar of Malvern Link.
1950, Canon R. B. Lunt, RD, Vicar of Malvern, resigned 1974.
1951, Christopher P. Norbury, Sherridge, Malvern, died 1975.
1952, Lady Dorothy Lygon.
1952, Mr J. Godfrey N. Russell, Holland House, Malvern, died 1975.
1952, Mrs Dyson Perrins, Little Davenham, Malvern, resigned 1966.
1955, Mrs D. E. Baker, JP, Lea, 5 Cing Lane, Malvern.
1956, Mrs Margaret Moore Ede, Southlea, Redhill, Worcester, died 1981.
1957, the Reverend J. R. Bamber, Vicar of Holy Trinity, Malvern.
1961, Lady Lettice Cotterill, The Old Rectory, Madresfield, resigned 1967.
1961, Lady Doris Eleanor Garrod, Lea, Sling Lane, Malvern, resigned 1987.
1967, Mr William Edward Charteris Watkinson, Tyre Hill House, Hanley Swan, died 1981.
1967, Lady Jean Marie Huntington-Whiteley, Ripple Hall, Tewkesbury, resigned 1996.
1967, Mrs Patricia M. W. Smith-Maxwell, Welland Court Farm, Upton-upon-Severn, resigned 2007.
1970, Mrs Agnithe De La Cour, Pickersley Court, Malvern, resigned 1993.

1974, Mr James G. Ruddock, Newland, resigned 1993.
1975, Mr Jeremy James Russell, Holland House, Malvern, resigned 1993.
1975, Miss Lettice Patricia Mary Lygon, Pyndar House, Hanley Castle, died 2007.
1977, Mr George Lodge, Madresfield Grange.
1981, Sir Berwick Hungerford Lechmere, Bart., Church End House, Hanley Castle, resigned 1996.
1982, Sir John Henry Geers Cotterell, Bart.
1982, Sir John Alexander Willison, Ravenshill Green, Lulsley, resigned 1994.
1990, Mrs Vera Rowberry, resigned 1993.
1992, Mr Thomas Richard Cotterell.
1993, the Honourable Lady Rosalind Elizabeth Morrison.
1996, Mrs Diana Margaret Rosalind Russell.
1996, the Honourable Marigold Webb.
2005, Mrs Lucy Chenevix Trench.
2007, Mr Nicholas A. Lechmere.
2007, Mr Philip Smith-Maxwell.

Vicar-Wardens, Chaplains and Families

Year	Name	Retired	Died	Age	Buried in Newland
1863	James Skinner	1877	1881	63	5 Jan. 1882
	Agnes Skinner, wife				
	Agnes Skinner, daughter		1868	18	12 Feb. 1868
	George Ure Skinner, brother		1867		
	Marguaretta Skinner, niece				
	Mary Skinner, niece				
	Katharine Green, sister-in-law				
	Agatha Skinner, niece				
	Mary Green, niece				
1877	George Cosby White	1897	1918	93	
	Harriette White		1890	69	9 May 1890
1897	Robert Wylde	1926	1927	83	
1927	Magdalen Wylde, sister				
	Mary Dorothea Wylde, daughter				
1927	Maurice Frederick Bell				
1929	Mrs Bell				

Year	Name	Retired	Died	Age	Buried in Newland
1929	Francis Wilfred Osborn	1938	1952	90	
	Mrs Osborn				
1937	Arthur Wilfrid Hatherly	1941	1941	69	
	Mrs Hatherly				
1942	John Hunt	1958	1974	87	
	Mary Hunt		1974		
1958	Francis Benjamin Darke	1963	1963	68	5 Sept. 1963
	Mrs Darke				
1963	Frederick Trevor Bott	1966	1987	84	
	Mrs Bott				
1967	Richard Arthur Charles Brodribb the last vicar-warden		1979	61	26 Oct. 1979
	Nancie Brodribb		1979	63	27 Apr. 1979
	Dorothy Brodribb, daughter				
1980	Hartley Brown		1982		1 June 1982
	Kathleen Frith, housekeeper	1982 to home	1983		1 July 1983
1982	Matthew William Hardwicke Nichols	1984	1985		
1984	John Arthur Arrowsmith Maund, Bishop	1988	1998	88	18 July 1998
1988	Clarence Simpson	1990	1997		
	Norma Simpson				
1991	Brian Gilbert Burr	1996	2004		
	Ruth Burr, wife		2011		
1997	Geoffrey John Marsh		1997	59	25 Sept. 1997
1998	Walter James Jennings	1999			
	Linda Jennings				
2000	John Mark Meredith Dalby	2007	2013		
2007	Hartley Roger Watson				
	Jane Watson				

Churchwardens

These have been obtained from a variety of sources but is incomplete.

1875–91, Mr Russell.

1906–07, J. Bourne and J. Meek.

1920–21, G. R. Lewis and Edward Whitehouse.
1921–22, Joshua Wilson and C. Wallace-Cox.
1928, B. Alder and H. C. Kings.
1930–37, H. C. Kings and A. R. Summers.
1944–47, T. W. Horton and Charles J. Smith.
1948–50, R. O. Allen and Charles J. Smith.
1954, Major Bridge and O. William Stokes.
1955, Charles J. Smith and O. William Stokes.
1963, Henry George Purser.
1962–63, A. H. B. Anson and Miss Dorothy Pembridge.
1965–67, Henry George Purser and C. Harry Holliday.
1967–80, A. E. Bullock and W. E. C. Watkinson.
1982–85, A. E. Bullock and Gordon L. Barnes.
1985–87, A. E. Bullock and Ronald Cheese.
1987–88, A. E. Bullock and Ronald Clay.
1988–90, A. E. Bullock and Michael Peach.
1991–97, A. E. Bullock and Mrs Jean Newton.

The post of churchwarden of Newland was now replaced by that of Madresfield with Newland.

Clerks to the Trustees

Clerks were appointed by the Trustees and normally employed and remunerated by them, but the Reverend J. W. Greaves was one of their number and was clearly 'honorary.' Appointments were normally recorded in the minutes of the Trustees, but there are some occasional omissions.

1859, Charles Bolton Edgecumbe.
1866, Ethelbert West (also organist and choirmaster).
    Elizabeth West, wife.
    Noreen West, daughter, acting for 6 months in 1871.
    Louisa West, daughter, acting for 1 month in 1871.
    Bertha West, daughter, acting for 2 months in 1871.
1878, William F. Cox.
1904–24, Miss A. W. Crompton.
1925, B. Amphlett; died same year.
1926, Mrs Amphlett.

1929–40, the Reverend J. W. Greaves, Rector of Madresfield.
1941–49, the Reverend J. G. R. Blackwell, Rector of Madresfield.
1949–60, Harry Percy Pembridge.
1961–63, G. L. E. Longman.
1963–70, E. A. Beale.
1970–80 Mrs Meriel Serjeant.
1980–99, Mrs Vera Rowberry.
2000+, Peter Hughes.

Curates

1861–1875 are from Assistant Curates of Newland 1861–77. All others from *Crockford's Clerical Directory* and from the parish registers.

1861–66, George Robert Adam, later Vicar of Sholden, Kent; came as deacon.

1864–67, Sidney Phillip, later Rector of Nuneham Courtenay, Oxon; came as deacon.

1867–?, Charles Henry Kennard, no further details.

1868–71, Arthur Middlemore Morgan, later Rector of Mucking, Essex.

1869–71, Charles Edward Taunton, later Vicar of St John the Baptist, Harlow, Essex.

1871–74, William Henry Harrison, later Curate of Laugharne.

1874–75, Alexander Barrington Orr, later Rector of St Palladius, Drumtochty.

1878, Edward John Eyre, later Vicar of Cleveland.

1877, Henry Holloway, buried in Newland 3 October 1904, aged 62.

1878–79, Francis E. W. Wilmot, later Vicar of Monnington-on-Wye, Herefordshire.

1879–91, Walter Consitt Boulter, later Vicar of Norton and Lenchwick.

1891–98, Gordon Charles Grist, later Vicar of Woolhope, Herefordshire.

1898–1900, Hubert Edgcombe Hadow, later Curate of Bisley, Stroud.

1901, William A. Norton, living with servant in Almshouse.

1902–04, Henry Holloway, buried in Newland 3 October 1904, aged 62.

1904–05, Charles Rowland Fowke, unofficial appointment.

1905–13, James Webb Cheshire, later vicar in Torquay.

1916, Reginald Margnie Foss, no further details.

1920–23, Arthur Theodore Tasker, later Vicar of St Andrew, Chippenham.

1923–25, A. E. Crowder, later Vicar of All Saints, East Clevedon

1925, C. Radford, no further details.

Lay Wardens

This post was created after the death of the last vicar-warden in 1979. It lapsed a year later but revived in 1987. Initially the Wardens then held office under the administrator, Mrs Rowberry, but on her retirement in 1999 they became the senior lay officers of the community.

1979–80, Mrs D. K. Beaumont.
1987–88, Mrs Lloyd.
1988, Mrs Mary Oseman.
1997, Mrs Johanna Flint, died 8 Dec. 2003.
2004, Mrs Jean Wild, died 13 Nov. 2010.
2007, Mrs Megan Burnett
2008, Mrs Lesley Lewis

Matrons, Sisters and Nurses

The Choir School had their own Matron. See separate list.

1864–65, Miss Barbara Fleetwood, after 1865 title 'Matron' was given to the senior Sister.
1865–80, Sisters of St Margaret's, East Grinstead.
1871, Betty Searle, widow, nurse, aged 41.
   Sister Matilda, Sister of Charity, aged 36.
1880, Sisters of St Peter, Kilburn (Sisters of Mercy).
1881–91+, Mary G. Cotterill, (Nursing) Sister of Mercy, CSP.
   Frances Heason, Second Sister, aged 29.
1891, Catherine E. P. Labgett, Nursing Sister, aged 58.
   Maria Baldwyn, Nursing Sister, aged 54.
1897, Sisters of St Mary the Virgin, Wantage.
1901, Charlotte Andrews, Sister of Mercy, aged 54.
   Margaret N. Wilson, Sister of Mercy, aged 33.
1911, Frances Cecil Richardson, Sister in charge of the infirmary, aged 31.
   Agnes Emma Bown, Sister in charge of Beauchamp Almshouses, aged 60.
1922, Sister Minna.
1926, Sisters of the Epiphany at Truro.
1939, Miss Bockett.
1942–53, Mrs M. C. Young.
1953–55, Sister Mildred Tunbridge, died 1955.

1955–69, Sister Olive Edwards, left or died 1987.
1969–71, Sister Elsie Mary Collins.
1971–77, Sister Archibald.

Medical Officers
The post lapsed after the creation of the National Health Service.

1864, Dr Alexander Weir, snr.
1894, Dr Alexander Weir, jnr.
1910–32, Dr Stevens, emigrated to New Zealand.
1932–43, Dr Jamison previously partner to Dr Stevens.
1943–49, Dr G. Waugh Scott.

Porters

Year	Name	Died	Buried in Newland	Age
1864	William Moulden inadequate; became ordinary pensioner		29 Mar. 1881	81
1865	John White inadequate; became ordinary pensioner	1875		
1865–66	Robert Laurence inadequate; became ordinary pensioner		17 Mar. 1883	93
1867–82	Thomas P. Hurd retired, then ordinary pensioner		26 Nov. 1883	82
	Elizabeth Hurd, wife moved after his death to Malvern Link		12 Mar. 1907	84
1883–89	John Butler			
	wife			
1889	George Wheeler retired Jan 1899, then ordinary pensioner		27 Jan. 1900	45
	Sarah Wheeler, wife, 1901, servant to curate			
1899	Henry J. F. Magdalinsky, dismissed 1901			
	Florence Magdalinsky, wife			
1901	John Cooper		11 Apr. 1917	70
	Sarah Ann Cooper, wife		13 Sept. 1928	83
1911	Mr Tucker			

Year	Name	Died	Buried in Newland	Age
1916	Mr Reed			
	Emily Reed, wife	1917		36
1923–42	Herbert John Cooper		2 Sept. 1947	73
	Caroline Cooper, wife		28 May 1948	68
1943–58	William Daffin, moved away		15 Oct. 1975	82
	Ann Elizabeth Daffin, wife, moved away		27 May 1986	92
1958–64	Henry George Purser, moved away	1985		
	Kathleen Purser, wife	1984		
	Dorothy Mary, daughter			
	George Oved, son	2012		
1964–78	Albert Edwin Bullock moved to Choir School	2006		
	Doris Kathlene Bullock moved to Choir School	2007		
1978–80	John Beaumont			
	Mrs D. K. Beaumont, wife			
1980–82	Eric Oseman			
	Mary Oseman, wife, remained resident			
1982	John Sims, moved away			
	Mildred Sims, wife, moved away			
1992–97	James Parker, moved away			
	Margaret Parker, wife moved away	2010		
1997–2004	John Flint, remained resident			
	Johanna Flint, wife	2003		
2004	Roger Hodkinson	2012		65
	Jenny Hodkinson, wife, remained resident			
2013	John Tinnion			
	Angie Tinnion, wife			

Servants and Domestic Staff

Year	Name	Position	Age
1871	Jane Mackie	general servant at Clerk's house	19
1881	Mary Allisterer	general and domestic servant in Sister's house	15
	Ellen Henderson, widow	domestic servant at Warden's lodge	40
	Mildred Glover	domestic servant at Warden's lodge	21

Year	Name	Position	Age
	Harriet Haynes	domestic servant at Warden's lodge	72
1881	Joseph Caswell	domestic servant at Warden's lodge	14
1881	Mary Griffiths	domestic servant, cook, at Warden's lodge	36
	Elizabeth Griffiths	domestic servant, housemaid at Warden's lodge	22
1881	Rebecca Wade	servant in Sisters' house	
1881–91	Annie Young	domestic servant, parlour-maid later cook at Warden's lodge	28
1886	Ann Jones	servant in Infirmary	52
1891	Clara Bunn	housemaid at Warden's lodge	30
	Eliza Lovatt	general and domestic servant in Sisters' house	26
1901	Kate Merratt	general and domestic servant at Warden's lodge	33
	Edith Newnham	general and domestic servant in Sisters' house	22
	Sarah Wheeler, widow	general servant to Curate	46
1901–11	Mary Louise Webb	general and domestic servant later cook at Warden's lodge	28
	Alice Waters	general and domestic servant, later housemaid at Warden's lodge	25
	Eliza Gertrude Bachelor	general and domestic servant at St Barnabas	27
	Sarah Ann Price, widow	general and domestic servant at St Barnabas	47
	Alice King	general and domestic servant at St Barnabas	16
	Annie Vanstone	general and domestic servant at St Barnabas	28
1907	Harriet Stinton	widow of cathedral verger, Wardens lodge	93

Organists and Choirmasters (O&C)

1864, Charles Bolton Edgecumbe, O&C of Choir School
1866, Ethelbert West, O&C of Choir School.
1897–1908, Dr E. T. Cook O&C of Choir School, became Organist of Southwark Cathedral.
1908–11, T. F. Bye, ex-Choir School Chorister, O&C of Choir School, Teacher Malvern College and Uppingham.
1911–19, Claude Joseph Biggs O&C of Choir School, Professor, Recitalist and Teacher Radley College.
1920, Ronald Biggs, O&C of Choir School, Teacher Malvern College, then BBC.

1921–81, A. T. (Bertie) Shaw, O&C of Choir School to 1945, Teacher Worcester Grammar.
1981–84, Gordon Lansdown Barnes, Organist.
1984–1987, Miss Dorothy Pembrudge, Organist.
1987–1997, Mrs Mary Overton, Organist.
1997–2001, T. Alan Gilbert, Organist.
2001, Charles Allsopp, O&C and founder of Beauchamp Community Adult Church Choir.

Choir School Matrons

There is no record of a Choir Matron in the earliest days, but there must certainly have been one.

*c.*1879–97, Mrs Caroline Jenkins, 1891 census.
1898, Miss Helena Salter, 1901.
  Miss Mary Edith Ray, 1911.
1926–37, Mrs Sanders, moved to Bournemouth.
1939, Mr and Mrs Young, Choir School Master and Matron.
1943, Miss Tonks resigned in 1943.

Choristers of the Choir School

Choir School records are reasonable up to 1882; thereafter various sources have been used to make a complete record as possible. Many additions, corrections and new information to this list have been undertaken by Colin R. Brownlee, as part of his research in the Choir School.

Year	Name	Home	Age at Joining	Left	Information
1864	William New		12	Dec. 1867	
	Charles Hill		12	May 1866	
	John Howse		12	May 1866	
	Herbert Vaile	Overbury	11	Apr. 1865	
	William Arkell		11	Aug. 1868	
	John Barnes		10		
	Alfred Tansley		9		
	William Stuart		8		
1865	George Hancock		10	Oct. 68	
1866	Fred E. Clarke		10		died 8 Aug. 1873 aged 16.
	Robert James		9	1867	
	Charles A. Arkell		12		
1879	Samuel Caswall	Guarlford	8	1887	assisted porter of the Almshouses: 1889 moved to Sussex.
	Albert Harry Mantell	Cricklade	7		apprentice to House carpenter of Madresfield Court: 1887 apprentice carpenter Worcester.
	Walter Dobbs	Huntley	11		Hall boy at Madresfield Court: 1887 Sergeant in Cavalry.
	Thomas Baker	Malvern	12	1882	Second Footman at Madresfield Court.
	Edwin Bales	Tenbury	12	1883	Royal Ordnance office at Southampton.
	John Price	Chislehurst	11	1884	provided for by uncle in Cheltenham: picture framer maker in New York.
	Frank Bolton	Chislehurst	11	1887	
	Charles Marshall	Over Whitacre	10	1887	Warden's under-gardener: 1889 gardener to House of the Good Shepherd.

Year	Name	Home	Age at Joining	Left	Information
1882	Walter Mantell	Cricklade	12	1884	apprentice to House carpenter of Madresfield Court: 1887 apprenticed to baker in Malvern Link.
?	Thomas Hutchings				removed by mother to help her on small farm.
1884	Gerald Slater				
1884	Frederick Overbury				dismissed for dishonesty.
(1891)	Edwin Righley		14		age as shown on the 1891 census, exact date of joining unknown.
	Charles Collins		14		age as shown on the 1891 census, exact date of joining unknown.
	Percy Greenland		11		age as shown on the 1891 census, exact date of joining unknown.
	Ernest Freeland		9		age as shown on the 1891 census, exact date of joining unknown.
	Willie Stafford		9		age as shown on the 1891 census, exact date of joining unknown.
	Walter Kite		13		age as shown on the 1891 census, exact date of joining unknown.
1894	Albert J. F. Berry		8	1903	Second Lieutenant, killed in action at Flanders, 1917, 31 years old.
1895	Arthur Mason		8	1901	'Good situation at High Wycombe' (Warden's Report).
1895	Gilbert Slater		8		Lieutenant, killed in action at Fonquevillers, 1916, 29 years old.
1895	Ralph Parry		8	1903	accounts office of SPCK, Northumberland St., London.
1896	Dudley F. Cox		9		Sapper, killed in action at Somme, 1916, 29 years old.
	Charles H. Green		12	1903	apprenticeship at Surgical Instrument Makers in London.
	Fred Woolridge		11	1903	
	Arthur A. Hornby		11		
	Charles E. Williams		11		
	Kenneth P. Volckmann		10	1903	adopted Mr Parker, uncle and MP for Lough, placed Wesleyan Kent College.
	Alfred C. Beard		10		

Year	Name	Home	Age at Joining	Left	Information
1904	Thomas Frederick Bye		11	1911	organist whilst still at the Choir School, 1908–11.
	Reginald A. James		7		Private, killed in action at Somme, 1917, 20 years old.
	Albert Rea		8		Bombardier, killed in action at Flanders, 1917, 22 years old.
1905	William Russell		7		Private, killed in action at Flanders, 1917, 19 years old.
	Harry Courtenay Evans		9		Gunner, killed in action, 1916, 23 years old.
1906	Henry Stride		8		Private, killed in action at Flanders, 1917, 19 years old.
1908	Ernest Bird		8		Private, killed in action at Flanders, 1917, 17 years old.
1910	Edward Nudds				
1910	Edwin Finch				
1911	James Lindsay Hamilton		14		age at 1911 census. Date of joining not known. Studied Medicine at Cambridge.
	Alfred William Beale		13		age at 1911 census. Date of joining not known.
	Ronald Brown		13		age at 1911 census. Date of joining not known.
	Charles Kingsley Adams		11		age at 1911 census. Date of joining not known.
	Joseph Stride		11		age at 1911 census. Date of joining not known.
	Bernard Harry Kimberley		12		age at 1911 census. Date of joining not known.
	John Charles Tainton		10		age at 1911 census. Date of joining not known.
1911	Knowsley Wallis		9		
1912	Sydney Denyer		10		
1920	E. Clarabutt				sometime vicar of Lostwithiel
	James Arthur Croft		9		King's School Worcester; Priesthood at Kelham; Vicar of All Saints. Bromsgrove, retired on health grounds to become vicar of Alfrick and Lulsley. Died 1962.

Year	Name	Home	Age at Joining	Left	Information
1924	Cyril Penson	Penge		1929	ordained priest.
1923	Alan Partridge				twins.
1925	Ernest and Bernard Partridge				
1928	Leonard Hunt	Bucknall	11	1932	Royal Air Force.
1928	Peter Carpenter	London SW4	9	1931	
	Victor Nigel Caple	Wallington	10	1931	
	John Matthews	Fladbury	10	1934	
	Marmaduke Matthews	Fladbury	8	1934	
	Horace V. G. Edwards	Edgware	11	1930	
	George M. B. Piers	Abingdon	10	1933	
	Michael Watson	Reading	11	1931	
1930	William John Inman	Bristol	10	1931	
	Hubert Stead Salisbury	Elmley Castle	8	1935	Brother of Harold H.
	Robert C. MacWilliams	St Agnes	10	1931	
1931	Paul Lancelot Cooper	Hereford	8	1937	
1933	John Comper	Stockbridge	8		
	Peter Eric Roberts	Kenton	8	1935	
	Jeremy Henry Barkway	Camberley	9	1933	
1934	John Constantine	Kenton	11	1937	
	Alfred E. H. Sammons	Wembley	11	1936	
1935	Dennis A. J. Wren	Harrow	12	1938	
	Patrick C. Bagnall	Malvern Link	10	1935	
	Geof. Wm. Constantine	Kenton	8		

Year	Name	Home	Age at Joining	Left	Information
1935	Peter Neville Arnold	Kenton	11		
	Keith C. D. Watson	Kenton	10	1938	
1936	Peter R. Johnson	York	10	1938	
	Michael B. V. Jones	Harrow	8	1937	
1937	Ivor Maxwell Perren	London EC1	11		
1938	Peter Wm. Janes	Coventry	9		

Sometime between 1938 and the closure in 1945, these boys were at the Choir School.

Raymond, Frank and Leslie (Buddy) Hutchinson.
William (Billy) Parish, adopted by a naval officer in Plymouth.
Dennis Bratchford.
Jimmy Smith.
George Day.
Alfred Youdell.

Pensioners and General Residents

A largely, though not wholly, complete register was kept from the foundation until *c.*1900, and this has been supplemented by censuses and by funeral and burial books. The register was discontinued *c.*1900 until a new register was created for 1928–80. Other sources, primarily again censuses, funeral and burial books have been used for 1900–27, but there are inevitably many gaps. From 1981 onwards there are electricity payments, TV records and a variety of other sources including oral tradition, though there are still some gaps. Records of Lygon Lodge residents, who initially were recipients of a separate charity, are particularly scant. Information on the previous place of residence ceases about 1910.

Abbreviations used in this section:
Q   Quadrangle Flat
CSH   Choir School House
WLA   Warden's Lodge Flat A
WLB   Warden's Lodge Flat B
WL1   Warden's Lodge Flat 1
WL2   Warden's Lodge Flat 2
CSF   Choir School Flat

Year	Name	Residence	Election age	Year of death	Age died	Date of burial in Newland Churchyard	Length of stay in years
1864	Thomas Barker	St John's	?	1864	died before arrival		
	Jane Barker	St John's	78	1867	81	31 Aug. 1867	3
	Francis Barnes	Madresfield	75	1877	88	10 Oct. 1877	13
	Mary Barnes	Madresfield	76	1875	81	18 Feb. 1875	11
	John Batchelor	Newland	74	1865	75	13 Feb. 1865	1
	Sarah Batchelor	Newland	74	1865	75	13 Feb. 1865	1
	James Biscoe	Eldersfield	72	1875	86	31 Mar. 1875	11
	Sarah Biscoe	Eldersfield	81	1866	82	20 Nov. 1866	2
	Anne Boulton	Forthampton	79	1865	79	buried at Forthampton	1
	Elizabeth Bruton	Madresfield	75	1865	76	3 Apr. 1865	1
	William Cooper	Crowle	74	1868	78	23 Jan. 1868	4
	Sarah Cooper	Crowle	59	1875	70	25 Mar. 1875	11
	James Drinkwater	Newland	78	1869	82	25 Feb. 1869	5
	Maria Drinkwater	Newland	68	1878	84	23 Dec. 1878	14
	Thomas Fowler	Powick	80	1868	86	26 Feb. 1888	4
	William Griffiths	Claines	69	1864	69	22 Sept. 1864	0
	Dorothy Griffiths	Claines	72	1868	79	2 Nov. 1868	4
	William Heaven	Bromsberrow	72	1872	80	5 July 1872	8
	Jane Heaven	Bromsberrow	71	1868	76	13 Nov. 1868	4
	Margaret Howells	Leigh	86	1865	87	11 June 1865	1
	Sarah Jones	Claines	63	1890	88	16 Aug. 1890	26
	Samuel King	Powick	58	1867	60	1 Feb. 1867	3

Year	Name	Residence	Election age	Year of death	Age died	Date of burial in Newland Churchyard	Length of stay in years
1864	Elizabeth King	Powick (left for Powick)	57	(1880, Powick)	72	20 Aug. 1880	11
	Michael Stallard	Powick	77	1867	80	20 May 1867	3
	Mary Stallard	Powick	75	1866	76	27 Oct. 1866	2
	James Stokes	Gt. Malvern	79	1865	80	22 June 1865	1
	Catherine Stokes	Gt. Malvern	79	1867	80	7 Dec. 1867	3
	Isabella M. Walker	Cheltenham	78	1865	76	30 June 1865	1
	John Williams (married Sept. 1866 Anne 1870)	Newland	75	1870	81	1 Feb. 1870	6
	William Moulden (married Jan. 1871 Mary Ann Turner)	Hanley Castle	64	1881	81	29 Mar. 1881	17
	Sarah Moulden	Hanley Castle	80	1870	86	5 May 1870	6
	Anne Bowcott	Madresfield	62	1885	81	6 Jan. 1885	21
	James Charles	Leigh	65	1882	82	14 Nov. 1882	18
	Anne Charles	Leigh	60	1894	89	5 Mar. 1894	30
	Sarah Cooper	Jersey	62	1875	70	25 Mar. 1875	11
	William Shailes	Powick	75	1872	83	2 Mar. 1872	8
	John Tudge	Leigh	88	1865	89	17 Sept. 1865	1
	Elizabeth Tudge	Leigh	78	1874	88	13 Jan. 1874	10
	Robert Lawrence	Gt. Malvern	75	1883	93	17 Mar. 1883	18
	Sarah Lawrence	Gt. Malvern	75	1876	86	19 Apr. 1876	11
	Ruth Cook, daughter, laundress, aged 49 in 1871						
1865	Richard Pritchard	Clevelode	74	1877	84	20 June 1877	12

Year	Name	Residence	Election age	Year of death	Age died	Date of burial in Newland Churchyard	Length of stay in years
1865	Eleanor Pritchard	Clevelode	67	1872	73	5 July 1872	7
	Hannah Mervis, grand-daughter, aged 11 in 1871						
	Mary Wigley	Redmarley	67	1878	82	23 July 1878	13
	John (or James) Body	Powick	81	1877	94	5 May 1877	12
	Louise Walker	Cheltenham	77	1875	83	4 Dec. 1875	10
	John White, porter	Shelsey Beauchamp		1875			10
1866	Anne Williams	Claines	53	1906	90	5 Dec. 1906	40
1867	Nancy Bayliss	Staunton	74	1882	82	8 June 1882	15
	James Mason	Spetchley	83	1873	84	16 Jan. 1873	6
	Mary Mason	Spetchley	74	1876	83	1 July 1876	9
1868	Elizabeth Caswall	Newland	74	1887	91	23 Jan. 1887	20
	Frank Caswall, grandson, aged 7 in 1881						
	John Holt	Gt. Malvern	79	1874	87	10 Aug. 1874	6
1869	Elizabeth Adams	Speenhamland	63	1886	81	14 Dec. 1886	18
1871	Mary Ann Moulden	Powick		1892	82	22 Oct. 1892	21
1872	William Jones	Gt. Malvern	76	1876	81	22 June 1876	4
	Hannah Jones	Gt. Malvern	65	1881	78	22 Oct 1881	9
1873	Charles Bennett	Powick	71	1876	75	4 Mar. 1876	3
	Sarah Bennett	Powick	69	1883	81	23 Apr. 1883	10
1874	John Kings	Madresfield	75	1885	86	14 Nov. 1986	12
	Anne Kings	Madresfield	73	1892	90	5 Jan. 1892	18
	Sarah Kings, daughter, laundry maid, aged 48 in 1881				54	Aug. 1889	

Year	Name	Residence	Election age	Year of death	Age died	Date of burial in Newland Churchyard	Length of stay in years
1874	William Rogers	Tibberton	73	1875	73	25 Mar. 1875	1
	Hannah Rogers	Tibberton	68	1880	74	8 Apr. 1880	6
1875	William Yeomans	Guarlford	77	1891	93	9 July 1891	16
	Elizabeth Yeomans	Guarlford (left for Powick)	79	(1884, Powick)	89	17 May 1884	9
	Edward Phillips	Ombersley	73	1878	76	21 Feb. 1878	3
	Sarah Phillips	Ombersley	71	1883	78	11 Apr. 1883	8
	Joseph Trapp	Madresfield (married May 1876 Drusilla Cole)	74	1889	88	2 Nov. 1889	14
1876	Drusilla Trapp	Tibburton	70	1903	97	27 Apr. 1903	27
	Samuel Horniblow	Whittington	79	1878	82	20 Aug. 1878	2
	John Corbett	Ombersley	69	1881	73	5 Nov. 1881	5
	Mary Corbett	Ombersley	73	1879	76	4 Dec. 1879	3
1877	Elizabeth Drinkwater	Madresfield		(died 1877 before arrival)			
	Samuel Willis	Warndon	69	1878	70	20 Nov. 1878	1
	Hannah Willis	Warndon	69	1889	81	2 Feb 1889	12
	James Jones	Welland	71	1884	74	19 Apr 1884	7
	Elizabeth Jones	Welland	71	1883	70	21 July 1883	6
1879	William Philpott	Powick	81	1881	82	7 Feb. 1881	2
	Charlotte Philpott	Powick	71	1885	77	28 Apr. 1885	6
	Thomas Raine	Leigh	74	1882	79	11 May 1882	3
	Mary Raine	Leigh	66	1894	84	8 Mar 1894	15

Year	Name	Residence	Election age	Year of death	Age died	Date of burial in Newland Churchyard	Length of stay in years
1879	Jane Foxhall	Newland	79	1885	85	2 May 1885	6
	Thomas Gittins	Powick	88	1884	94	31 Dec. 1884	5
	Anne or Ellen Gittins	Powick	80	1883	86	16 June 1883	4
1881	Louisa Perrins	Hanley Castle (left for Powick)					
	James Stallard	Powick	72	1883	72	22 Feb. 1883	2
	Harriet Stallard	Powick	72	1895	77	25 May 1895	14
	Richard Barber	Gt. Malvern	77	1883	80	20 Nov. 1883	2
	Lucy Barber	Gt. Malvern	79	1882	79	19 June 1882	1
	Miles T. Chandler	Malvern Link	71	1881	72	17 Dec 1881	0
	Eliza Chandler	Malvern Link	63	1896	81	23 Oct. 1896	15
1882	Thomas Hurd (late porter)	(left after 1883 for Malvern Link)		1883	82	26 Nov. 1883	15
	Elizabeth Hurd			1907	84	12 Mar. 1907	15
1883	Samuel Bridges	Malvern Link	69	1888	74	25 Jan. 1888	5
	Anna Bridges	Malvern Link	61	1886	63	7 July 1886	3
	Joshua Drew	Dymock	70	1883	71	15 Dec 1883	0
	Hannah Drew	Dymock	79	1886	85	8 June 1896	3
	John Maskell	Pyecombe, Surrey	73	1903	92	27 Jan. 1903	20
	Mary Maskell	Pyecombe, Surrey	64	alive 1901			
	William and Edith Lucas, grandchildren, aged 9 and 6 in 1891						
1884	Sarah Procter	Inkberrow	72	(no further information)			
	William Hyde	Powick	67	1885	76	25 Aug. 1885	1
	Harriet Hyde	Powick	70	1904	96	1 Feb. 1904	20

Year	Name	Residence	Election age	Year of death	Age died	Date of burial in Newland Churchyard	Length of stay in years
1884	Miles Morris (married Oct. 1891 Mary Ann Grundy)	Hanley Castle	69	1897	84	9 June 1887	13
	Hannah Morris	Hanley Castle	68	1891	78	24 Jan. 1891	7
	John Groves	Claines	77	1886	78	18 Aug. 1886	2
	Mary Groves	Claines	76	1888	80	24 Nov. 1888	4
1885	Edwin Smith	Ledbury	70	1888	74	17 Aug. 1888	3
	John Holtam	Claines	70	1899	85	29 Apr. 1899	14
	Elizabeth Holtam	Claines	70	1891	78	8 June 1891	6
	Thomas Farrant	Madresfield	74	1898	86	27 Oct. 1898	13
	Ann Farrant	Madresfield	75	1888	75	22 Feb. 1888	3
	Thomas Harsnell	Newland	76	1889	80	9 Apr. 1889	4
1887	Joseph Matthews	Newland	75	1891	76	24 Jan. 1891	4
	Susannah Matthews	Newland	66	1891	69	12 Dec. 1891	4
	Charles Drew	Upton-upon-Severn	72	1893	80	28 Dec 1893	6
	Elizabeth Drew (married 27 Mar. 1897 Thomas Greenhill)	Upton-upon-Severn	65	1906	84	9 Nov 1906	19
1888	Thomas Winwood	Hartlebury	69	1889	73	25 May 1889	1
	Elizabeth Winwood (resigned 25 Mar. 1890)	Hartlebury	60				2
	William Farnham	Hallow	70	1896	80	6 Jan. 1896	7
	Henry Stokes	Winchcombe	80	1892	86	23 Jan. 1892	4
1889	Thomas Moore	Ripple	79	1892	86	18 June 1892	3
	Mary Ann Moore	Ripple	72	1896	82	5 May 1896	7

Year	Name	Residence	Election age	Year of death	Age died	Date of burial in Newland Churchyard	Length of stay in years
1889	John Barratt	Lathbury	65	1915	89	23 Nov. 1915	26
	Matilda Barratt	Lathbury	63	1904	77	21 May 1904	15
	Matthew and Jane Barratt, children, aged 35 and 40, porter and porteress at Thornbury Union, in 1891						
	John Haytor, grandson, aged 20, footman at Madresfield, in 1901						
	Samuel Hewer	Wanborough	64	1902	76	27 Mar. 1902	13
	Elizabeth Hewer	Wanborough	60	1910	80	13 Apr. 1910	21
	Sarah E. Hewer, daughter, aged 36, church embroidress, in 1901; still resident in 1911						
1890	Charles Best	Longdon	85	1898	93	9 July 1898	8
	Benjamin Brown	Salwarpe	76	1896	83	26 Sept. 1896	6
	Elizabeth Brown	Salwarpe	69	1905	85	25 Feb. 1905	15
1891	Mary Ann Morris	Newland	61	(no further information)			
	Eliza Wasgeant	Lygon		1904	85	28 May 1904	13
1892	William Roberts	Leigh		1896	80	2 Nov. 1896	4
	Mary Roberts	Leigh		1909	91	17 Mar. 1909	17
	George Randle	Malvern		1894	76	2 May 1894	2
	Elizabeth Randle	Malvern		1902	85	17 Feb. 1902	10
1893	Joseph Protheroe	Dymock	69	1907	82	11 Nov. 1907	14
	Hannah Protheroe	Dymock	59	1910	78	9 Apr. 1910	1
	William White	Severn Stoke	68	1895	70	1 June 1895	2
	Harriet White	Severn Stoke	68	1912	87	18 Jan. 1912	19
1895	William Hughes	Worcester	74	1901	81	9 Feb. 1901	6
	William Jones	Hanley Castle	68	1899	79	26 July 1899	4

Year	Name	Residence	Election age	Year of death	Age died	Date of burial in Newland Churchyard	Length of stay in years
1895	John Peart	Kemerton	72	died 1895 before arrival			
1897	James Evans	Severn Stoke	71	1899	74	30 Mar. 1999	2
	Thomas Greenhill	Oddingley	73	1906	83	29 May 1906	9
	Richard Pember	Ashperton	74	1898	76	27 Apr. 1898	1
	William Preece	Leigh	77	alive 1901			
	Mary Preece	Leigh	72	1901	78	2 May 1901	4
1899	Thomas Brookes	Oddingley	84	1900	86	30 Apr. 1900	1
	Mary Brooks	Oddingley	80	1912	94	5 Mar. 1912	13
	Charles Hinds	St Johns	71	1912	85	30 Sept. 1912	13
	Adelaide Hinds	St Johns	74	1912	81	27 Feb. 1912	13
	Joseph Mitchell	Leigh	70	1919	91	20 Feb. 1919	20
	Elizabeth Mitchell	Leigh	71	1918	90	4 Jan. 1918	19
	George Wheeler (late porter)			1900	45	27 Jan. 1900	11
	Sarah Wheeler (1901 servant to curate)						
	Martha Chamberlain	Lygon		1900	53	16 Aug. 1900	1+
1900	William Jones	Leigh	66	1911	77	2 Dec. 1911	11
	Eliza Jones	Leigh	63	1921	80	23 May 1921	21
	Charles Neal	Upton-upon-Severn	66	1919	85	17 Apr. 1919	19
	Caroline Neal	Upton-upon-Severn	67	1919	87	19 Apr. 1919	19
	Arthur Kemp	Iardebigge	72	1910	79	17 Nov. 1910	10

THE BEAUCHAMP ALMSHOUSES AND ST LEONARD'S CHURCH, NEWLAND 1864–2014

Year	Name	Residence	Election age	Year of death	Age died	Date of burial in Newland Churchyard	Length of stay in years
1900	Ellen Maria Kemp	Iardebigge	67	1901	68	5 Oct. 1901	1
	William Taylor	Severn Stoke	76	1911	87	2 May 1911	11
	Sarah Taylor	Severn Stoke	73	1908	79	24 Nov. 1908	8
1901	Jane Chamberlain	Lygon	60	1906	71	15 Sept. 1906	5+
	George Summers	Lygon	73	1906	78	5 June 1906	5+
	Emma Symes	Lygon	62	1935	98	13 Dec. 1935	34+
	Mary Turner	Lygon	75	1905	80	16 Aug. 1905	4+
1902	George Mitchell	Leigh		1908	85	25 Aug. 1908	6
	Emma Mitchell	Leigh		1908	82	2 May 1908	6
	Joseph Sadler	Dymock		1902	62	11 Dec. 1902	0
	Maria Sadler	Dymock		1913	72	29 Jan. 1913	11
1906	Miss Sarah Sutton	Lygon		1907	56	8 July 1907	1
1907	William Crump	Newland		1908	79	26 Aug. 1908	1
	Mary Crump	Newland		1915	85	1 Jan. 1916	9
	Edward Grubb	Leigh		1908	75	23 May 1908	1
	Mary Elizabeth Grubb	Leigh		1935	92	10 June 1935	28
	John Edwards	Powick	70	1915	79	20 Dec. 1915	8
1909	William Savory		67	1910	70	28 Dec. 1910	1
	Jane Savory		64	1912	69	20 Nov 1912	3
	William Reynolds		81	1915	88	22 Sept. 1915	6
	Anne Reynolds		77	1919	85	4 Nov. 1919	10
	Thomas Gilson		66	1915	75	12 Feb. 1915	6

Year	Name	Residence	Election age	Year of death	Age died	Date of burial in Newland Churchyard	Length of stay in years
1909	Mary Gilson		66	1912	75	31 Aug. 1912	3
	Elizabeth Phillips		78	1912	85	15 Feb. 1912	3
1911	John Cooper (late porter)			1917	70	11 Apr. 1917	16
	Sarah Ann Cooper			1928	83	13 Sept. 1928	27
	Frances Batchelor	Lygon	82	1915	86	13 Mar. 1915	4+
	Mary Ann E. Wisdom	Lygon	66	1914	69	2 Feb. 1914	3+
		(left for Laburnum House, Upton)					
1912	James Gunter			1922	86	14 Nov. 1932	20
	Mary Gunter			1922	75	9 May 1922	10
	Joseph Bridges			1912	72	26 June 1912	0
	Hannah Goode			1917	75	12 Nov. 1917	5
	George Crump			1936	80	4 Mar. 1936	24
	Susan Crump			1924	88	17 Dec. 1924	12
	Henry Burston			1926	84	25 June 1926	14
	Ann Burston	(left for Upton)		1941	97	17 May 1941	28
	William Jones			left or died Apr. 1928			
	Harriett Jones			alive at 87 in 1923			
	John Harben			1921	85	8 June 1921	9
	Esther Harben			1916	80	21 Sept. 1916	4
	Joseph Robinson	(left for Powick)		1915	77	20 Oct. 1915	3
	Ellen Robinson			1929	87	16 Mar. 1929	17
	Ellen Mary King			1934	89	10 Mar. 1934	22

Year	Name	Residence	Election age	Year of death	Age died	Date of burial in Newland Churchyard	Length of stay in years
1913	William Church			1929	76	22 Nov. 1929	16
	Alice Church	(no further information)					
	Miss Marianne Freeman			1943	94	20 Mar. 1943	30
	Jane Rowberry			1923	80	17 Oct. 1923	10
1917	Joseph Green			1923	79	12 Nov. 1923	6
	Anne Green			1925	80	21 Oct. 1925	8
	Thomas Nicholls	(asked to leave same year)					0
	Mrs Nicholls	(asked to leave same year)					0
	Emma Davis	alive at 76 in 1923					
	Thomas Reed			1924	80	3 Apr. 1924	7
	Caroline Reed			1923	67	5 Jun. 1923	6
1919	Benjamin Waters			1922	76	9 Feb. 1922	3
	Annie Waters			1925	68	2 Dec. 1925	6
	George Scrivens			1931	84	9 Sept. 1931	12
	Elizabeth Scrivens			1928	72	13 Apr. 1928	9
	Fanny Durrant			1921	73	11 Jan. 1921	2
1920	John Jarman Barnes			1938	85	13 July 1938	18
	(one of the first choristers who joined in 1864, then became assistant to the porter)						
	Alice Barnes			1926	77	21 Oct. 1926	6
1923	Elizabeth Payne			1926	79	25 May 1926	3+
1923	Anne Watson	(alive aged 65 in 1923)					
1925	George Hodgetts			1925	68	14 Mar. 1925	0

Year	Name	Residence	Election age	Year of death	Age died	Date of burial in Newland Churchyard	Length of stay in years
1925	Mrs Hodgetts	(no further information)					
	Theresa Tombs			1927	71		2
1926	Daniel Bartlett Hunt			1935	81	1 Nov. 1935	9
	Mrs Hunt			1935			9
	William Edwin Tustin	25Q		1947	82	31 July 1947	21
	Eliza Tustin			1940	72	7 Dec. 1940	14
	James Senter			1932	77	2 Apr. 1932	6
	Emily Senter	7Q		1955	89	19 Jan. 1955	29
	Thomas Newbury			1941	81	16 May 1941	15
	Mary Jane Newbury			1943	80	21 June 1943	17
1928	George Lock			1934	76	31 July 1934	6+
1928	Annie Elizabeth Lock			1928	72	8 Nov. 1928	0+
1928	Thomas James Corbett			1943	86	6 Feb. 1943	15+
1928	Ann Margaret Corbett			1929	75	12 Aug. 1929	1+
1928	Jane Devereux			1928	84	2 Aug. 1928	
1928	Emma Vaughan			1930	69	19 Aug. 1930	2+
1929	Matthew Hinton			1935	85	26 Feb. 1935	6
	Eliza Hinton			1939	86	25 Mar. 1939	10
1929	George Phillips	(1933 moved away)		(1937, Martley)	79	23 Feb. 1937	4
1929	Fanny Devereux	11Q		1949	77	24 Oct. 1949	20
	Helen Weeks	Lygon		1930	92	20 June 1930	

Year	Name	Residence	Election age	Year of death	Age died	Date of burial in Newland Churchyard	Length of stay in years
1929	Lucy Jane Turbott	Lygon		1938	76	27 Dec. 1938	
1930	Samuel Weaver			1933	71	3 Jan. 1934	4
	Clara Ellen Weaver	22Q (1952 left for Droitwich)		1955	90	22 Jan. 1955	22
	Joseph Cooper	(no further information)					
	Mrs Cooper	(no further information)					
1932	James Lane			(left or died Dec. 1933)			
	Charles Griffiths			1941	84	17 Nov. 1941	9
	Annie Griffiths			1943	83	22 May 1943	11
1934	Charles Denny Hughes	21Q		1947	74	21 Oct. 1947	15
	Mrs K. Hughes	21Q		(left or died Aug. 1961)			
	Mrs Ellen Maria Preston	19Q		1951	86	31 Jan. 1951	1
	Isaac Joseph Keyte			1939	79	28 Jan. 1939	5
	Elizabeth Keyte	6Q (1950 moved away)		1952	88	14 Feb. 1952	16
	Mrs Mary Ellen Stone	15Q (1952 moved away)					18
1935	John Herman			1940	79	31 Jan 1940	6
	Mrs Herman			left or died Jan. 1943			8
	Charles William Oliver	20Q (left 9 Jan. 1950)					15
	Frederick J. Wells	(left 1937)					1
1936	Mary Ann Chance	(1939 left for Upton)		1940	92	19 Oct. 1940	3
	Charles Fisher	(left Oct. 1937 1937)					1
	William Davenport			1937	65	Dec. 1937	0
	Mary Davenport	(left July 1938)					1

Year	Name	Residence	Election age	Year of death	Age died	Date of burial in Newland Churchyard	Length of stay in years
1936	Edwin Saxon	(no further information)					
	William Simmons	(no further information)					
1938	Beatrice Mary Poore			1938	72	14 May 1938	
1939	Mr Bridges	(left Mar. 1943)					4
	Harriet Bridges			1943	74		4
	Miss Anne Maria Brooke	18Q (1954 left for Droitwich)					15
1940	Miss Elizabeth Mary Evans	13Q (1960 left for Evesham)	68	1961	89	30 Jan. 1961	20
	Laura Elsie Brown	(if admitted, left after a week)	62				
	Miss Alice Dodd		55?	(no further information)			
1941	Mrs Gertrude Eaton	8Q (left for Avonside)	62	1962	83	2 Dec. 1962	22
	Mr Cockin	(left 13 July 1942)	74				1
	Mrs Cockin	(left 13 July 1942)	74				1
	Walter William Stephens	14Q	68	1947	74	20 June 1947	4
	Mrs Mary Stephens	14Q (left 21 Jun 1948; to Birmingham)	60	1975	94	11 Mar. 1975 (ashes)	7
	Herbert John Cooper (late porter)	4Q		1947	73	2 Sept. 1947	24
	Caroline Cooper	2Q		1948	68	28 May 1948	25
	Mary Griffin	Lygon		1941	68	4 Dec. 1941	
1943	Frank Troughton	16Q	78	1950	78		7

Year	Name	Residence	Election age	Year of death	Age died	Date of burial in Newland Churchyard	Length of stay in years
1943	Mrs Susan E. Troughton	14Q (1959 left for Evesham)		1959	90	18 July 1959	16
	Miss Emma Jane Hardy	(1947 left for Upton)	80	1949	87	June 1949	4
	William Hughes	5Q	67	1955	79	Aug. 1955	1
c. 1946	Miss Harriett May Shepherd	CS		1978	92	31 Oct. 1978	32
1947	Charles Henry Douglas	21Q		1947	74	21 Oct. 1947	
1948	Rachel Lillin Harvey	Lygon		1948	89	29 Mar. 1948	
	Miss Alice Maud Jackson	15Q (1970 left for Avonside)		1975	96		22
	Mrs Esther Frances Hooper	2Q		1956	84	1 Oct. 1956	8
	Mrs Alice Bowen (daughter of former porter Mr Cooper)	3Q		1973	95	4 Apr. 1973	25
	Mrs Smith (daughter of former porter Mr Cooper)			1968			20
	Miss Emma M. Caroline Hill	2Q (1957 left for Pershore Hospital)					9
	Mr W. A. Baker	9Q (left 4 Sept. 1948)					0
	Miss Dorothy Pembridge	9Q/2 Woodlands (left 1965–1994; 2001 moved away)		2004	89	6 Jan. 2005 (ashes)	24
	Mr C. E. Crump	10Q (left Sept. 1949)					1
	Alfred Edward Tillam	12Q		1965	70	12 Nov. 1965	17
	Esther Elizabeth Tillam	12Q (left for Ronkswood)		1971	81	4 June 1971	23
	Miss Annie Griffin	17Q (1978 left for Shrub Hill)		1980	93		30
	J. Neale	24Q (left Dec 1948)					0

Year	Name	Residence	Election age	Year of death	Age died	Date of burial in Newland Churchyard	Length of stay in years
1949	Mrs Grocock	10Q (left or died 1951)					2
	Mrs Ethel Tucker (daughter of former porter Mr Cooper)	19Q		1978	93	26 Aug. 1978	29
	Miss Amy K. Bullock, MBE	4 Lygon		1986 (obituary in Grapevine Jan. 198)	97	25 Nov. 1986	37
	Mrs Lottie Mary Churchfield	24Q		1958	73	15 July 1958	9
	Miss Wicketts	(no further information)					
	Harry Percy Pembridge (clerk)	1 Lygon		1960	80	13 Dec. 1960	11
	Katherine Ellen Pembridge	1 Lygon		1955	72	28 Aug. 1955	6
1950	Miss Alice Mary Hillier	20Q		1953	70	15 Aug. 1953	3
	Miss Martha W. Thomas	6Q		1963	78	28 Dec. 1963	13
1951	Mrs Mary Elizabeth Ibbotson	16Q		1953	83	2 July 1953	2
	Miss Ibbotson	16Q (admitted to vacant flat)					
1952	Mrs Hodges	10Q (left 1952)					
	B. J. Mantle	11Q (left or died 1954)					
	Archibald Cockerill	10Q		1960	71		8
	Mrs L. A. Cockerill	10Q (left or died June 1980)					
1953	Miss Annie Taylor	15Q		1961	71	6 Jan. 1961	8
	Miss Louisa Turner	16Q (left 1961)		1962	82		8
	Sidney Morse	22Q		1956	82		3
	Ethel Alice Morse	22Q		1970	87	(buried Colwall)	17
1954	J. Meredith (assistant porter; left 7 Nov. 195)	20Q					2

THE BEAUCHAMP ALMSHOUSES AND ST LEONARD'S CHURCH, NEWLAND 1864–2014

Year	Name	Residence	Election age	Year of death	Age died	Date of burial in Newland Churchyard	Length of stay in years
1954	Miss Ida Lilian Kay	11Q		1959	78	11 Apr. 1959 (ashes)	5
	Charles Boyt	18Q		1963	90	9 Jan. 1963	9
	Edith Ellen Boyt	18Q		1962	85	14 June 1962	8
1955	Mrs Louisa Morley	7Q (left 21 Aug. 1964)					9
1956	Mrs M. C. Phillips	5Q (left 1956)					0
	Harry F. J. Green	20Q (left 1957)					1
	Mrs Green	5Q (left 1957)					1
1957	Miss Elizabeth E. Kemp	4Q		1961	61		4
	Norah Lyons	Choir School		1957	79	15 June 1957	
1958	Mrs Ethel Mary Franklin	5Q		1967 (killed in road accident)	86	6 Dec. 1967	9
	Miss F. M. Diaper	24Q		(left or died 1960)			2
1959	Miss Catherine Hackett	20Q (1972 left for Avonside)		1975	82	7 Feb. 1975	13
	Miss Ethel Shepherd	11Q (1979 moved away)		1979	88	1 Nov. 1979	20
1960	Charles James Bryan	8Q (moved to 3 Council Houses)		1963 (Powick)	72	24 Dec. 1963	3
	Mrs Rose Lilian Bryan	8Q (left May 1969)		1977 (died Howsells)	89	14 Feb. 1977	9
Pre-60	Arthur H. B. Anson	CSH		1979	83	5 Apr. 1979	19+
	Mrs Josephine Anson	CSH (1990 moved away)		1992	83	14 Feb. 1992 (ashes)	30+
1961	Arthur Francis Nelson	2Q		1969	77	15 Aug. 1969	8
Pre-63	Mrs Mary Grizzell	WLB (left 1978)					15+
	Elizabeth Bough	1L		1964	81		

267

Year	Name	Residence	Election age	Year of death	Age died	Date of burial in Newland Churchyard	Length of stay in years
1964	Mrs Hephzibah Fletcher	4Q (1975 left to live with daughter)		1976	86		11
	Miss Margaret Alice Lowndes (missionary in Zanzibar)	6Q (left July 1969)		1973	83		5
	Mrs Evelyn Powell	13Q		1965 (buried Hatherley)	69		1
	Miss D. Nora Hatherley	14Q (1966 left for Oxford)					2
	Miss Alice Maud Viggers	16Q		1972	72	16 Aug. 1972	8
	Miss Winifred Barron Anslow	18Q		1978	88		13
	Miss Enid Jane Robertson	21Q (1966 left for Bristol)		1972	82		2
	Mrs Margaret Grace Smith	23Q		1968	86	23 Dec. 1968	4
	Mrs Alice Wilson	24Q (1969 left for Isabel Harrison Gardens)					5
1965	Deaconess D. G. Burlingham	11Q		1986	87		22
	Miss Rosa Benson	7Q		1974	73		9
	Miss Hilda Watson	9Q		1979	80	23 May 1979	14
	Mrs Alice Maud Nottingham	13Q		1976	78	21 June 1976	11
1966	Miss Mary Grace Corbett	12Q		1966 (died hospital)	73	28 Dec. 1966 (ashes)	0
	George Mason	21Q (1972 left for Ronkswood)		1973	74		6
	Sidney George Bradford	3 Lygon		1969	92		3

THE BEAUCHAMP ALMSHOUSES AND ST LEONARD'S CHURCH, NEWLAND 1864–2014

Year	Name	Residence	Election age	Year of death	Age died	Date of burial in Newland Churchyard	Length of stay in years
1966	Mrs Louisa Frances	12Q (1970 left for home)		1970	92	(buried Madresfield)	4
1967	Miss Annetta W. Andrews	14Q (1976 left for Avoncroft)		1975	74		3
	Miss Elsie M. A. Partington	5Q		1977	87	14 June 1977	9
	Mrs Ann M. Jackson	23Q (1978 left for Avonside)		1977	85		10
1969	Miss Cicely Taplin Crawford	(left Sept. 1971)		1981	61		9
	Sister Elsie Mary Collins	WLB(1969 left for Birmingham)					0
	Mrs F. Smith	24Q (1974 left for Solihull)					5
	Miss Mercia D. Cluley	6Q (1970 left to live with daughter)					1
	Victor Alfred Merrell	6Q (moved 1970)					1
	Mrs Agnes Merrell	2Q (left or died 1987)			32		
	Sister Olive Edwards	St Christopher's		1974	66	1 Nov. 1974	5
	Miss Florence Emma Ibbotson	8Q (left or died 1990)					21
	Mrs May Elizabeth Griffiths	3 Lygon		1973	78		3
1970	Mrs Lucy Little	7Q		1977	84		7
	Mrs Sarah Jane Bick	15Q		1976	90	16 Aug. 1976	6
	Mrs Susannah B. Edwards	21Q (1975 left to live with friends)			81	Feb. 1980	5
	Miss Nella Amy Barnard	20Q					13
1972	Thomas Laver (UMCA missionary; left or died 1985)	16Q (left or died 1985)					13
	Mrs Rosemary G. Purry (USPG office worker)	2 Lygon		1977	81		5
	David Owen						

269

Year	Name	Residence	Election age	Year of death	Age died	Date of burial in Newland Churchyard	Length of stay in years
1972	Mrs Cissie Gertrude Owen	2 Lygon		1988	85		12
1973	Mrs Annie May Bailes	3 Lygon		1973	74		0
	Mrs Annie Brown	3Q (left 1982)					9
	Miss Agnes Evetts	3Q (left for council flat 1978)					5
1974	Miss Mary Emeline Warren	2Q (left for Perrins 1993)		1996	82	31 May 1996 (ashes)	19
	Miss E. H. Nesta Bough	4 Lygon		2003	89	31 May 2006 (ashes)	29
1975	Miss Alice F. Bendall	4Q		1987	67		12
	Miss Georgiana Meyrick-Jones	15Q (left 1991)		1998 (Worcs.)	72		16
	Mrs Alice B. Wood	21Q		1990 (there in 1989)			15
	Mrs Elizabeth Blades	15Q		1980	72		5
	Miss Ada Smith	18Q		1980	68	6 Aug. 1980 (ashes)	5
	Mr Jack Bennett	7 St Barnabas (1979 left for Worcester)					4
	Mrs Edna Bennett	7 St Barnabas (1979 left for Worcester)					4
1976	Miss Nellie Louisa Lloyd	13Q		1986	78	3 Dec. 1986	10
1977	Miss Grace Jackson	5Q		(alive in 1982)			
	Mrs Helen Mary Bell	7Q		1982	75	4 Dec. 1982	5
	Harold Cook	14Q (left Mar. 1978)					1
1978	Mrs Ethel Smith	6Q (moved to Woodlands)		1987		21 Apr. 1987	
	Mrs Emma Victoria Hoult	WL1		1987	86		9

Year	Name	Residence	Election age	Year of death	Age died	Date of burial in Newland Churchyard	Length of stay in years
1978	Miss Kathleen I. Haines	WLB		(alive 1982)			
1979	Albert Edwin Bullock	CSF ground floor		2006	91		42
	Mrs Doris Kathlene Bullock	CSF ground floor		2007	89		43
	Mrs Lilian Isabel Drinkwater	17Q (left 1997)		1998 (Evesham)	90		18
	Mrs Georgina Browne	5Q (2003 moved away)		2005	93		24
	Mrs Marjorie Clarke	16Q (left or died 1993)					14
	Mrs Beatrice M. Mathews	11Q		1983	89	5 Sept. 1983	4
c1979	Mr William R. Stapleton	2 Lygon		1981	65	24 Aug. 1981	2
	Mrs Muriel Irene Stapleton	3 Lygon		1994	76	31 Oct. 1994	15
1979	John H. L. Beaumont	WLB (left 1980)					0
	Mrs Beaumont	WLB (left 1980)					0
	Edward Phillips	15Q (15Q became Guest Floor) (left 1983)					3
	Miss Florence Mary Piller	18Q (left c.1989 for Springfield)		1993	94	11 Mar. 1993	9
1981	Miss Dorothy M. Bater	24Q		1987	76	23 Jan. 1987	4
	Dr Barbara Boal	WLB (2001 left for home)					20
	Mrs Edith Clements	10Q (left or died 1994)					13
	William Quin	7 St Barnabas (left 2000)					19
1982	Mrs Annie Hazeldine	3Q (still there in 1999)		2004 (Pershore)	94		
	Mrs Jean St Maur Newton	14Q		1999	82		17
	Mrs Edna I. Curtis	22Q (left or died 1987)					5

Year	Name	Residence	Election age	Year of death	Age died	Date of burial in Newland Churchyard	Length of stay in years
1982	Miss Lilian Louise Haines	15Q		1988	77	24 June 1988	6
1984	Mrs Jane Haynes	23Q		(alive 1998)			
1985	Anthony Kennington Leefe	9Q (USPG, 2005 to home)		2005	86		20
	Miss Edwina Roberts	7Q		1998	84		13
	Eric Alfred Oseman	(1991 left for Somerset)					
	Mrs Mary Oseman	6Q (2013 moved away)		2000	82		
	Claude Elliott Reeves	6SB (1999 moved away)		2004	86		13
	Mrs Joan Reeves	6SB (1999 moved away)		2005	87		13
1987	Thomas Keegan	20Q		1995			8
	Mrs Margaret W. Adams	22Q		2000	78	(ashes)	13
	Miss Ivy Gwendoline Field	13Q (1999 moved away)		1995			2
	Mrs Joan Pile	4Q		1995			8
	Frederick William G. Prime	8Q (moved away)		1998	91		13
	Mrs Dorothy M. Prime	1 Lygon		(alive 1989)			
1987	Norah Elizabeth Smith	6Q (moved away)		1998	87	29 May 1998	11
	Mrs Lee Wheeler	24Q (moved away)					23
	Mrs Edith Taylor	24Q (left or died by 1990)					3
1988	Andrew James	2 Lygon (left 1989)		(alive 2012)			
	Mrs Pat James (warden of Pyndar)	2 Lygon (left 1989)		(alive 2012)			
1988	Mrs Dorothy S. Lethbridge	WL2		1998	90		10

Year	Name	Residence	Election age	Year of death	Age died	Date of burial in Newland Churchyard	Length of stay in years
1988	Mrs Pat Harrod	WL2 (2013 moved away)					
1989	Mrs Irene Tawse	15Q (moved away)		2012	88		
1990	Mrs Gwendoline Hill (deputy-warden)	13Q		2000			10
	Mrs Mary Bennett	7Q (2013 moved away)					22
1991	George H. Collier-Baker	1 Lygon (2003 moved away)		2003	76		12
	Miss Eileen M. Samuels						
	Mrs Noreen Iris Pope	2 Lygon (2007 moved away)		2011	96		16
1992	James Bryans			1998	73		6
1992	Mrs Delia Bryans						
1993	Mrs Dorothy McCaig						
1994	Miss Juliet Lygon	12Q (2012 moved away)					18
	Mrs B. C. C. (Pamela) Moger	10Q (left or died 1995)					1
	Mrs Mary Louise Overton	3 Woodlands (1998 moved away)		2010	89		4
	Miss Dorothy Pembridge	2 Woodlands (2001 moved away)		2004	89	6 Jan. 2005 (ashes)	24
1995	Miss Charlotte Stoddart	6Q (left or died 1995)					0
	Mrs Yvonne Clarke	1 Woodlands (2003 moved away)		2004	81		8
	Mrs Pauline Houlding						
	John Joseph Lomasney	20Q		1997	68		
	Mr E. Pettitt	11Q	(no further information)				1
1996	Mrs Jean Wild	5Q		2010			14
1996	Guy Phillips						

Year	Name	Residence	Election age	Year of death	Age died	Date of burial in Newland Churchyard	Length of stay in years
1997	Alan Gilbert	8Q (2001 moved away)					4
	Mrs D. Sam. Crump	(2004 moved away)					7
	Jim Parker	CSF (2007 moved away)					15
1997	Mrs Margaret Parker	CSF (2007 moved away)		1910			15
	David M. Annett	St Christopher's		2004	86		7
1998	Mrs Ronnie Whitford						
1999	Bernard Reginald Webber			2002	76		3
	Mrs Carol Webber						
2000	Raymond Emlyn James	3Q		2000	62		0
	Mrs Thelma Bailey						
	Chris Bassett	7 St Barnabas (2001 moved away)					
	Jacqueline Bassett	7 St Barnabas (2001 moved away)					
	Mrs Diana Crews						
	Mick Furlong						
	Tom Hickson	(2010 moved away)					10
	Mrs Vera Hickson			2002	72		2
	Ms Pat Hipwell						
	Peter James						
	Mrs Olive Hampson			2007	86		7
	John Orange						
	Mrs June Schuil						
	Mrs Barbara Williams						
2001	Norman Mills						

Year	Name	Residence	Election age	Year of death	Age died	Date of burial in Newland Churchyard	Length of stay in years
2003	Charles and Julie Allsopp						
	John and Jean Cowell						
	John and Olwyn Craze						2
2004	Mrs Kath Graty						
	John Flint	from Porter's Lodge					
	Mrs Betty Terrington						
2005	Mrs Ann Bingham	(moved away)					
2006	Mrs Sylvia Mair						
	Mrs Dawn Trevou						
2007	Maurice Brady	(moved away)					
	Mrs Paula Brady						
	Mrs Megan Burnett						
2008	Gerald Campbell						
	Mrs Sheila Campbell						
2010	Charles Hines						
	Mrs June Tilt						
2011	Colin R. Brownlee						
	Mrs Jill Coleman						
2012	Miss Jackie Simmons						
2013	Mrs Jenny Hodkinson	(from Porter's Lodge)					
	Mrs Diana Quinney						
2013	Tony Prescott						
	Mrs Pat Prescott						

Priests in the Community (other than Wardens and Chaplains)

These date only from the opening of St Barnabas in 1901, and records are very sparse. The list draws on the 1901–11 censuses, on funeral and burial registers, on electors registers and a variety of miscellaneous sources. It includes priests who for whatever reason were accommodated elsewhere in the community, but there are still many gaps.

Year	Name	Room	Additional information	Date died	Age died	Date of burial in Newland Churchyard	Length of stay (years)
1901	Frederick Lacon		Vicar of Headless Cross, Redditch an overseas bishop	19 Dec. 1906			5
c. 1907	Thomas Humphris Clark		Vicar of Heybridge, Essex	1913	86	7 Nov. 1913	
	Miss Clark		daughter				
c. 1907	Thomas Hoyle Compton		Vicar of Woodlands St Kath, Somerset	1913	85	31 July 1913	
	Emma Sarah Compton						
	Agnes Winifred Compton		daughter				
1911	Lorenzo Clutterbuck		Rector of Teversham, Cambridge	1913	79	9 Jan. 1913	
	Lucy Deborah Mary Clutterbuck			1911			
	Cecilia Clutterbuck		daughter				
	James Taylor		Canon; SPG missionary in Bombay	1918	77	26 Apr. 1918	
	Kate Mary or Mercy Taylor			1917	57	July 1917	
?	James Coles		SPG missionary in Andovovanto	1917	64	4 May 1917	
?	William James Courtenay			1919	70	11 July 1919	
1919	Alfred Harry McLaughlin		Vicar of Much Birch, Hereford	1935	82		16
	Jessie Mabel McLaughlin			1943	77		
	Father Warner						
	Miss Warner		sister				
	James Edward Griffen	2SB	Archdeacon of Zanzibar	1940	88		
?	William Ismay			1922	76	15 May 1922	
	Florence Ismay					Jan. 1943	
?	Frederick William Fremantle Bishop	1SB		10 June 1925	65		

Year	Name	Room	Additional information	Date died	Age died	Date of burial in Newland Churchyard	Length of stay (years)
?	Lorna Bishop	1SB		1924	55	14 Oct. 1924	
?	Marian Hanbury	4SB		28 Nov. 1924	78		
?	Mary Leader	4SB		1926	68	3 Mar. 1926	
?	Alfred Hawker	4SB		8 Apr. 1929	71	15 Apr. 1929	
?	Lydia Henrietta Hawker			23 Aug 1928	62	29 Aug. 1928	
?	Alfred Thomas Greanstreet	2SB		1927	74	1 Oct 1927	
1922	William Weber						
1923	William James Worster	3SB	Vicar of St Barnabas, Rainbow Hill	1947	91	10 Mar. 1947	24
	Kate Worster	3SB		1946	89	7 Jan. 1946	23
	Mrs Dorothy Margaret Worster			Jan. 1985			
1928[?]	Edgar Alfred Reader	1SB	Vicar of Bradpole	1947		10 May 1947	
	Emma Minchin Reader			1946	76	1 Apr. 1946	
c.1931	Frank Percival Downman		Org. Sec. CETS	1937	85	Dec. 1937	6
1939	Francis Murray Downton		Curate of Temple Balsall	1941	64	3 May 1941	2
1940	Alan Moultine Myone	2SB	Archdeacon of Matabeleland	1944	59	10 Mar. 1944	4
	Dorothy Mylne			1953			
1942	Alfred Henry Gillard	4SB	Rector of Rackenford, Devon	1946	72	4 June 1946	4
	Gertrude Annie Gillard			1944	65	30 May 1944	2
	Mr Hughes	2SB	ex-missionary	1943/44?			
1946	Cecil John Wood	2SB	Bishop of Melanesia, 1912	1957	82		11
	Mrs Marjorie Allen Wood		moved to Bromley College, Nov. 1957	11 May 1972			
	Jasper Stoneman Caiger	3SB		17 Dec. 1955	83		

Year	Name	Room	Additional information	Date died	Age died	Date of burial in Newland Churchyard	Length of stay (years)
1946	Edith Mary Maud Caiger		moved to Gt. Malvern	1957	85	31 Oct. 1957	
	Henry Whalley Ellwood	2SB	Vicar of St Chad, Gateshead	1965	91	July 1965	19
	Henry or Herbert Foley Napier	2SB		1946	73	26 July 1946	
	Mrs Napier						
	Albert Ernest Dudley	4SB	UMCA missionary in central Africa	17 Feb. 1966	87		20
	Mrs Anna Dudley		moved to Lymington in 1966	Nov. 1989			
1947	Marmaduke Warner	1SB		15 Sep. 1957	79		10
	Mrs Warner			c.1955			
?	Mary Andrews Warren	1SB		1951	82	26 Feb. 1951	
1957	Frank Greville Horth	3SB	moved to home	Feb. 1980	95	18 Feb. 1980	
	Maud Mary Horth		moved to home in Gloucester	1988	91	5 July 1988	
1957	John Reginald Weller	2SB	Bishop of Falkland Islands, then Argentina	26 Oct. 1969	89	30 Oct. 1969	12
	Mrs Frances Weller	12Q (1970)	1978 to Kent; later Perrins	1992	83	15 Dec. 1992	21
	Elizabeth, aged 16		daughter				
	John, aged 12		(Capt. John P. Weller married Jan 1976)				
1959	Douglas Frederick Coles	3SB	Vicar of Oldbury-on-Severn	1965	77		6
	Mrs Coles	3SB	left 1966				7
1964	Frederick J. Newson	CSF	Vicar of Guarlford; Jan. and Feb. 1991	1965	82		1
	Mrs Frances May Newson	CSF	cf. *Grapevine* Feb. 1997 p.8	1996	94		30
1968	Bernard John Flavell	7SB	Vicar of Haselbury and, Somerset 1979 to Droitwich				11

Year	Name	Room	Additional information	Date died	Age died	Date of burial in Newland Churchyard	Length of stay (years)
1968	Robert Harry Pilbeam	5SB	Rector of Ashbrittle, Somerset 1969 to Somerset	1975			
	Mrs Pilbeam						
1969	Samuel Wynne Davies	8SB	Rector of St Giles, Wimborne 1979 to Wales	1980	81	1 Nov. 1980	10
	Richard Clement White	6SB	Rector of Great and Little Packington	Aug. 1985			16
	Mrs Joyce Isabel White	6SB		1974	74		5
	Canon Arthur Charles Knights	5SB	ex-Bulawayo; 1969 to home in Knutsford left April 1970	May 1971			
	Mrs Knights			1974/75			
1970	William Henry Davies	5SB	Vicar of Whittington, Lichfield to Avonside	1976		17 Aug. 1976	6
	Mrs Davies		c. 1977 to Wales				
1979	Ernest Roy Bowdler	5SB	Canon of Langley Marish, Berkshire left 1985				6
1980	Reginald Stanley Lansdown	8SB	Rector of St Bede, Nelson, Lancashire	1986		30 Aug. 1986	6
1982	E. Baker	23Q		Mar. 1984			
1983	Stanley Chapman Pickard, CBE	6SB	Bishop of Lebombo; to Redmarley Bishop	Apr. 1988		19 May 1988	5
?	Pritchard						
	Maurice James	WLA	Archdeacon of South Basuto	1993			
	Mrs Mary James	2Q	2003 to Watlington	2012			
1985	Alan Bacchus Gordon	20Q	Vicar of Old Brampton, Chesterfield	Feb. 1988	89		3
	R. L. P. Milburn,	5SB	Dean of Worcester; left 1996				11
	Mrs Marjorie Milburn						

280

Year	Name	Room	Additional information	Date died	Age died	Date of burial in Newland Churchyard	Length of stay (years)
1987	John Watkin Aubury	8SB	Canon; Rector of Colyweston and Peterborough; left 1999				12
	Mrs Pam Aubury		left 1999				12
	Walter Richard Iliffe	11Q	Rector of Broome, Worcestershire	1992			5
c. 1989	George Cardell Briggs, CMG		Bishop of Seychelles; left c. 1999 for home	2004	93		10
1995	Henry M. Deane-Hall	WLA	Rector of the Donheads, Somerset; left 1997				
	Mrs Kathleen A. Deane-Hall	WLA	left 1997				
	Alasdair J. MacKeracher		Vicar of Swimbridge, Devon; left that year				
	Mrs Elizabeth M. MacKeracker						
	Stephen B. Oliver		Archdeacon of Cape Town; left 1996				1
	Mrs Oliver						
1996	Albert Woods		Vicar of Upper with Nether Swell				
	Mrs Woods						
	Bryan Hall		St Christopher's, left same year				
1997	Douglas Edward Green	21Q	Honorary Canon Minsterley c. 2009 to home				12
1998	Dennis Gordon Griffin	20Q	Vicar of Christ Church, Pendlebury	April 2006	82		8
2000	Harry Ogden		Rector of Christ Church, Moss Side 2005 to home	2012			5
2002	John Catling Allen		Honorary Canon Great and Little Torrington				
2003	Gordon Mitchell Ikin		Vicar of St James, Thornham				
2007	Andrew Gibson Williams		Rector of Whimple, Talaton, etc.; moved away 2013				
	Mrs Pat Williams						

Year	Name	Room	Additional information	Date died	Age died	Date of burial in Newland Churchyard	Length of stay (years)
2010	Martin James Baddeley		Archdeacon of Reigate; 2012 moved away				2
2011	John Vickerman		Canon; Vicar of King Cross, Halifax				
2013	Graham Oakes		Rector of Holy Trinity, Bath, and Chaplain Royal United Hospital, Bath				
	Mrs Judith Oakes						
	Ian Corbett		Hon. CE Clevedon with Clapton in Gordano				

Altar Servers

No records were kept of the names of the servers. These are the names we know; there will have been many more.

1864–1945	Choir school choristers served at the said eucharists. Local boys served at the sung eucharists.
1920–c. 1935	Reginald J. H. Hewer, became merchant sailor in WWII, lost at sea, 1940.
1925–c. 1940	C Wallace-Cox* Churchwarden (1921–22).
1923–c. 1975	Ted Bullock, Boy and Man, with intermittent gaps, Porter (1964–78).
1930s	Reginald King
1939–c. 1944	George Purser, Porter (1958–64), Churchwarden (1958–63).
1940s	Tommy Hunt.
	Pat Dixon.
	Freddy Jones.
	Jonathan Morris.
	David Morris.
	Jonathan Poper.
	Jonny Goode.
	Ronald Tongue.
	Billy Taylor.
1943–c. 1958	Bill Daffin*, Porter (1943–58).
1944–c. 1952	Tony Bullock, son of Ted Bullock.
1949–c. 1953	David Leonard Jones, christened in St Leonard's (now Sir David Jones). Four of his friends were also servers.
1961–c. 1968	Andrew Burrow, nephew of Ted Bullock.
1986–c. 2004	Tony Leefe.*
2003–2011	James Allsopp.*
2006–2011	Roger Hodkinson.*
2008	Alex Brodie.
2011	Colin Brownlee.*
2012	Catherine Brodie (the first girl ever to serve at St Leonard's).
2012	William Waite.
2012	Jon Goldswain.*
2013	Gabriel Waite.
2013	David Russell.*

All names are for boy servers, except when marked '*' which indicates an adult.

Appendix II
Church Ritual, Liturgy and the Altar Servers

On ritual and liturgy Skinner's preference was for the Sarum use, adopted from pre-reformation times, rather than the 'Western' use which followed contemporary Roman Catholic practice. His altar book, which still survives in the sacristy, was *The Priest to the Altar*,[1] the first of a series of books which supplemented the text of the Prayer Book with private devotions for the priest.

Notes by a member of the congregation from an instruction on ritual given by him in 1874 were published posthumously. These imply the use of incense, vestments and biretta, the preparation at the foot of the altar and the kissing of the altar, though some of these may have represented his ideal rather than what actually happened at Newland. In general the *Book of Common Prayer* was followed faithfully, though at choral services the Benedictus and the Agnus Dei were added. In the creed there was kneeling at the Incarnatus, and after the consecration there was a silent memento. The priest said

---

[1] Skinner used the first edition of this, privately printed in 1861. Its compiler was P. G. Medd.

silently a threefold 'Lord I am not worthy' before communicating and also said silently 'Behold the Lamb of God' as he invited the communicants. He performed the ablutions after the blessing, but then read the last gospel from John 1:1–14.[2]

In 1888 'in loving memory of one in Paradise' White gave a new altar book, superbly printed, hand-bound and decorated with silver embroidered covers,[3] but sadly we do not know which this was. Another book was given in 1931, though again we do not know which it was. In 1948 a new and very definitely anglo-catholic book, *The English Missal*, was given as a thankoffering, and in 1964 there was a gift of *The Altar Missal*, a slightly more moderate book produced by the Cowley Fathers. These two books remained in use till 2007, though it is not clear how much was imported from them. Hunt, for example, still felt like Skinner that loyalty to the prayer book required that he should still take the ablutions after the blessing, but thereafter he still recited the last gospel which was not in the prayer book.

For the choir, Newland's books of Sunday introits and sequences were deemed to be worn out in Osborn's day and the sequences were reprinted, though not the introits which were included in *The English Hymnal*.

For the laity, in January 1983 Mr Martin replaced Newland's traditional interim rite with Rite B from the *Alternative Service Book* at the 8 a.m. Sunday 'parish' service. This was similar to the older rite and in one respect—the Gloria at the beginning rather than at the end—more 'catholic.' He had hoped that this would also be adopted for the 11 a.m. 'community' service and had provided copies accordingly, 'but Father Nichols spirited them away.'[4] The community

---

[2] *Instructions on the Ritual of the Altar,* Bath, 1877.

[3] It was presumably heavily used, and sometime after 1961 the covers were placed around another altar book, the third (1914) edition of *The English Liturgy,* edited by Percy Dearmer and others; this was a more 'moderate' book than Skinner's.

[4] Manuscript diary of Hilda Coe. In her working life Hilda (1894–1983) had edited the women's page of the *Daily Express.* When her sister died she became companion and housekeeper to her London neighbour Gordon Barnes. From their arrival in

[*See p.290 for n.4 cont.*]

still stuck to its traditional rite, though Bishop Maund also moved the Gloria to the beginning of the service. In 1993 when the green booklets were out of print Father Burr had them reprinted (with blue covers) for the community, and they were reprinted again in 1999. By this time, however, all midweek celebrations were according to the modern Rite A of the *Alternative Service Book*.

Some slight updates to the Sunday liturgy were made in the early 2000s, and in 2005 the three-year lectionary was introduced at the 11 a.m. Eucharist with lay people reading the Old Testament lessons and epistles. Further changes followed, and in 2011, when new service books were donated by Jill Coleman in memory of her husband, the rite was the Common Worship form in traditional language. For weekday celebrations, in 2001 Rite A of the Alternative Service Book was replaced by the modern language version of Common Worship in a suitably enriched form.

In 1893 White held five services on Ash Wednesday, including commination and sermon. Ashing was not mentioned explicitly till 1980, but it may well have been practised earlier and it quickly became the norm. Under Osborn and Hatherly there were often weekly mission services in Lent, evensong and address, or stations of the cross, and Hunt held an afternoon service on mothering sunday, with an address to the parents. In the 1990s there was often a Wednesday afternoon service in Lent. This was replaced in 2001 by an address after the Wednesday eucharist and more recently by a house-group 'York' course on Wednesday evenings. Also from 2001 to 2007 there was compline in the chapel on Saturday evenings, while more recently the stations of the cross have been revived on Sunday afternoons in Lent.

Malvern Link in 1975 till her death aged eighty-nine she kept a daily diary in which—among many other things—visits to St Leonard's on Sundays and holydays are duly recorded along with occasional information about parish life and people. Initially her accounts of Sunday lunch were longer than those of Sunday Mass, but gradually her comments on the services and in particular the sermons (and the clergy!) became longer. Her diaries were kindly donated to the archives by the Reverend John Guise.

Wylde observed the blessing and distribution of palms on Palm Sunday and this has been observed ever since. Until quite recently Maundy Thursday was observed only by the usual morning eucharist, but in 1980 there was a sung mass on the evening of Maundy Thursday and this was the first time that an evening eucharist was celebrated at Newland. This evening celebration quickly became the norm, and it was followed from 1982 by the watch of the passion.

On Good Friday Wylde held the Three Hour Devotion among other services, while Osborn had matins and litany at 8 a.m., stations of the cross at 9 a.m., the 'altar service' (ante-communion) at 10 a.m., followed by the singing of the reproaches and the veneration of the cross, then the Three Hours Devotion from 12 noon to 3 p.m., and evensong said at 6.30 p.m. Hunt in 1951 had ante-communion, veneration of the cross and reproaches before the Three Hours, while Bott added a children's service. The stations, reproaches and veneration were gradually dropped, but from 1980 to 1984 Good Friday still began with matins, litany and ante-communion sometime between 9 a.m. and 11 a.m., and this was normally followed by the Three Hours Devotion and in 1980 by a later evening devotion.

From 1985 the earlier service was abandoned, and the Three Hours tended to begin with matins and litany, which were followed by the liturgy of the day (which now included the administration of communion) and meditation or homilies. From 1988 there was matins and sometimes litany at 9 a.m., with devotional addresses and liturgy later but no 'three hours.' In 1992 Father Burr reverted to matins and litany at 12 noon and 'The Last Hour', a devotional service at 2 p.m. The liturgy with its veneration of the cross and administration of communion was revived in Father Marsh's brief chaplaincy when there was matins and litany at 9 a.m., and the liturgy (including communion) at 2 p.m. Under Father Dalby there was a watch of prayer from 12 noon till 2 p.m., and this was followed by the full liturgy including the reproaches, veneration of the cross and communion. The full liturgy is now the norm.

On Easter Eve White or Wylde introduced a short service in the churchyard, followed by solemn matins of Easter. Under Hatherly Easter Eve was marked by 'the accustomed Procession to the Churchyard, where prayers for the Departed were read', and this was followed by the blessing of the holy fire and the paschal candle and the first evensong of Easter. From 1980 to 1984 Easter Eve was observed by what was variously described as the vigil ceremonies, the blessing of the Easter candle, and the service of light and liturgy of the word. From 1981 to 1983 there was also mention of the blessing of the churchyard, but thereafter this seems to have lapsed. It was not until 1997 that Father Marsh added the first communion of Easter to the vigil ceremonies, but this was a 'one-off' until Father Watson also included it. Again, this is now the norm.

On Easter Sunday Wylde had holy communion at 7 a.m. and 8 a.m., procession, sung mass and sermon at 10.45 a.m. and evensong and sermon at 6.30 p.m. In 1930 there was a record number of communicants at 7 a.m. and 8 a.m. 'and at the sung Service at 11 the Church was so crowded that chairs had to be brought in from the Library and Board Room.' In the afternoon there was a children's festival service with a procession into the Quadrangle, and the day finished with evensong. From 1942 to 1951 Easter communicants ranged from 104 to 134. Evensong (or vespers) continued till 1988, and in 1982 it was solemn. In 1997 Father Marsh held evening prayer and benediction.

At Christmas Osborn introduced the midnight mass but warned, 'Those who desire to make their Communion at this hour should obtain cards from the Clergy, and will be expected to observe the Fast from 6pm.' As in many parishes, Christmas soon became more popular than Easter, and from 1942 to 1951 Christmas communicants ranged from 129 to 168.

Osborn always observed the Feast of Corpus Christi, and he noted in brackets in the calendar the 'Falling Asleep of the Blessed Virgin Mary' on 15 August. Brodribb observed this latter as the Assumption of the Blessed Virgin Mary. Later, Father Nichols observed the Immaculate Conception on 8 December. In 1984 candlemas ceremonies were first mentioned explicitly in the registers, and these have been observed ever since.

In May 1982 a ward of the Guild of the Servants of the Sanctuary visited the church for their office and benediction (probably the first time this service had been held at Newland), and in the following month the diocesan branch of the Confraternity of the Blessed Sacrament celebrated sung mass, procession and (again) benediction and in June 1985 there was pontifical mass (with Bishop Maund as celebrant), sermon and benediction for the Worcester Deanery CBS. St Leonard's had always been firmly anglo-catholic, but 'Prayer Book Catholic' not Roman; however, it was now beginning to move beyond this.

Dean Milburn's obituary indicates his dislike of what he deemed the narrow anglo-catholicism which prevailed in his day, and a 1997 letter sent by Mrs Rowberry to chaplaincy applicants stated that 'The worship is Anglo-Catholic, although other forms of service may be used on week-days in the chapel.' But the anglo-catholic tradition continued on weekdays as on Sundays and, while successive chaplains have moved slightly 'up' or 'down', it can be fairly claimed that the worship is consistently and recognisably that of the catholic tradition in the Church of England.

The Altar Servers

No records were kept of the Altar Servers so the information we have is very scant indeed. The church has a superb collection of ceremonial equipment and up to the closure of the choir school in 1945 there was a large team of Servers and Altar Boys. They would be in attendance for all Sunday services, Feasts and Festivals, with the choir school choristers acting as servers at the daily said eucharist.

A large team of boys were still present in the 1950s, serving on Sundays and Festivals; but by 1969 the last boy had left and most of the ceremonial equipment was packed away. Over the next few decades, one or two adult servers was the norm.

The start of the twenty-first century saw the gradual resurgence of anglo-catholic ritual when Father Mark Dalby was appointed as chaplain in 2000. The use of incense was revived for major festivals with the Father Harry Ogden, one of the priests in residence, acting as Thurifer, followed a few years later by Father Gordon Ikin; there being only one other server at that time. Roger Hodkinson then took over as Thurifer between 2006 and 2011, being joined by James Allsopp as a Server. On Christmas Eve 2008, Alex Brodie became the first boy server since the 1960s and now, at the age of seventeen, is the senior server and Thurifer.

In 2011 Colin Brownlee became Master of Ceremonies and since then a serving team of eight has been built up. On Sundays, Feasts and Festivals the full panoply of anglo-catholic ceremony has been reinstated as it was for most of St Leonard's history.

Appendix III
The Church Organ

In August 1878 White asked the Trustees to authorise £22 to be spent on the cleaning of the organ by Nicholson since it had not been cleaned since its erection. For some years there is silence, but in June 1936 it was cleaned and overhauled, an electric blower was fitted, and a new stop—15th on Great—replaced an unsatisfactory clarinet.[1]

In 1986 an archdeacon's certificate was granted for organ repairs according to the plans of Nicholson and Co. in Worcester. Over the next two years, at a cost of £11,510 met from the bequest of Gordon Barnes, the organ was completely dismantled by Trevor Tipple to enable the rotten floor under it to be replaced. Twenty-four pipes were added, along with a closed horn stop in memory of John Valentine Hewer by his son. Trevor Tipple wrote at this time,

> The Swell organ pipework was short compass (the lowest octave missing) and the Pedal organ compass was two octaves as opposed to the usual two and a half octaves, now standard. The work recently

---

[1] This work was paid for from Miss Gillham's legacy.

carried out has involved a new electric action bass system for the Swell organ, the introduction of 224 completely new pipes, enlargement of the Swell box to accommodate the new pipework and the provision of a new Balanced Swell pedal to operate the shutter mechanism, replacing the old hook-down lever: also refurbishment of action mechanisms.

Specification
Manual compass, 56 notes. Pedal compass, 30 notes

Great Organ		**Swell Organ**	
Open Diapason	8	Open Diapason	8
Dulciana	8	Viol da Gamba	8
Stopped Diapason Bass	8	Stopped Diapason	8
Stopped Diapason Treble	8	Principal	4
Principal	4	Mixture	15-19-22
Flute	4	Trumpet	8
Fifteenth	2		

Pedal Organ		**Couplers**
Bourdon	16	Swell to Pedal
Fagotto	8	Swell to Great
Fagotto	16	Great to Pedal

Three composition pedals to Great Organ. Balanced Swell Pedal

The renovations of 2008 were in memory of Pamela Bulmer.

Appendix IV
Churchyard and Community Burials

In 1931 the warden spoke of the urgent need for the enlargement of the churchyard, and in 1932 an extension on land conveyed by Lord Elmley was duly consecrated. In February 1937 the paths, then in a bad state, were put into good condition thanks to a gift from Miss Agatha Skinner, niece of the first warden; the work involved 31 tons of gravel and sand. In 1973 the churchyard paths were again resurfaced, and in 1986 the PCC resolved, subject to a faculty being granted,

> To remove to the perimeter of the churchyard gravestones occupying the oldest section of the churchyard where no burials have taken place since the early years of this century, and level all burial mounds thereon in order to make the land available for new burials.

As usual in these situations, objectors were invited to inform the PCC secretary 'stating the grounds of their objection and what interest they have in the graves concerned.' The Trustees asked Mrs Rowberry to approach the archdeacon 'with a view to a specific portion of the land being set aside for the Community use' (even though such use was more and more rare). But nothing came of the PCC proposals. Ted and Doris Bullock continued to do mowing and trimming, and in 1988 a working party sought to improve the oldest section, but in 1989 the Bullocks retired. The 1997 pastoral scheme left the churchyard in the hands of the PCC, which lacked the financial resources to maintain it and, despite the Trustees' best endeavours, it exuded a rather forlorn and neglected appearance. Happily it is now in much better condition. But the churchyard is not as central to the community (or to the parish) as once it was. Burials reached their peak in 1940–49. Thereafter there was a decline, most marked from 1990.

Originally community burials, at the expense of the Trustees, had been almost invariable, but later these ceased to be the norm. One reason may be because at some point the Trustees decided no longer to meet the expenses. Another may be that fewer people died while resident in the community. Yet another was the increasing popularity of cremation. The first instance of the burial of ashes in the churchyard is recorded in 1946 and the movement towards cremation was furthered by the opening of Worcester crematorium in 1960. The number of Beauchamp interments per decade was usually in the twenties (though it twice exceeded this) until 1960, but again from 1990 it declined vastly. The percentage of Beauchamp interments was between 39 per cent and 69 per cent until 1920. Thereafter this too has steadily declined.

The Newland Burial Registers

Years	Numbers in Register	Total	Numbers of Beauchamp	Others	Percentage in Beauchamp
1816–61	1–107*				
1862–69	108–194	87	44	43	51%
1878–97	195–317	123	73	50	59%
1897–1919	318–464	147	67	80	46%
1920–29	465–544	80	26	54	32%
1930–39	545–610	66	20	46	30%
1940–49	611–693	83	22	61	27%
1950–59	694–764	71	18	53	25%
1960–69	765–800, 1–14	50	15	35	30%
1969–79	25–83	59	21	38	36%
1980–89	84–135	52	19	33	37%
1990–99	136–163	28	10	18	36%
2000–09	164–181	18	2	16	11%
2010+	182–184	3	1		

* *These presumably took place at Great Malvern.*

Appendix V
The Grounds

Hunt tried to picture the original setting, 'The Almshouses are surrounded by tastefully laid out lawns, terraces, gardens and shrubberies and flower borders, overlooking fields to the horizon.' In the early days the porter seems to have had overall responsibility for the grounds, and residents and choirboys were required to assist in their maintenance. But little is known in detail about them except that the lawn mowers were pulled by a donkey, and Ted Bullock remembered doing this.

If we approach the grounds today and pass through the main entrance to the great gate, the gardens are mostly lawns with a wide border along the road side adjacent to the railings. This has been largely undisturbed as there is a lot of regeneration towards the back.

To the left there are lawns and a column, with a small cross at the top. At first sight the column could be taken as a war memorial but in fact it is a private memorial erected in Canon Wylde's time and attributed by Bertie Shaw to 'Mr Tapper', presumably the later Sir Walter Tapper, who had already designed the church of the Ascension in Malvern Link. The persons commemorated are a Henry

Slater and his wife Charlotte Isabel who were devout anglo-catholics and members of the Newland congregation where they esteemed Wylde as 'our dear priest.' The Latin inscription[1] gives no personal details other than their names, but Henry was born in Manchester, and Charlotte nee Watson in Cheltenham. They married in Holborn in 1880, and in 1901 they were living in Marple, Cheshire, where Henry was director of a paper staining works. Sometime thereafter they moved to Summerfields in Lower Howsell, Malvern Link. Henry died on 19 June 1909 aged seventy, and it was after this that the pillar was erected—to the alleged sorrow of Cosby White who regretted the displacement of some ash trees. Charlotte lived on at Summerfields until her own death on 5 April 1927 aged seventy-nine. They do not appear to have had any children, and presumably the addition of her name was undertaken by other family members and/or their godchildren.[2]

To the right, holly and ivy together with yew trees form a tunnel. There is a flower border in front, and this leads first to the car park and then to an avenue of flowering cherries and a woodland area planted with spring bulbs, including some of the rare fritillaries; these give a lovely display early in the year. There is also a pumping station erected by the-then Upton RDC. On the other side are various outbuildings—a boiler house, laundry, car port and storerooms. Meanwhile, near this avenue a tin garage adjacent to St Barnabas has recently been dismantled and a new green walkway created under

---

[1] 'Orate pro anima Domini Henrici Slater Etiam pro anima Carlottae Isabellae Slater. Te precor O benedicte salvum me fac crucifixe per crucem tuam Domine libera nos.' This may be roughly translated, 'Pray to the Lord for the soul of Henry Slater, also for the soul of Charlotte Isabel Slater. I beseech you, O blessed crucified one, to save me, and by your cross, O Lord, deliver us'

[2] Henry had a nephew, Gilbert John Leigh Slater, who was lodging with Charlotte in 1911. He was later commissioned as a lieutenant in the Worcestershire regiment, and was killed in action in France on 20 April 1916. He is among those mentioned on the war memorial 'who served in this choir and sanctuary'. As he was a boy at the choir school, this may have influenced Henry and Charlotte in their choice of Malvern for their retirement.

the yew trees with hostas, ivies and ferns. The yew hedge has been trimmed and a border of yellow and pink carpet roses has been planted by the lawn. A new heather garden has been created at the end of this walkway with a small pond, and this leads to the beautiful flower borders at the back of the buildings. Water butts have been installed along the laundry wall and several potentillas have been planted. Two difficult dark corners have been gravelled with pots, planted with greenery on one side and flowers on the other, and all this has made a great improvement. The borders have been planted with roses and clematis, also herbs with a seat placed in a quiet sunny corner. Lots of summer bedding plants in pots make this an attractive place.

In 1984 trees were planted along the length of the new gardens leading to Woodlands, and residents were encouraged to contribute to the cost. In August 1993 the road from the car park to Woodlands was resurfaced with tarmac and the driveways inside the Quadrangle with tarram and chippings at a total cost of £17,500. Mrs Rowberry also hoped to 'clear a large area of wilderness and make it into lawned and shrubbed gardens', and this was duly done.

The main archway opens onto the quadrangle which is divided by gravel paths into four lawns with a fountain in the centre and a tree on each lawn. One of these was planted by the American Ligons in 1973 in memory of the Honourable Richard Lygon, but shortly afterwards two elm trees there, each 110 years old, fell victim to Dutch Elm disease, and Brodribb commented, 'The Quadrangle will never be quite the same without them.' They were quickly replaced, though not with elms. There are three limes, but it is the catalpa (sometimes known as an Indian Bean Tree) on the lawn nearest the church which is beautiful in blossom and arouses most interest from visitors though they can rarely identify it . It was planted to mark the Queen's Silver Jubilee by Councillor John Guise on behalf of Newland Parish Council but we can never explain why it was chosen. We have always understood that it is of South American origin, though Wikipedia states that it is 'native to warm temperate regions of North America, the Caribbean, and East Asia'.

After the death of Countess Beauchamp a small sundial dated 1705 was erected in her memory in the middle of the Quadrangle, but it was later felt that this was too small for such a vast expanse, and at the millennium it was moved to a corner of the Quadrangle and replaced by a large fountain which is now a major feature.

To the right of the Quadrangle are the residents' flats, and the small gardens attached to them are planted individually and with their own choice of plants. This makes a colourful display for most of the year. One resident has an unusual garden of very good topiary.

To the left, the borders have recently been pruned and tidied. The walls and windows of the church are now visible again and will no longer be damaged by climbing plants. Camellias, mahonias, hebes, spirea and thymes have been planted and roses tied to wires where they can be trained to a pleasing shape. A scented garden has been planted by the cloisters and includes hamamelis (witch hazel), mahonia, japonica, Christmas box, vibernus pinks and scented geraniums. The more unusual black-stemmed bamboo also grows here.

To the south of the Quadrangle is the Long Walk and here we actually have some historical information in that in 1977, to mark the Queen's Silver Jubilee, twelve different trees were planted alongside it, as well as the catalpa referred to above. A prunus Kansan was planted just to the east of the iron gates on behalf of the community by its oldest resident, Mrs Ethel Tucker. Next in order were trees given by Mrs F. Newson in memory of her husband who had been vicar of Guarlford for fifty-one years; Mrs Anne Dudley in memory of her husband Father A. E. Dudley, formerly of St Barnabas; Mr and Mrs R. J. Clay and Mr and Mrs S. James in memory of Mr and Mrs Randall, parents of Mrs Clay and Mrs James; Mrs A. A. Evetts, in memory of her husband, Mr John Evetts; Mrs L. A. Cockerill in memory of her husband Mr Archibald Cockerill; and Miss D. Pembridge in memory of her parents Mr and Mrs H. P. Pembridge. To the west of the gates were trees given by Mrs K. I. E. Davies and family in memory of Father W. H. Davies; Mrs F. Weller and family, in memory of Bishop J. R. Weller; Mrs and Mrs Smith in memory of Mrs Smith's son, Colin John Gent; Mrs Thyrza Mc Collum, a member of the American branch of the Lygons; and Mr and Mrs G. J. Lewis of Powick. Finally, on the lawn nearest the church Councillor John Guise planted a catalpa (sometimes known as an Indian Bean tree) on behalf of Newland Parish Council.

Only a handful of these 1977 trees survive, and the wall and flower beds are being slowly restored and planted with perennials to reduce the amount of maintenance needed. Care is being taken to use insect friendly plants, and there is now a large variety of birds, butterflies and bees.

The western end of the walk is lawn, and an urn planted with a cordyline has been placed in the centre to enhance the view. An old plough and tools will be made into a feature near the horse chestnut tree. At the eastern end, the garden around St Christopher's is being restored with the removal of a rockery and the creation of a longer grassy area.

To the south of the Long Walk is the paddock, originally known as Chapel Meadow. Over the years residents have planted fruit trees—apples, pears, damsons and plums—but in general the area was neglected. Recently, however, a local youth group, HOPE, has worked hard clearing the undergrowth, especially around the impressive cedar. The Woodland Trust has given young trees of different varieties and a nursery bed has been established for them. The paddock is now being made into a meadow with wild flowers; seeds were planted early in 2012 and gave a colourful display in the summer while the wild flowers are now establishing themselves among the grasses. It is intended to preserve the Paddock's wilder nature in contrast to the main grounds, but simple paths are also being created and kept mown, benches have been provided, and it is hoped—as is already happening—to make it a place where residents can enjoy a meandering walk or a peaceful rest.

Meanwhile an oak tree has been planted to commemorate the Queen's Diamond Jubilee. Bee hives are now kept in the meadow and delicious honey is extracted. Another area has been set aside for composting, and cold frames are being installed for cuttings from the various shrubs to be grown on ready for planting in the flower borders.

In the recent past, residents undertook the mowing and in most cases took great pride in the small gardens by their flats or cottages but it was still necessary at some times for the Trustees to employ an external gardener on a part-time basis. But now everything is done by the residents, one of whom wrote of the 'complete transformation' of the grounds in recent years.

In 2010 'the Heart of England in Bloom—It's Your Neighbourhood Campaign' reviewed sixty-two local entries and deemed the Beauchamp Community 'Outstanding' (a category for those marked eighty-six to one hundred per cent). The assessor noted:

> The grounds of the Beauchamp Community are outstanding with their wealth of mature trees, shrub borders, manicured lawns, focal points and an over 'the wall' large wild garden, which houses the communal compost area and two bee hives. The wonderful mix of style, design and plant choice to residents' own front garden areas. The exacting standard of maintenance to the grounds carried out by volunteers, residents of the Beauchamp community. The summer fête raising funds for the buying of trees. The 'over the wall' wild area—activities involving the local youth groups.

He added that 'This must be one of the best kept secret gardens in Worcestershire', and noted just one area for development: 'Suggest carrying out a tree audit—then record, label all trees and produce a list for visitors.'

In 2011 the grounds were again deemed 'Outstanding', and the assessor suggested the formation of a garden club. This suggestion was taken up eagerly, and the club now meets monthly under the able chairmanship of John Craze, though some of its members are active every week. The club has significantly enhanced the sense of community, while it is to him and to the members that we owe the ongoing improvements to the grounds. In 2012 the grounds were again deemed 'Outstanding.'

Work continued apace in the grounds and in 2013 not only were they deemed 'Outstanding' yet again, but were also awarded a shield for 'Gardening Excellence.' The Garden Club has embarked on a programme of shrub replacement, planted over eight hundred more daffodils and five hundred crocuses. Fund raising events, such as a Christmas raffle, lunches and strawberry tea are always well attended. In July 2013 the grounds were opened to the public for the first time and the event was a great success; particularly popular was the two-acre wildlife paddock which is an ongoing project.

Further nest boxes for birds and bats have been added to the grounds, together with other measures to encourage wildlife. Future plans for the paddock include a pond. Residents work hard in their own particular gardens where they install features such as small ponds and fountains, together with seating and other ornamentation in keeping with the grounds. Eighteen species of butterflies and twenty-three species of birds have been recorded in the ongoing project to chart wildlife.

The grounds are undoubtedly the finest they have been in our 150 year history and the hard work of the Garden club and residents will ensure they remain so for another 150 years!

Appendix VI
The Chapel at Newland

The early history of Newland is closely involved with Great Malvern Priory. According to legend, when the monastery at Deerhurst in Gloucestershire was sacked by the Danes in 1016, the monk Werstan escaped and fled to the Malvern Hills where he established a hermitage and chapel. This later became a monastery and received a charter from King Edward the Confessor, though shortly afterwards Werstan was murdered. This legend was so treasured by the later monks of the Priory that they commemorated it in a series of panels in a fifteenth century stained glass window in the north clerestory of their choir, but unfortunately the oldest documents make no mention of Werstan and he is generally regarded nowadays as 'medieval fabrication.'

We are on firmer ground with the monk Aldwyn who, according to William of Malmesbury writing in the early twelfth century, was sent by Wulfstan, Bishop of Worcester, to establish a cell at Malvern. In time Aldwyn gathered thirty monks round him, and in 1085 this community was established by Wulfstan as the Benedictine Priory of Great Malvern. The Priory, dedicated to the Blessed Virgin and St Michael, was always subject to Westminster Abbey on one of whose estates it was founded. To the north of the Priory, and almost adjacent to it, there was built between 1170 and 1217 the parish church of St Thomas à Becket which seems to have been a modest building. At the dissolution of the Priory in 1541 the parishioners boldly bought the priory church for £20 to take the place of St Thomas's which was then allowed to fall into ruin.

The manor of Newland, a fief of Westminster Abbey, was given to the Priory by Gilbert, Abbot of Westminster (died 1117) and this was confirmed by King Henry I and by Pope Honorius III in 1217. Newland is not mentioned by name in Henry's charter, though Windeff (Woodsfield in Powick) and Limberga (Limberrow at Pinn's Green) are, but 'illa nova terra assarta' (that newly cleared land) is generally taken to refer to Newland and, being more cultivable than the slopes around the Priory, it was presumably 'assarted' from the forest some time around 1100. Before the dissolution the Prior of Great Malvern granted the manor of Newland to his nephews William and John More But the Mores held it only till 1568. It then passed through at least five families till it was acquired by Earl Beauchamp in 1809

The monks of the Priory established a grange at Newland, probably the site of the present Grange Farm, and nearby they built a small chapel first mentioned in the 1217 papal confirmation; it was possibly rebuilt in the fifteenth century In the medieval period it was taxed with the church of Great Malvern, and until the dissolution a monk from the Priory said Mass alternately at Newland and at Woodsfield chapel. In 1540 the stipendiary curate of Newland, William Robyns, is mentioned among the monks of Great Malvern and he was still curate there in 1552 when an inventory carried out by order of Edward VI indicates that its possessions, which included two copes and three chasubles, were, as Brian Smith described them in *A History of Malvern*, 'more and richer' than those of the Priory It is said that the chapel would have been destroyed had it not been for the happy intervention of John More. In 1554 its advowson was granted to Lord Lumley along with that of Great Malvern. Sometime later it acquired the twelfth century font from the old parish church of St Thomas. In 1608 there was mention of the Church House at Newland, and until its demolition *c.*1958 there was a half-timbered thatched cottage at the southeast corner of Newland Green which belonged to the benefice and was known as the Old Vicarage. *The Victoria County History* states that 'It was undoubtedly the Priest's House when Newland was served by Malvern Priory, and may be identical with the church-house mentioned above'; Hunt states that it was bought for the benefice, along with other glebe land, in 1730.

The 1552 inventory, the earliest known source to mention the dedication of the chapel, gives this as St Michael. In 1881 G. S. Munn, rector of the adjacent parish of Madresfield, noted that 'it is unusual to find a dedication to St Michael in so low a condition' and suggested that 'it may have followed the dedication of the mother church.'[1] Eighteenth century sources still give it mostly as St Michael and the earliest noted reference to St Leonard is in 1782 when the historian T. R. Nash mentioned 'the chapel of Newland dedicated to St Leonard' This last dedication prevailed, and became the norm in the nineteenth century. In his notes Annett, who published a scholarly booklet on church dedications in the diocese of Hereford, commented, 'What an extremely tricky subject this is, and how often dedications were changed.'

Smith reckons that after the dissolution the chapel soon fell into decay, and also that few sacramental functions took place there. He notes that 'The baptismal register does not start until 1596, which may be an indication of when the St Thomas's font was moved there, but a few marriages were held from 1562'; also, 'despite the presence of a cemetery in 1610 burials were normally still made in the parish graveyard at Great Malvern'

For the next two centuries the chapel was probably content with its lot, while its incumbents, appointed by the vicar of Great Malvern, were often non-resident and frequently held other appointments

---

[1] 'Madresfield Church, Worcestershire', *Worcester Architectural Society,* 1881 p.119. Churches dedicated to St Michael were traditionally built on higher ground.

Documents of 1741 and 1809 were signed by the 'chapelwardens', and a 1743 document speaks of 'the chapel of Newland in the parish of Great Malvern.' In the banns book residents were normally described up to 1795 as 'of this chapelry', while marriages up to 1805 were described as having taken place in the 'chapel' of Newland. Now, however, it seems to have aspired to a higher status: in 1799 the banns book replaced 'this chapelry' by 'this parish', and in 1807 the marriage register replaced 'chapelry' by 'church.' But there is no evidence that it formally attained a higher status at this point. A marriage licence granted in 1832 referred to it as the chapel and chapelry of Newland, and Cassey's 1860 directory speaks of it as 'a chapelry in the parish of Great Malvern' and of its living as 'a perpetual curacy.'

The chapel's appearance in the mid-nineteenth century is well documented. There are five measured architect's drawings by W. J. Hopkins, as well as water-colours and drawings of both the exterior and the interior. Copies of most of these are hanging in the cloister of the Beauchamp Community. Internally it measured only about 55 feet by 14 feet, and in 1854 J. Noake described it as a 'humble little church', though 'one of the few remaining wooden-framed' ones:

> The building is merely an oblong room, with wooden porch on the north side, and bell cot of the same material above, surmounted by a kind of branch-spire a diminutive specimen, covered with sheet iron or some similar metal. On the N.W. there is a vestry, which was an addition to the church, originally intended as a stable for the curate's horse, but about the year 1833 it was enlarged and taken into the church for the accommodation of the inhabitants of the Link, and consecrated by the bishop. At the time of the erection of the new church at the Link, this additional room being no longer required, it was converted into a vestry.
>
> In the year 1846 the church was restored . . . The panels formed by the wood frame-work, which were formerly filled with lath and plaster, have of late years been repaired with brick in many of the lower compartments,. The windows are of two lights, with wood

frames. Formerly the walls were covered with scrolls and texts in old black letter; these are now removed, but on the edge of the low chancel roof, facing the congregation, is the inscription, on zinc—"You shall keep my sabbath, and reverence my sanctuary: I am the Lord"; and over the interior of the entrance door—"Holiness becometh thine house, O Lord, for ever". On the wall near this door is the record of the following charities . . . The font is as ancient a specimen as I have ever seen in the county, being a plain circular basin, devoid or ornament except a rude kind of star moulding running round the upper edge. When the church was repaired in 1846 the font was also restored by the incumbent, and a cover presented by the Reverend G. S. Munn."

Noake also mentions that in the vestry there was a chained copy of the *Paraphrase of Erasmus* dated 1522

Smith thought the old Newland chapel must have been 'one of the most remarkable churches in the county' and mentioned that the fittings had included ten high-backed pews and a fine late eighteenth century three-decker pulpit and reading-desk. He added that the roof had originally been thatched, and that a south door had been blocked about the turn of the eighteenth century, and a porch added instead on the north side. He also states that after St Matthias Malvern Link was built and consecrated in January 1846 'the little church was again hardly used.' But this seems dubious, and it may be that the 1846 repairs were Newland's response to the building of St Matthias. J. Severn Walker in 1862 suggests that among items not mentioned by Noake 'a gallery was removed' and 'new windows were also inserted, the eastern one being filled with painted quarries.' Since then, he added, 'the sanctuary walls have been enriched with hangings and an embroidered dossel' Its condition was now deemed highly satisfactory.

An 1855 article in the *Ecclesiologist* praised it as 'an excellent model for a church, of the simplest type, in many colonial situations, or for a temporary church at home' and added, 'After the lapse of probably five centuries, it remains in good substantial repair, and seems likely yet to outlast many fabrics of brick and stone—ostensibly more durable works of the present day' Walker also stated that 'the little edifice has been well cared for of late years, and is in a better state of repair than many buildings erected at the same or even a much later period, with far more substantial materials.'

Appendix VII
Principal Sources

Apart from the two books mentioned in the preface, there are a number of good sources for the early period. There are printed copies of the 1859 Scheme and its various revisions up to 1875, there are the voluminous papers of the sixth Earl, and there are also several printed pamphlets by Skinner:

Newland Accounts 1861–77.
The Newland Almanack with the Vicar's Pastoral Letter, 1869.
The Newland School. A Pastoral Letter to his Parishioners and Friends, 1875.
Newland Parish Church and the Beauchamp Community, 1877.
Instructions on the Ritual of the Altar, 1887.

There are also a good number of Orders of Service for special occasions and a mass of press cuttings; both of these range from the earliest days almost to the present day. But apart from a 1921 typescript *Notes on the Life of the Reverend George Cosby White 1825–1918 by a Priest* [Canon J. G. Griffin] *of St Barnabas' Hostel,* the general material now becomes sparse and, such as there is, requires considerable further work. Little has been preserved from the beginning of Cosby White's ministry in 1877 to Father Brodribb's death in 1979 (though occasionally one comes across a few gems). More happily, much has been preserved for period from 1980.

The four volumes of the Trustees' Minutes (1859–1889, 1890–1980, 1980–89, 1990–2012+) are invaluable. Volumes one and two are mostly in script, while volumes three and four are typed. The first volume covers only thirty years—these were the formative years when so much was happening. The second volume covers ninety years—these were the solid but less exciting years of consolidation. The third volume covers only ten years—these were years of much activity. The fourth volume covers twenty-one years—years partly of activity and partly of consolidation. But, as in most minutes, there are surprising omissions, and it is a pity that the wardens' reports, which dealt with the 'nitty-gritty' of community life, are often not appended, though a few have survived in the general archives.

The parish registers for baptisms and marriages relate more to the wider parish, but the burial register and the churchyard records are an important source for the community as well.[1]

The Parish Magazine is another important source, but there are many gaps and the only ones which have been preserved are 1893, 1897–1907,[2] 1930–37, 1965–74. There were times when it was not published, e.g. it came 'to an untimely end' as a result of the First World War and was not resumed till 1930, but it was probably published from 1938 to 1964 and from 1975 to 1980, but no copies have been traced. More happily most issues of *Grapevine*, survive from 1982.[3]

---

[1] The parish registers up to 1901 are obtainable from the Birmingham Archives.

[2] From April 1906 to December 1907 and possibly later, the magazine was a joint venture with Guarlford and Madresfield—a precursor of things to come.

[3] The first issue I have consulted was August 1984. Thereafter I have consulted all, except for September 1986, February 1990, June 1994 (no. 142), October 1994 (no. 146), July–December 1997 (no. 170–171) and March 1978 (no. 173).

The PCC came into being only in 1920, but four volumes of useful minutes survive, 1920–41, 1941–44, 1944–59, 1959–67.

As indicated in the first appendix, a largely, though not wholly, complete register of the community was kept from its foundation until *c.* 1900 but was discontinued until a new register of pensioners covered the period 1928–80 Choir school records are reasonable up to 1882; thereafter they are good only from 1928 to 1938. Lygon Lodge and St Barnabas records are both very meagre.

Unfortunately, apart from the records of the sixth Earl referred to above, the community's own archives have been in a chaotic state. Work is now in hand to order them chronologically, but in the meantime the reference 'BCA' indicates that the information has been obtained from these archives but it is impossible to supply a more helpful reference.

One source I have shirked. In 1974 Godfrey Russell, whose firm had acted for the Trustees since at least 1943 and probably much earlier, referred to about thirty-five files relating to the charities. The number doubtless became much larger.